Regulation of Sexual Conduct in UN Peacekeeping Operations

Olivera Simic

Regulation of Sexual Conduct in UN Peacekeeping Operations

Springer

Olivera Simic
Law School
Griffith University
Nathan Campus
Nathan
Queensland
Australia

ISBN 978-3-642-28483-0 ISBN 978-3-642-28484-7 (eBook)
DOI 10.1007/978-3-642-28484-7
Springer Heidelberg New York Dordrecht London

Library of Congress Control Number: 2012939489

Printed on acid-free paper

Springer is part of Springer Science+Business Media (www.springer.com)

Endorsements

This book presents the human side of the debate over whether there should be a "zero tolerance" policy towards sexual relationships between peacekeepers and the people they are mandated to protect. Olivera Simic's research confounds the stereotype of women as victims in times of conflict and challenges the wisdom of blanket policies about human relationships. This is a bold and confronting analysis.

Prof. Hilary Charlesworth, Australian National University

Olivera Simic's new book "Regulation of Sexual Conduct in UN Peacekeeping Operations" is a bold and much needed intervention into debates around Sexual Exploitation and Abuse (SEA) involving UN peacekeepers and Bosnian women. Given that current UN policies to protect women from SEA are overprotective and informed by gender and imperial stereotypes, Simic argues that they are in tension with the human rights of those involved. This book promises to broaden and deepen debates that go to the very heart of gendered relations in peacekeeping operations (PKO), and in turn, provide policy makers with a more enlightened and realistic agenda with which to facilitate change in the challenging environment of the PKO.

Dr. Paul Higate, University of Bristol

I have worked on issues of sexual violence including trafficking for many years, a great deal of it in Bosnia. Sometimes what seems to be an obvious solution, such as a zero tolerance policy has unintended consequences because it was designed from a male perspective with the conduct of men in mind. Olivera Simic has looked from a different perspective and reached conclusions by actually talking to women and translating their experience. This is not the whole story, but it is a reminder that we women cannot be boxed in by the male, and sometimes the female gaze! An important and provocative book.

Madeleine Rees, WILPF Secretary-General and the former Head of Office of the High Commissioner for Human Rights in Bosnia and Herzegovina

> Women are not only victims of war. They are also agents who make their own decisions and choices.

This politically correct declaration has been rehearsed many times in policy worlds as well as in feminist studies. Still, in the last two decades there is little evidence that it actually informs international interventions into the lives of women in war, or inspires a broad range of feminist studies on women and war.

This book is an exception. In it, women's capacity to act and make informed choices—even under the gravest of war circumstances—is not just a principal consideration but also a methodological standpoint.

Taking up the topic of sexual relationships, sexual exploitation and prostitution in the peacekeeping context, Olivera Simic examines UN policies that, more or less, collapse those three phenomena into each other and ban all sexual encounters between local women and peacekeeping (predominantly male) personnel. Simic argues against such policy, noting its denial of sexual agency of women, its adherence to dominant gender stereotypes of women's multiple vulnerabilities and men's sexual predation, as well as its imperialist undertones. Rather, she argues, one has to distinguish between an adult and a child, consent and force, voluntary and involuntary actions. Those arguments are supported with empirical study with local women in Bosnia and Herzegovina, and peacekeepers with broad international experiences.

Arguing for "sex positive" approach to prostitution and sexual relations will, undoubtedly, be seen as controversial. And for sure, this book will raise many brows, for many different reasons. Nevertheless, without engaging with those questions head-on, as openly as possible, and without giving lived realities as much consideration as feminist politics and the politics of peacekeeping, all we will be left with are politically correct declarations.

Dr Dubravka Zarkov, Associate Professor, International Institute of Social Studies, The Hague

Preface

Why do many feminists feel uncomfortable talking about consensual sex in times of war? Why is it hard to imagine consensual states of desire during warfare? Is all sex under coercive circumstances rape? These questions haunt me because I know of other stories, other experiences, that tell of consensual sex during the siege of Sarajevo as well as in other cities in Bosnia and Herzegovina (BH) during the war. I have a close friend who lived under the siege in Sarajevo, had sex with her then boyfriend and conceived her son in 1994, an unthinkable year in Sarajevo to have sex. I know of many other babies conceived and born during the war, babies born from love not rape. I know of consensual sex between women and men belonging to different ethnic groups; people who should have been 'enemies'.

All of this knowledge was on my mind when I attended the Women's Worlds 2011 Conference held in Ottawa, Canada. It was truly a wonderful event in which almost 2,000 women from 92 countries came to exchange ideas, network, 'connect and converse'.[1] Each day featured as many as 20 parallel sessions where almost 800 women presented their papers covering the issues of concern for women: refugee women, women in prostitution, women in politics, poor women, women in war and many others. The plenary as well as some parallel sessions were conducted in three languages: English, French and Spanish. Women from all age groups were there and from various social, cultural and economic backgrounds. I particularly enjoyed the plenary sessions where women from marginalized and under-represented communities, such as indigenous, transgendered and women with disabilities featured. In many respects such a gathering was a historic event since many feminists work in isolation, under political and economic pressure and in life-threatening situations. The congress was an opportunity to gather women from around the world and to share women's accomplishments as well as the struggles and challenges they face in the twenty-first century.

[1] Women's Worlds 2011, http://www.womensworlds.ca/.

The conference also gave me a chance to meet the women behind the articles and books I had been reading. The presence of famous feminist scholars such as Cynthia Enloe and Kathleen Barry meant a lot to me. Because I come from a country wretched and destroyed by civil war, because I experienced war first hand and know what it means to lose one's country of birth, to lose family and friends, to be a refugee and to search and reinvent one's identity,[2] being present at an academic conference such as this and presenting my work surrounded by such well known feminist thinkers brought many contradictions and pleasures. My long-term academic interest has been in UN peacekeeping operations and peacekeepers in particular in the region of former Yugoslavia, the region I was born in. I did my research on peacekeepers and sexual violence, initially focusing on their involvement in trafficking in women.

However, in my PhD thesis I focused on something quite different. While my thesis focused on peacekeeping, it did not concern sexual abuse but consensual sexual relationships between peacekeepers and local women in BH. I interviewed Bosnian women who had consensual sexual relationships with peacekeepers during the war and in its aftermath. We talked about their desires, experiences and opinions of the UN 'zero tolerance policy' on sexual abuse and sexual exploitation which also 'strongly discourages' sexual relationships.[3] I analysed this rich empirical data and was excited about the prospect of presenting the Bosnian women's voices in front of this array of feminist scholars.

But when it was my time to enter this international conversation, I faced something I had not expected. The subject of my paper "Policing the Peacekeepers Sex: The Regulation of Sexual Relationships between Local Women and UN Peacekeepers" seemed to disappoint, because it did not reinforce the prevailing image of the Bosnian woman in war-time; the image of the victim. I was daring to speak of sexual agency during this devastating time of war. I said that the Bosnian women that I interviewed told me that they had various motivations for engaging in sexual relationships with peacekeepers, and that these ranged from love to sex for fun. Maybe love could be imagined as a reason, but who could imagine a Bosnian woman having sex for fun during the war?

My writing is about war, its consequences and the ways in which people are trying to make sense of a violent past, face it and move forward. I have been inspired by feminist thinkers, such as Enloe, Otto, Vance and others who each in their own way talk about women, sex, pleasures and dangers. I know the dangers part very well. Feminist thinking has been an important part of my personal and academic life because of the insights and concern for women victims of war,

---

[2] See for example, 'Speaking the Unspeakable, Remembering the Whished to be Forgotten' (2011) 3 (2) *International Feminist Journal of Politics* 247.

[3] *Secretary-General's* Bulletin, *Special Measures for Protection from Sexual Exploitation and Abuse*, ST/SGB/2003/13 (9 October 2003). Sec 3.2 (d): 'Sexual relationships between United Nations staff and beneficiaries of assistance, since they are based on inherently unequal power dynamics, undermine the credibility of the UN and are strongly discouraged'.

particularly the victims of the war in my country and its horrendous rape camps. Rape has always been part of war and BH is no exception to it.[4] I spent several years researching the sexual abuse of women in the wars in the former Yugoslavia, but then I decided to shift my concern to agency and women who were not victims of sexual abuse but had consensual sex in times of war. I became interested in the contrasting world of consensual sex going on at the same time in BH. I had become overwhelmed with the feminist literature on rape in BH[5] and the overwhelming image and assumption that Bosnian women are only victims. I do not attempt to deny the fact that women are being taking advantage of in times of peace and war and that they are vulnerable. However, assuming, positioning and constructing women in war as nothing but victims is also harmful to women. What is happening to women during war? Rape, yes, but not only.

I am not the only scholar who is questioning the totalising narrative of victimization that grows out of war. Jasmina Husanovic, suggests that the central question of feminist politics in BH is how to deal with 'loss, rupture, break—mend it, repair it, restore it, repoliticize it, reimagine it, make it creative, politically productive, turn it into the politics of hope, of emancipator politics'[6] at the same time. Studies on sexual violence against women in wars have contributed hugely to our understanding of the intersections between gender, sexuality, collective identities and violence. However, feminist studies of Yugoslavia, followed by those of the Rwandan war in the late 1990s, largely focused on studies of war rape.[7] Zarkov suggests that agency and victimisation should be only two of the many possible narratives of the positioning of women within a violent conflict. Instead of assuming the presence of either agency or victimisation, a feminist studying a violent conflict should rather ask when and how agency and victimisation are prioritised in the experiences and representations of war, what other narratives of women's and men's positioning within the war there are, and how they are obscured or denied.[8]

Scully also argues that the rhetoric of the sexual vulnerability of women and girls has serious implications for women's leadership in post-conflict societies. She raises important questions such as the implications of defining a female subject as requiring sexual protection in the context of building a post-conflict society[9]. Her point is that an exclusive focus on sexual violence against women during war and

[4] Susan Brownmiller has documented this in 1975 in her groundbreaking book *Against Our Will: Men, Women and Rape* (Bantam Books, 1976).

[5] See generally, Alexandra Stiglmayer (ed), *Mass Rape: The War against Women in Bosnia-Herzegovina* (University of Nebraska Press, 1994).

[6] Jasmina Husanovic, 'The Politics of gender, witnessing, postcoloniality and trauma: Bosnian feminist trajectories' (2009) 10 (1) *Feminist Theory* 113.

[7] Dubravka Zarkov, 'Towards a new theorizing of women, gender and war' in Mary Evans, Kathy Davis and Judith Lorber (eds), *Handbook of Gender and Women's Studies* (SAGE, 2006) 231.

[8] Ibid 233.

[9] Pamela Scully, 'Vulnerable women: A critical reflection on human rights discourse and sexual violence' (2009) 23 *Emory International Law Review* 113.

on their vulnerability in post-conflict reconstruction may hinder the objectives of human rights.[10] Zarkov is also concerned that classical feminist studies of women and war shifted from the conceptualisation of agency and empowerment to a theoretically and politically much more problematic conceptualisation of sexual victimisation and victimhood of civilian women.[11] She argues that Eurocentrism, racism and Orientalism have ensured that there have always been women and regions that have been seen as more empowered and emancipated than others. Thus, it has also been very easy to perceive some of them entirely through the prism of victimisation. Not surprisingly, women in the Balkan and African wars have been seen as belonging to the latter group and their sexual victimisation has been seen as the ultimate destiny of women in war.[12] Because of such positioning of BH, there has been no discussion about sexual relationships in war and in the peace-keeping context. The former Yugoslav feminist scholars have focused on rape and sexual violence instead. While this is a fact I am aware of, I was still not prepared for the reactions that followed the presentation of my paper.

I presented my paper on the third day of the conference on a panel dedicated to women and post conflict resolution. Since I have done previous research into peacekeeping and trafficking in women, whenever I presented papers on this topic at feminist conferences, I have always had the full attention of the audience. My talks about sexual abuse, trafficking and peacekeeping were always welcomed and praised. However, this time while I was introducing myself and my research to a room full of international feminists, I started to second guess myself. I soon became aware of unrest in the room. It was almost as if my research into stories about Bosnian women making decisions to enter into consensual/romantic relationships with peacekeepers was 'out of place.' I had never had this feeling before although I had presented this particular research a few times to different audiences in Australia. I tried to shake off my growing sense of discomfort and continued to explain why I had undertaken this work–I was driven to do so by the injustice I felt that was produced by the UN's 'zero tolerance policy' that bans almost all sex between women and peacekeepers. While I was saying this I could not help but think that if I were speaking about trafficking instead of peacekeeping, I would not be getting the same feeling of discomfort. I reminded myself that as a Bosnian woman I had a right, a legitimacy, to explore sexual agency and not just focus on being a victim.

Despite this internal dialogue and struggle to stay optimistic, the more I spoke, the less comfortable I felt. While I continued reading my paper I could see that a few women were expressing quiet anger at what they were hearing. I began to understand a little better about what was happening. Many of my listeners did not want to hear another story that went against how they were used to seeing Bosnian

[10] Ibid 120.

[11] Zarkov, above n 7, 230.

[12] Ibid.

women. However, the point of my work was to show the supremacy of the narrative which totalizes women's experiences to 'war kills everything' including sexual desire, further dehumanized women and men already victimized. My work was shattering the image of Bosnian women as only victims of rape and trauma. I was trying to show that, even during war-time, some Bosnian women had sexual agency with a freely expressed sexuality and a greater sense of bodily integrity then had been discussed before. I even dared to say that some women had told me that they had wanted 'only sex' and nothing else from the peacekeepers. This revelation seemed like a revolution, like something unbelievable, unimaginable. How could we imagine Bosnian women during the bloodiest war in Europe since WWII as having a desire to enjoy sex under the bombs and the bullets? Even as I said the words, I heard with their ears and could understand why such an image sounded unreal, distorted, even insulting. To imagine something so intimate in times of destruction is hard but it nevertheless is a fact of life. The desires for love and sex do not stop with the beginning of war but they become wretched and intermingled with war. Lepa Mladjenovic, a well known feminist activist from Serbia, in her 1998 letter to Women in Black activist Joan Nestle writes:

> From the beginning of wars in this region from '91 I felt that I have to invent 'Ten thousand ways' to let my lesbian desire breathe. At some moment during the last eight years it was not easy for me to put in words how do I feel when making love with a woman and in the back there is a radio with the news of war. Killed, or expelled or other fascist acts. In my room, I would not be able to stand up from the bed, leave the desired bodies and switch off the news, also because I thought the respect to the killed I will show by not switching off the radio.[13]

This powerful excerpt from Lepa's letter to her friend is telling us that war is destructive but it does not stop all lives. The living continue to have ordinary sexual desires. In times of war people have a greater desire to live and learn to appreciate and not take for granted every day they awake. In a classic, 'A woman from Berlin', a woman who wrote a diary during the fall of Berlin in 1945 writes,

> There is no doubt that the threat to life enhances the will to live. I myself am burning with a more intense and larger flame than before the war of bombs. Each new day of life is a day of triumph.[14]

I, however, began to understand more about the complexities and problems presented by my paper as the day progressed. During question time, one woman asked me where I included trauma and victimhood in my work on Bosnian women. I answered,

> Yes, I know that the vast majority of Bosnian women were victimized and many raped during these times, I am not trying to deny that, but I am trying to explore other moments as well, to see if moments of agency can exist in such a place and time and what we can learn from this. Can these women despite trauma have consensual sex in times of war and its

---

[13] The email correspondence between Lepa and Joan on the file with author.

[14] Anonymous, *A Woman in Berlin* (Secker and Warburg, 1955), 27.

> aftermath? Does the fact that the vast majority of Bosnian women are victimized and many of them raped diminish expression of their agency?

I was struck by this exchange, because I had never before seen Bosnian women only through this lens of victimhood. Maybe this is because I am Bosnian, and I don't see my friends and other women only as victims. I know many of them are, but they are also courageous women who keep struggling to make life, to keep loving. Why is it so uncomfortable to talk about Bosnian women as women who made decisions to have sex with peacekeepers or local men, and some of them not for long-term commitment but just for their pleasure? I believe that we need to allow these 'other' voices to be listened to too.

Another response from a woman in the audience showed me how deep these questions can go. She commented that European women are 'certainly different' from African woman and that African women need 'more protection.' Are all African women victims? Where does the discussion of agency come here? Are we going to homogenize all women on the African continent as victims who need protection or at least more protection than European girls and women? Are we going to compete for victimhood status? Of course, women do need protection from sexual violence, but not from consensual sex. I am not convinced that European girls are 'less vulnerable' then African girls in times of war and that their experiences are so vastly different when it come to consensual sex but only more research and thinking beyond the box of victimhood will give better answers.

I understand I am walking that famous tightrope between pleasure and danger spoken about in Carole Vance's classic anthology, but I did not think talking about agency would be heard and felt as diminishing the trauma that Bosnian women suffered during and after the war. I was learning that it sounded almost indecent to talk about these women as something other than victims of rape. Some of the feminists hearing my paper were not used to or perhaps had never heard anything else about Bosnian women except the history of victimization. As I have indicated previously, there is a huge body of scholarly literature on Bosnian women as victims and in some way, this has helped to create this almost stereotypical thinking—there is only one Bosnian woman, the victim. Any attempt to discuss her in other ways is seen as rude, indecent and damaging. Any attempt to broaden the discussion, to 'unpack' the Bosnian woman subject from the existing framework is a dangerous and thankless task. This is why it is important to continue to keep questioning the many hidden and precious Bosnian women identities that will shed light on their agency, resilience and courage despite the horrors they faced.

On the last day of the conference, I was attending a session organized about Bosnia, Somalia and the subject of rape. A woman sitting in front of me seemed rather surprised when I told her that I was not raped or sexually assaulted during the war. I was shocked to think that this woman and probably other women in the room thought of me as a possible victim of rape only because I had introduced myself as a woman originally from Bosnia. Whenever I spoke, women would look at me with empathy and understanding and that sort of silent respect we show towards victims.

It is difficult to escape from the prism of victimhood and be seen as more than a victim. I do not exist in a vacuum and it is not enough that I don't see myself as victim. I may decide not to identify as such, but I cannot stop others from viewing me in this way. Yet I want Bosnian women to be seen as something more than creations of the war. I respect our victimhood, but at the same time, with this book I want to dismantle the prevailing power of this image and show the complex lives that coexist with it.

Brisbane Olivera Simic

10 February 2012

Acknowledgements

I am grateful to all those who have stood by me and supported me throughout the book writing process. This book builds upon a doctoral thesis undertaken at the University of Melbourne, Law School. My greatest appreciation is for my two supervisors, Professor Dianne Otto and Associate Professor Michelle Foster, whose knowledge, wisdom and guidance have been invaluable and integral to the completion of this book. I am also very grateful to my examiners, Professor Hilary Charlesworth and Dr Paul Higate, who provided thoughtful and constructive comments, which I found most useful in improving my book.

Appreciation also goes out to Professor Carolyn Evans, Dean of Melbourne Law School, and to the Institute for International Law and the Humanities staff for all the instances in which their assistance helped me along the way. I would also like to express my gratitude to the Melbourne Law School who provided me with a comfortable intellectual and environment in which I could thrive, study and write.

I recognise that this research would not have been possible without the financial assistance of the Melbourne International Research Scholarships, Melbourne International Fee Remission Scholarships, and express my gratitude to those agencies.

I am in particular thankful to my principal supervisor, Professor Dianne Otto, whose dedication to my research and insightful comments have challenged me intellectually and stimulated my thinking and growth during the doctoral process. Her encouragement, support and feedback after reading numerous drafts were extraordinary. I doubt that I will ever be able to convey my appreciation fully, but I own her my eternal gratitude.

Special thanks to my husband Stojan Ignjatovic who has been a steady source of support and encouragement throughout the ups and downs of the doctorate research process. I am very grateful for the friendship and hospitality of Yoriko Otomo, Iva Puker, Lia Kent, Nesam MacMillan, Joan Nestle, Fayen d'Evie, Katsuhiko Suganuma, Terry Martin, Zala Volcic, Daniel W Muriu and Takele S Bulto. I also thank Madonna Adcock for her fantastic technological help, and to the Griffith Law School and its staff who helped me to get through the final stages in completion of this book. I am also grateful for the assistance of the team at Springer, especially Anke Seyfried and Manuela Schwietzer.

My sincere thanks and deepest gratitude are owed to the women from Bosnia and Herzegovina, and the peacekeepers who shared their perspectives and experiences with me. This book would not have been possible without their openness and generous contributions of time. I hope that I have done justice to their courage and integrity.

Last, but not least, I wish to thank my family and friends who have shown their immeasurable support and encouragement in all aspects of my life. I dedicate this book to my parents, Desimirka and Milenko Simic, for giving me the space and opportunity to go where I want to in life and for providing the unconditional love, confidence and support to get there.

Contents

Abbreviations

BH	Bosnia and Herzegovina
CDU	Conduct and Discipline Unit
CEDAW	Convention on the Elimination of All Forms of Discrimination against Women
DHA	Department of Humanitarian Affairs
DPA	Department of Political Affairs
DPKO	Department for Peacekeeping Operations
DRC	Democratic Republic of Congo
ECPS/ECHA	Executive Committees on Peace and Security and Humanitarian Affairs
HRW	Human Rights Watch
IASC	Inter-Agency Standing Committee
ICCPR	International Covenant on Civil and Political Rights
ICESCR	International Covenant on Economic, Social and Cultural Rights
IDPs	Internally Displaced Persons
IFOR	Implementation Force
IOM	International Organisation for Migration
IPTF	International Police Task Force
MINUGUA	United Nations Mission in Guatemala
MONUC	United Nations Mission in the Democratic Republic of Congo
NATO	North Atlantic Treaty Organization
NGOs	Non Governmental Organisations
ODIHR	Office for Democratic Institutions and Human Rights
OGA	Office of Gender Affairs
OHCHR	Office of the High Commissioner for Human Rights
OHR	Office of the High Representative
OIOS	United Nations Office of Internal Oversight Service
ONUC	UN Peacekeeping Operation in the Congo
ONUMOZ	United Nations Mission in Mozambique

ONUSAL	United Nations Observer Mission in El Salvador
OSCE	Organization for Security and Cooperation in Europe
PKOs	United Nations Peacekeeping Operations
SEA	Sexual exploitation and abuse
SEA	Sexual exploitation and sexual abuse
SFOR	NATO-led Stabilization Force
SGB	Secretary-General's Bulletin on Special Measures for Protection from
SRSG	Special Representative of the U.N. Secretary-General
STOP	Special Trafficking Operations Program
UDHR	Universal Declaration of Human Rights
UN	United Nations
UNAIDS	Joint UN Programme on HIV/AIDS
UNDP	United Nations Development Programme
UNEF I	United Nations Emergency Force
UNESCO	United Nations Educational, Scientific and Cultural Organization
UNFICYP	United Nations Peacekeeping Force in Cyprus
UNHCR	United Nations High Commissioner for Refugees
UNHCR/SC-UK	United Nations High Commissioner for Refugees/Save the Children United Kingdom
UNICEF	United Nations Children's Fund
UN GA	United Nations General Assembly
UNIFIL	United Nations Interim Force in Lebanon
UNMEE	United Nations Mission in Eritrea
UNMIBH	United Nations Mission in Bosnia and Herzegovina
UNMIL	United Nations Mission in Liberia
UNPROFOR	United Nations Protection Force in the Former Yugoslavia
UNTAC	United Nations Mission in Cambodia
UNTSO	United Nations Truce Supervision Organization
WFP	World Food Programme
WHO	World Health Organization
ZTP	Zero tolerance policy

Chapter 1
Sexual Conduct and Peacekeeping

This book critically analyses the United Nations (UN) Secretary-General's Bulletin on Special Measures for Protection from Sexual Exploitation and Sexual Abuse (SGB) which was promulgated in 2003 to address the problem of 'sexual exploitation and abuse'[1] within the context of peacekeeping operations (PKOs).[2] The book is concerned with the broad definition of sexual exploitation provided by the SGB, which includes most sexual relationships and prostitution. This research project was prompted by my apprehension that, following application of the SGB, local women who entered into sexual relationships with peacekeepers[3] were being identified as victims of sexual exploitation, and unfairly banned from engaging in such relationships. I also became concerned that the SGB might reinforce the stereotype that all women working in prostitution are victims, and that all peacekeepers engaged in prostitution or sexual relationships are sexual predators who cannot treat local women with respect. In light of these concerns, I decided to undertake qualitative empirical research to determine whether it was justified in the context of PKOs for the UN's zero tolerance approach to sex between peacekeepers and local people to include sexual relationships and prostitution.

To answer this core question, the book employs primarily qualitative research. The research involved interviewing three groups of participants: Bosnian women who had engaged in sexual relationships with peacekeepers during the UN's

[1] Since the promulgation of the SGB, the term 'sexual exploitation and abuse' has become widely used in official UN documents, often as an acronym: SEA.

[2] The UN, scholars and researchers interchangeably use terms such as: UN peacekeeping operations, peacekeeping missions, missions and operations. For clarity within this book, I will use the term 'peacekeeping operations' to refer to the broad range of UN peacekeeping operations from 1948 until the present.

[3] For the purpose of this research, the term 'peacekeepers' will be used to refer to any uniformed service member serving as the UN military component, UN civilian police officers and military observers, UN volunteers, and individual contractors and consultants working on behalf of peace support operations.

O. Simic, *Regulation of Sexual Conduct in UN Peacekeeping Operations*,
DOI 10.1007/978-3-642-28484-7_1, © Springer-Verlag Berlin Heidelberg 2012

Mission in Bosnia and Herzegovina[4] (UNMIBH) (Group A), Bosnian women who had worked within the UNMIBH (Group B), and peacekeepers in general (Group C). The interviewees were asked about their understanding of the SGB provisions, in particular with respect to sexual relationships and prostitution. Most significantly, Group A provided first-hand insight into the experiences of women who had sexual relationships with peacekeepers. The qualitative research is supported by feminist analysis of radical and 'sex positive' perspectives, which provide conceptual tools to evaluate the SGB and its effects, and the responses of the interviewees. It also evaluates the SGB in relation to previous empirical studies on sexual exploitation in peacekeeping contexts and through the lens of international human rights law.

My personal experiences with the UNMIBH, both as a Bosnian citizen and as an employee with the UN's Children's Fund (UNICEF), and the increasing reports of 'sexual exploitation and abuse' in PKOs, drove me to examine what the UN perceived to be the problem of sexual exploitation within the peacekeeping context. In 2001, I began to wonder about the extent and number of reported 'sexual exploitation and abuse' allegations that had emerged in both UNMIBH and PKOs around the world. At that time, the sex industry was thriving and Bosnia and Herzegovina (BH) was considered the main destination country in South Eastern Europe for women trafficked from the former Soviet Union bloc. Although it was clear that the country needed to deal more effectively with trafficking, I was concerned that all of the women who were found in the underground brothels and night clubs during police raids were being, *a priori*, identified as 'victims' of trafficking.

The fact that prostitution was illegal in BH at the time of UNMIBH (and still is) made it difficult for women who were voluntarily working in the sex industry to identify themselves as sex workers, since they ran the risk of being detained and left without any of the assistance that was provided to victims of trafficking. Under such circumstances, it was not surprising that women did not formally identify themselves as prostitutes, which further contributed to the marginalisation and invisibility of women voluntarily working in the sex industry. This also led to the apparent nonexistence of prostitutes in BH, and a lack of interest on the part of both local and international governmental and non-governmental organisations in acknowledging the reality of voluntary prostitution.

Gradually, I became more interested in researching the various types of sexual relationships that had developed between local women and peacekeepers during PKOs. I knew a number of local women who were having sexual relationships with peacekeepers and had heard rumours of local women engaging in prostitution. Although a wide range of sexual activities, such as consensual sexual relationships and voluntary adult prostitution, were flourishing in BH between peacekeepers and local women, they were never the subject of public UN policy discussions or

[4] UNMIBH 1995-2002.

scholarly research in BH. It seemed that everyone was preoccupied with trafficking in women, so all other sexual activities between peacekeepers and local women were being ignored.

Due to the intensity of the trafficking problem in BH, and as someone who was involved in programs aimed at preventing trafficking in women, I expected the UN to assist in developing strategies to curb the problem. However, I did not envisage that the UN would try to regulate all sexual conduct in PKOs in order to prevent trafficking and other sexual abuse. It was a surprise when the UN responded with a zero tolerance approach, prohibiting almost all types of sexual encounters between peacekeepers and local women. In order to prevent sexual exploitation and abuse, the UN has developed policies that not only prohibit such conduct, but also ban sexual relationships and adult voluntary prostitution. It was this expansion of UN policy regarding sexual exploitation that triggered this research project.

This introductory chapter sets the scene for the exploration of my research question. The first part of the chapter provides a brief overview of the perceived problem of sexual exploitation in PKOs that eventually prompted the zero tolerance policy (ZTP). The second part of the chapter outlines the purpose and scope of the book. The third part describes the methodology adopted in the empirical research, while the final part outlines the structure of the book and provides a brief overview of each chapter.

1.1 Background to the Research

There was a dramatic increase in PKOs in the early 1990s with the end of the Cold War. The increase in the number of PKOs was accompanied by the first reports expressing concern about sexual activities between peacekeepers and local women and girls. These reports appeared as early as 1995.[5] Soon after, reports began to proliferate about the sharp rise in prostitution as well as trafficking in women that accompanied PKOs in Somalia and BH.[6] These were followed by reports from later missions that alleged the involvement of peacekeepers in sexual exploitation and abuse in West Africa (Liberia, Sierra Leone and Guinea), the Democratic Republic of Congo (DRC), Eritrea and East Timor.[7] Indeed, links between the presence of

[5] Kien Serey Phal, 'The Lessons of the UNTAC Experience and the Ongoing Responsibilities of the International Community in Cambodia' (1995) 7(2) *Pacifica Review* 129.

[6] Natalia Lupi, 'Report by the Enquiry Commission on the Behavior of Italian Peacekeeping troops in Somalia' (1998) 1*Yearbook of International Humanitarian Law* 375; Human Rights Watch, 'Hopes Betrayed: Trafficking of Women and Girls to Post-conflict Bosnia and Herzegovina for Forced Prostitution' (2002); Sarah Martin, 'Must Boys be Boys? Ending Sexual Exploitation and Abuse in Peacekeeping Missions' (Refugee International, 2005).

[7] United Nations High Commissioner for Refugees and Save the Children UK (UNHCHR/STC-UK), 'Sexual Violence and Exploitation: The Experience of Refugee Children in Liberia, Guinea and Sierra Leone' (2002); Paul Higate, 'Gender and Peacekeeping Case Studies: The Democratic

peacekeepers and sexual exploitation and abuse of women have been documented across the full range of PKOs.

Although allegations of sexual exploitation and abuse surfaced in the early 1990s, it was not until 2002 that UN policies began to address the issue in a comprehensive way. However, despite these efforts, reports of sexual exploitation and abuse by peacekeepers have continued[8] and no real progress has been made towards resolving the problem and preventing its recurrence.[9] I will argue that the majority of the studies that have identified the problem of sexual exploitation and abuse within peacekeeping contexts, and which have informed policy development, have not critically examined the definition of sexual exploitation.[10] They have failed to recognise that the term sexual exploitation has included the whole range of sexual interactions between peacekeepers and local people, including sexual relationships and adult voluntary prostitution, which suggests that the researchers have failed to distinguish between exploitative and non-exploitative sex. As a result, the allegations, and investigations that have followed have not been limited to sexual exploitation and abuse, but have included consensual sexual activities as if 'they were of the same ilk'.[11] This lack of clarity was embedded in the comprehensive policy that was formalised in the SGB in 2003.

This book argues that a major problem with the approach of the SGB is the lack of clear differentiation between sexual relationships and sexual exploitation, and between prostitution and sexual exploitation. The SGB follows the broad definitions of sexual exploitation used by radical feminist scholars and most researchers, which include such diverse sexual conduct as rape, trafficking for the purposes of prostitution, sex with minors, voluntary prostitution, and almost all modes of consensual sexual relationships between peacekeepers and beneficiaries. The book argues that such broad definitions of sexual exploitation are over-inclusive because they encompass sexual activities that the participants would not

Republic of the Congo and Sierra Leone' (Pretoria, Gender and Peacekeeping, Institute for Security Studies, 2004) 91 Monograph Series; East Timor Institute for Reconstruction Monitoring and Analysis 'Commentary: International Security Forces and Sexual Misconduct', The La'o Hamutuk Bulletin (online), August 2001 <http://www.laohamutuk.org/Bulletin/2001/Aug/bulletinv2n5.html>; Deutsche Presse Agentur, 'U.N. Investigates Alleged Sexual Abuse by Peacekeepers in Eritrea', 14 April 2005 <http://www.reliefweb.int/rw/rwb.nsf/db900SID/ACIO-6BFN5E?OpenDocument>.

[8] Dianne Otto, 'Making Sense of Zero Tolerance Policies in Peacekeeping Sexual Economies' in Vanessa Munro and Carl F. Stychin (eds), *Sexuality and the Law: Feminist Engagements* (London, GlassHouse Press, 2007) 259.

[9] Machiko Kanetake, 'Whose Zero Tolerance Counts? Reassessing a Zero Tolerance Policy against Sexual Exploitation and Abuse by UN Peacekeepers' (2010) 17(2) *International Peacekeeping* 200.

[10] Paul Higate and Marsha Henry, 'Engendering (In)security in Peace Support Operations' (2004) 35(4) Security Dialogue 482; Daniel Gustafsson, *Peacekeeping and Prostitution: A Case Study of the Swedish Experience from Kosovo and Bosnia* (Masters Thesis, University of Lund, 2005); Martin, above n 6.

[11] Otto, above n 8, 262.

themselves perceive or experience as sexually exploitative. I contend that this is inconsistent with international human rights law, denies agency to women and automatically misrepresents the peacekeepers involved as perpetrators.

1.2 Purpose and Scope of the Book

This book is concerned with the broad definition of sexual exploitation provided by the SGB, which covers sexual relationships and prostitution. It focuses on the SGB provision 3.2 (c) which prohibits prostitution[12] in the context of PKOs, and provision 3.2 (d) which 'strongly discourages' sexual relationships between local people ('beneficiaries') and peacekeepers.[13] Although prostitution is banned and sexual relationships are 'strongly discouraged', they are both considered by the SGB as manifestations of sexual exploitation which 'violate universally recognised international legal norms and standards'.[14] The book argues that such a statement by the SGB is incorrect as international human rights law differentiates between coercion and voluntary behaviour in sexual conduct, distinguishing criminal and exploitative sexual activities as non-consensual and coercive.

The book examines the assumptions underlying the SGB, in particular in relation to the women the SGB claims it is most concerned about. The book does so by analysing perspectives on sexual relationships and prostitution that were elicited from Bosnian women and peacekeepers from a range of PKOs. The central aim of the book is to inform UN policymakers interested in developing strategies to address sexual exploitation by drawing their attention to the personal experiences of Bosnian women who had sexual relationships with peacekeepers and to the views of peacekeepers about the approach taken by the SGB.

It is as necessary to specify what this book does not deal with, as it is to say what it does deal with. Although the SGB was drafted primarily as a response to the study published by the UN High Commissioner for Refugees (UNHCR) and Save the Children UK about sexual exploitation of refugee children in Western Africa,[15] it is not confined to children, but covers adult women as well. However, this research is

[12] *Secretary General's* Bulletin, *Special Measures for Protection from Sexual Exploitation and Abuse*, ST/SGB/2003/13 (9 October 2003) sec. 3.2 (c): 'Exchange of money, employment, goods or services for sex, including sexual favours or other forms of humiliating, degrading or exploitative behaviour, is prohibited. This includes any exchange of assistance that is due to beneficiaries of assistance'.

[13] Ibid sec 3.2 (d): 'Sexual relationships between United Nations staff and beneficiaries of assistance, since they are based on inherently unequal power dynamics, undermine the credibility of the UN and are strongly discouraged'.

[14] Ibid sec 3 (1).

[15] UNHCR/STC-UK, above n 7.

limited to adults, defined as persons 18 years and over.[16] I decided to exclude children from my research project since discussion of children and sexual conduct draws on different legal norms and principles than those that apply to adults, and which are beyond the scope of this book. The book is also limited to heterosexual relationships, since different research strategies would need to be applied for same-sex relationships in the context of PKOs. This is not to suggest that such research is not warranted. Rather, I suggest that such research is long overdue since there are no empirical data about same-sex relationships in the context of PKOs.

This book is limited to qualitative research into sexual relationships between Bosnian women and male peacekeepers. While I am aware that there have been sexual relationships between Bosnian men and female peacekeepers, I decided to exclude analysis of such relationships, again to focus the book. The book also only explores Bosnian women's personal experiences with sexual relationships and not with prostitution. I did not undertake empirical research into Bosnian women's experiences with prostitution primarily because of the difficulties involved in locating willing interviewees, since the Bosnian women prostitutes who worked during UNMIBH, as I have mentioned, remain largely invisible because prostitution is illegal in BH.

Lastly, the focus of this book is on sexual exploitation rather than sexual abuse. I decided to explore sexual exploitation in PKOs since it is the SGB definition of sexual exploitation that includes consensual sexual relationships and prostitution. Sexual abuse involves coercion and the absence of consent.[17] A victim's choice, agency and consent are clearly absent when considering sexual abuse. However, choice, agency and consent are pertinent when discussing consensual sexual relationships and prostitution, although the SGB's definition of sexual exploitation seems to deny the relevance of these factors. For that reason, discussion of sexual abuse by peacekeepers is beyond the scope of this research project.

This book will demonstrate that the SGB's approach to sexual exploitation is problematic for two key reasons. Firstly, it employs a broad definition of sexual exploitation that includes sexual relationships and prostitution. I will argue that the SGB is driven by 'sexual negativity',[18] which treats all sexual activity as having negative consequences for 'beneficiaries'.[19] Secondly, the SGB treats 'beneficiaries'

---

[16] *Convention on the Rights of the Child*, opened for signature 20 November 1989, 1577 UNTS 3 (entered into force 2 September 1990) art 1.

[17] Secretary General's Bulletin, above n 13. Sexual abuse means 'the actual or threatened physical intrusion of a sexual nature, whether by force or under unequal or coercive conditions', para 1.

[18] Gayle Rubin, 'Thinking Sex: Notes for a Radical Theory of the Politics of Sexuality' in Carole S. Vance (ed), *Pleasure and Danger: Exploring Female Sexuality* (Routledge and Kegan Paul, 1984) 278.

[19] 'Beneficiaries of assistance' is a term officially used in UN policies, defined as follows: 'the entire population that we [UN peacekeeping forces] serve are considered beneficiaries of our assistance.' Department of Peacekeeping Operations, Challenges in Peacekeeping Operations, Year in Review 2005 <http://www.un.org/Depts/dpko/dpko/pub/year_review05/duty_of_care.htm>.

For the purpose of this research I have used the terms 'beneficiaries' and 'local populations' interchangeably to describe people under the protection of peacekeepers.

as passive and helpless and lacking the agency to decide whether to be involved in sexual relationships or prostitution with peacekeepers. Likewise, the SGB denies the agency of peacekeepers to decide for themselves about whether to become involved in sexual relationships with local women, or to engage the services of prostitutes. It also wrongly portrays all peacekeepers as sexual predators who prey on local women.

The book concludes that the inclusion of consensual sexual relationships and prostitution in the definition of sexual exploitation is not supportable. It argues that the policy is overprotective, relies on negative gender and imperial stereotypes, and should be revised in consultation with local women and peacekeepers affected by the policy.

1.3 Methodology

As an empirical study, this book explores the personal experiences of Bosnian women, as well as the views of women who worked in UNMIBH and peacekeepers from a range of PKOs. These experiences are examined in the context of the policy response to sexual exploitation adopted in the SGB. As a Bosnian woman who was born in the former Yugoslavia and who lived there for most of her life, I decided to use the BH context as my case study in order to analyse local women's perspectives on the SGB. I interviewed Bosnian women who had sexual relationships with peacekeepers, and Bosnian women who were working for UNMIBH between 1992 and 2002. Due to my familiarity with the region, its cultural context and language, I was well placed to undertake such research. While Bosnian women are a specific cultural group whose experiences do not necessarily reflect the experiences of other women who live under UN peacekeeping protection, I argue that women elsewhere may hold similar views and that my research project may inform broader policymaking. This similarity is due to the common experiences of women in war and post-conflict societies where PKOs are present. These experiences include similar socio-economic conditions, lack of employment opportunities, widespread poverty and high vulnerability to sexual exploitation. On the other hand, the peacekeepers who participated in this research included both men and women of diverse nationalities who had served in various PKOs around the world in different capacities. They included soldiers, civilian police officers and civilians. Thus, the views of the peacekeepers detailed in this book reflect the diversity and multi-nationality that is a feature of modern PKOs.

I have placed my empirical research in the context of other empirical studies, and have employed a feminist theoretical framework to critically assess the SGB and the responses of interviewees. Thus far, few feminists have been critical of the ZTP[20] and a majority of feminists have reacted positively to the

[20] One critique, developed by Dianne Otto, argues that the SGB treats almost all sex as coercive, and completely ignores the environment that is concerned with agency and survival. See, Otto, above n 8. Jennine Carmichael also argues that grouping sex with 'humiliating or exploitative

policy.[21] The question of whether (hetero)sexual relationships and prostitution are sexually exploitative is at the core of a longstanding division between feminists. For those who argue that heterosexuality under conditions of patriarchy and prostitution are forms of sexual exploitation, the ZTP seems to be well designed, as it reflects the radical feminist position, which claims that inequality between women and men in sexual relationships and prostitution degrades, objectifies and exploits women.[22] For 'sex positive' feminists who do not agree with this position, the ZTP is seen to perpetuate a conservative agenda that frames all women as victims and sex as 'harmful and dangerous'.[23]

While there are several empirical studies examining sexual exploitation in PKOs, only one of them considered consensual sexual relationships between local women and peacekeepers,[24] and none have sought opinions about the SGB from local women who have been directly affected by the UN's policies. Therefore, this research fills a void in the existing body of knowledge on sexual exploitation in PKOs by undertaking qualitative research exploring the importance of differentiating between sexual relationships and sexual exploitation, and between prostitution and sexual exploitation. This research project sheds light on the complexity of sexual relationships between Bosnian women and peacekeepers, and seeks their views on the question of prostitution in the context of PKOs. It has three key objectives. Firstly, it explores the realities of the lives of people affected by the SGB policy. Secondly, it reflects on the responses of Bosnian women and peacekeepers to the SGB inclusion of sexual relationships and prostitution in its definition. Thirdly, it seeks the views of interviewees about how future policy

behaviour' implies that all sex is harmful 'particularly when a transactional exchange is involved'. See Jennine Carmichael, *First, Do No Harm: Addressing the Problem of Sexual Exploitation and Abuse by International Aid Workers and Peacekeepers* (MA Thesis, The University of Melbourne, 2006) 29.

[21] Sheila Jeffreys, *The Industrial Vagina: The Political Economy of the Global Sex Trade* (Routledge, 2009)124; Vanessa L Kent, 'Peacekeepers as Perpetrators of Abuse: Examining the UN's plans to eliminate and address cases of sexual exploitation and abuse in peacekeeping operations' (2005) 14 (2) *African Security Review* 85; Elisabeth Defeis, 'U.N. Peacekeeping and Sexual Abuse and Exploitation: An End to Impunity' (2008) 7 (2) *Washington University Global Studies Law Review* 185; Muna Ndulo, 'The United Nations Responses To The Sexual Abuse And Exploitation Of Women And Girls By Peacekeeping Missions' (2008) 27(1) *Berkley Journal of International Law 127*.

[22] Catharine A MacKinnon, *Are Women Human? And Other International Dialogues* (The Belknap Press of Harvard University Press, 2006); Sheila Jeffreys, *The Idea of Prostitution* (Spinifex, 1997) Laurie Shrage, 'Comment on Overall's "What's Wrong with Prostitution? Evaluating Sex Work"'(1994) 19(2) *Signs: Journal of Women in Culture and Society* 564; Kathleen Barry, *The Prostitution of Sexuality* (New York University Press, 1995).

[23] Rubin, above n 19; Carol S. Vance, above n 19; Alice M. Miller, 'Sexuality, Violence Against Women, and Human Rights' (2004) 7 (16) *Health and Human Rights* 5; Dianne Otto, above, n 8; Dianne Otto, 'The Sexual Tensions of UN Peace Support Operations: A Plea for Sexual Positivity' (2007) XVIII *Finnish Yearbook of International Law* 33.

[24] Kathleen M. Jennings, 'Protecting Whom?: Approaches to Sexual Exploitation and Abuse in UN Peacekeeping Operations' (Fafo report, 2008).

guidelines should address prostitution and sexual relationships between peacekeepers and local women. The methodology employed in this empirical research is discussed in greater detail in Chap. 4.

1.4 Structure of the Book

The book has seven chapters. Following this introductory chapter, Chapter 2 provides an overview of the history of PKOs, focusing on challenges faced by PKOs since the early 1990s when the first serious allegations of sexual exploitation by peacekeepers emerged. Since 1990, the multi-dimensional nature of PKOs has involved large numbers of participants, including members of national contingents, civilian police, military observers, UN volunteers, consultants and individual contractors.[25] Changes in the scope and mandate of PKOs, which expanded to include peace building as a major component, have brought peacekeepers into almost daily contact with local populations. After profiling peacekeepers and the people who are beneficiaries of PKOs, and discussing the increased interaction between these two groups, the chapter introduces the problem of sexual exploitation as it emerged in the context of PKOs. The early reports alleging sexual exploitation of local women by peacekeepers are examined. The chapter concludes with the observation that serious allegations of sexual exploitation by peacekeepers have continued into the twenty-first century. These allegations have included involvement in trafficking women for the purposes of forced prostitution, rape and sexual assault, and the exchange of food and other humanitarian aid with beneficiaries in return for sex, known as 'survival sex'.

Chapter 3 examines responses to the allegations of sexual exploitation by individual PKOs as well as the institutional responses of the Department of Peacekeeping Operations (DPKO) and the Secretary-General (SG). It describes and analyses these responses in three stages, tracing the gradual increase in rigidity in approaches taken to prevent sexual exploitation. During the first stage, ad hoc responses were undertaken at the mission level, due to the unwillingness of senior UN peacekeeping officials to accept the emergence of problems of sexual exploitation and abuse in peacekeeping missions. The second stage saw more coordinated actions through the efforts of the DPKO and the SG, as well as senior peacekeeping personnel deployed in individual missions. The third stage commenced with the adoption of the ZTP on sex. This was elaborated in the SGB in 2003 when it became clear that allegations of sexual exploitation and abuse were threatening the reputation of the UN. Although the SGB was a reaction to sexual exploitation against children, the policy prohibits almost every kind of sexual activity between local

[25] Prince Zeid Ra'ad Zeid Al-Hussein, *A Comprehensive Strategy to Eliminate Future Sexual Exploitation and Abuse in United Nations Peacekeeping Operations*, UN GA, 59th sess, A/59/710 (24 March 2005) 4.

women and peacekeepers, regardless of age, consent and mutual agreement. This chapter analyses the wording of SGB provisions on prostitution and sexual relationships in order to identify its underlying assumptions and inform the framework for the empirical research analysis that follows in the next two chapters. It also deconstructs the SGB's feminist theoretical framework and questions the idea that it is based on human rights law. I argue that the ZTP is inconsistent with international human rights law, in particular the rights and freedoms related to sexuality and privacy, and that it is largely driven by radical feminist thinking, which considers prostitution and (hetero)sexual relationships to be forms of sexual exploitation. Finally, the chapter provides an overview of existing research into allegations of sexual exploitation by peacekeepers while on mission. It shows that there has been an overwhelmingly positive response to the SGB's approach from scholars and researchers. The chapter concludes that most researchers have not questioned the broad prohibitions of the SGB, nor sought the views of local women about the SGB.

Chapter 4 provides an overview of the research methodology and describes the aims and methods of the empirical research, which is the heart of the book. It introduces the local context of BH and outlines the interview methodology with the three groups of interviewees: BH women who had sexual relationships with peacekeepers (Group A); BH women who worked within the UN mission in BH (Group B); and peacekeepers in general who were bound by the SGB (Group C). The Chapter has two main parts, each of which is divided into several subsections. The first part begins with a brief introduction to gender politics in BH and a short historical background to the country. After this general overview, the chapter traces shifts in the status of women in BH before the 1990s, during the war, and in post-conflict BH. I also position myself, as a BH woman, within the research. The second part of the chapter explains the research aims and methods in more detail. The process of designing the interview questions for all three groups of interviewees is discussed, and the ethical issues raised by the research are identified. The methods applied to locate and select interviewees are described, as well as how the interviews were conducted with each of the three groups. Finally, the challenges and limitations of the research are identified.

Chapter 5 turns to an analysis of the interviewees' views about sexual relationships in the context of PKOs. Liberal use of direct quotations is made in order to ensure that the voices of the interviewees are the primary driver of the analysis. The chapter then analyses the responses to the SGB approach of strongly discouraging sexual relationships. Two competing views emerge. The first view, expressed by the overwhelming majority of interviewees in Group C (peacekeepers) and by one other interviewee (from Group B), was in favour of the SGB policy. The rationale behind this support for the SGB was the perception that local people in post-conflict societies are vulnerable, powerless and traumatised, and live in a highly insecure context. Thus, it was argued that local people need protection from any sexual encounter that may be exploitative, including sexual relationships with peacekeepers. The second view, held by all but one of the respondents in Groups A and B (BH women), disagreed with the SGB 'strong discouragement' provision. Several rationales for this position were voiced, relating to concerns about sexual autonomy, agency, and the sexual rights and freedoms of the participants in such relationships. Concerns were also raised about the patronising and imperial language that the SGB employs, and the stigma such language can attach to local women. It is notable that, despite their institutional views and general support for the SGB, two peacekeepers from Group C expressed similar concerns about the policy. Based on the empirical findings, the chapter concludes that the SGB provision on 'strong discouragement' of sexual relationships relies on a radical feminist perspective, is over-protective and is out of step with international human rights law.

Chapter 6 examines the interviewees' views on whether prostitution in the context of PKOs should be treated as sexual exploitation and consequently prohibited. As with sexual relationships, two distinct views emerged. One view, expressed by a minority of interviewees from all three groups, was supportive of the SGB view of prostitution as a sexually exploitative practice that should be banned. The second view, voiced by the majority of interviewees from all three groups, was that sex with minors, survival sex and trafficking in women for forced prostitution are forms of sexual exploitation that should be banned, while voluntary adult prostitution with fair remuneration is not sexually exploitative and therefore should not be included in the ban. Although consent and age do not appear in the SGB definition of sexual exploitation, for the interviewees they were crucial factors in distinguishing sexual exploitation from prostitution. By ignoring consent and age, the SGB embraces the radical feminist view which focuses on women's structural inequality, doubts the reality of women's sexual agency and is inconsistent with international human rights law. The chapter concludes that the interviewees make a strong case for distinguishing between prostitution and sexual exploitation in the UN policy. The policy should therefore reflect these views by not encompassing adult, voluntary and adequately remunerated prostitution in the definition of sexual exploitation, and therefore bring the policy into step with human rights law.

Chapter 7 concludes that, driven by radical feminist thinking, the SGB definition of sexual exploitation is over-inclusive in its 'strong discouragement' of sexual relationships and prohibition of prostitution, regardless of consent, age and fair remuneration. I argue that, as presently formulated, the SGB undermines women's agency and sexual autonomy, and blurs important distinctions between consensual sex and sexual offences. Because the SGB relies upon and perpetuates negative gender stereotypes and imperial hierarchies, it encourages stigmatisation and discrimination. It casts women as victims, and peacekeepers as sexual predators who cannot treat women as equals. My empirical findings reveal that the 'strong discouragement' of sexual relationships and the ban on prostitution can have very serious negative consequences for the UN, since these provisions may encourage racism, discrimination and stigmatisation. Furthermore, they suggest that imposing a blanket ban on prostitution may not contribute to its prevention or decline, as the UN hopes, but rather push the practice underground. It also has to be acknowledged that prostitution is a viable and legitimate economic option for women in post-conflict societies.

Following on from the perspectives of many interviewees, the book suggests that rather than focusing so heavily on the idea that sexual relationships and prostitution threaten the reputation of the UN, the UN should place more emphasis on reconsidering the breadth of immunities that peacekeepers enjoy while on mission. Such immunities contribute to the fact that peacekeepers committing most sexual offences act with impunity. This creates a general sense of imperial power which plays a significant role in undermining UN credibility in local communities. The book concludes that the SGB rules should treat both local women and peacekeepers as entitled to human rights and freedoms, and should consult both groups in order to reformulate its regulations. Furthermore, the UN should shift its rhetoric from patronising and imperial language to language of agency and gender equality, and view women as capable participants in their own lives whose perspectives should be taken seriously.

Chapter 2
UN Peacekeeping Operations: The Emerging Problem of Sexual Exploitation

2.1 Introduction

This chapter explores the origins and development of Peacekeeping Operations (PKOs)[1] during the Cold War and in the post Cold War period, with a view to providing a context for my discussion of perceived sexual exploitation in current PKOs. The chapter will examine the academic literature on early concepts of PKOs, as well as bedrock principles and mandates. Furthermore, it will highlight the main differences between Cold War traditional peacekeeping and the PKOs developed after the 1990s, as well as challenges that PKOs have faced in their evolution. The chapter will illustrate the multi-dimensional nature of contemporary PKOs with a particular reference to the UN Mission in Bosnia and Herzegovina (UNMIBH). Next, the chapter will develop a profile of peacekeepers and 'beneficiaries of assistance' and outline the types of interactions that have developed between peacekeepers and beneficiaries during PKOs. Lastly, the chapter will introduce the perceived problem of sexual exploitation in order to provide a framework for Chap. 3, which will examine the evolution of UN responses to sexual exploitation in the peacekeeping context through the lenses of feminist theory and international human rights law.

While issues of sexual exploitation were not raised during PKOs in the Cold War period, during the 1990s, as peacekeeping became more ambitious, the first reports expressing concerns about sexual interactions between peacekeepers and beneficiaries appeared in almost all countries where PKOs had been established. Accordingly, UN policies and codes of conduct have sought to more closely regulate relationships between peacekeepers and local populations.

---

[1] I am aware that this term was not used after World War II, but only at the beginning of the 1990s. However, it is used here to refer to all UN Peace Support Operations, from 1948 till the present.

O. Simic, *Regulation of Sexual Conduct in UN Peacekeeping Operations*,
DOI 10.1007/978-3-642-28484-7_2, © Springer-Verlag Berlin Heidelberg 2012

2.2 The Origins and Development of UN Peacekeeping Operations from the League of Nations Through to the End of the Cold War

This section briefly outlines the core principles that were established in the early period of peacekeeping development. In addition, it explores institutional developments related to PKOs, as well as the nature and scope of PKOs. Finally, it outlines the emergence of racial issues in PKOs during the Cold War era, while noting that gender concerns were overlooked.

The practice of 'peace observation' began under the League of Nations (the League), which laid the groundwork for the later development of explicit peace-keeping operations by the UN Security Council. The early peacekeeping initiatives carried out by the League aimed to prevent unrest and violence in the aftermath of World War I.[2] Although the Covenant of the League of Nations did not mention 'peace observation', article 11 authorised the Council of the League to 'take any action that may be deemed wise and effectual to safeguard the peace of nations'.[3] During the 1920s the League exercised its authority by supervising the international administration of the German industrial centre, the Saar region, where French, British and Belgian forces had policing roles.[4] In 1933, with the impending plebiscite in this region and mounting fear from the international community that the vote could provoke political violence, the League deployed 3,300 troops, comprising British and Italian soldiers supported by small contingents of Dutch and Swedish troops.[5] The international troops were guided by two key principles: that the consent of the host state was required for the operation, and that the use of force was permitted only in self-defence.[6] The League also supervised the post-war plebiscite held in the Basin region, supported by international military forces made up of around 3,000 British, French and Italian troops.[7]

Although the League's 'peace observation' efforts enjoyed success, there were also signs of fundamental weakness.[8] For example, in cases where disputants did not consent to intervention, the UN found it difficult to have an impact.[9] Moreover, in the mid 1930s the League proved incapable of organising collective security when its own members flouted their Covenant commitments by invading other

[2] Alan James, *The Politics of Peacekeeping* (London, Chatto and Windus, 1969) 11.

[3] *The Covenant of the League of Nations*, opened for signature 28 June 1919 (entered into force 10 January 1920) art 11.

[4] Alex J. Bellamy et al, *Understanding Peacekeeping* (Polity Press, 2004) 68.

[5] James, above n 2, 76.

[6] Ibid 77.

[7] Ibid 29.

[8] Bellamy et al, above n 4, 69.

[9] James, above n 2, 33.

states.[10] By the end of the 1930s, the League had become completely ineffective, with Japan, the United States of America (US), Germany and the Soviet Union refusing to participate in its activities.

In 1945, following World War II, the UN was established as a successor to the League in a new effort to foster a collective approach to international stability and peace. Consequently, the main purpose of the UN was 'to maintain international peace and security'.[11] The organ to which the UN Charter (the Charter) assigned primary responsibility for maintaining international peace and security was the Security Council.[12] Although the Charter laid down principles for the peaceful resolution of disputes, as well as enforcement action,[13] the term 'peacekeeping' was not used. Yet, PKOs were to become one of the Security Council's most important activities.

The initiative to establish a PKO may come from UN member states or from the Secretary-General. Proposals are then referred to the Security Council for consideration, and missions may be authorised or refused.[14] When the Security Council authorises a mission, it defines an operational mandate by its resolution. In the late 1950s, Secretary-General Dag Hammarskjold[15] referred to 'peacekeeping' as belonging to 'Chapter Six and a Half'[16] of the Charter, placing it between traditional methods of resolving disputes peacefully, such as mediation and fact-finding (Chapter VI), and more forceful action, such as embargoes and military intervention (Chapter VII).

The first PKO, the UN Truce Supervision Organization (UNTSO), was established by the Security Council in the Middle East in 1948.[17] Unarmed military observers continue to this day to help stabilise the region.[18] With the eruption of further crises in the Middle East, the first UN emergency force (UNEF I) was deployed in the region in 1956 after Egypt nationalised the Suez Canal.[19] Both UNTSO's role in implementing Palestinian-Israeli peace agreements and UNEF I's success in defusing the Suez crisis led to further demands for peacekeeping

---

[10] Bellamy et al, above n 4, 70.

[11] *Charter of the United Nations*, opened for signature on 26 June 1945, (entered into force 24 October 1945) art 1.

[12] Ibid Chapter V, art 23.

[13] Ibid Chapter VI and Chapter VII.

[14] Department of Peacekeeping Operations, *United Nations Peacekeeping Operations: Principles and Guidelines* (March 2008) 16.

[15] The former UN Secretary-General 1953–1961.

[16] Terence O'Neill and Nicholas Rees, *United Nations Peacekeeping in the Post-Cold War Era* (Routledge, 2005) 5.

[17] Sec Res 50, S/801, 310th meeting (29 May 1948).

[18] See, United Nations Truce Supervision Organisation, 13 January 2011. rg/en/peacekeeping/missions/untso/.

[19] Agostinho Zacarias, *The United Nations and International Peacekeeping* (1996) 32.

services.[20] UNEF I endorsed the principles for PKOs already laid down by the League, since it carried out its mandate with the consent of the parties to the conflict. Although armed, UNEF I units were only allowed to use their weapons in self-defence and even then with the utmost restraint.[21] Indeed, UNEF I set the scene for future PKOs as it was the first time UN forces were interposed between two warring parties.[22]

Since then, the principle of consent has become a key condition for the deployment of any peacekeeping force, making the deployment of PKOs dependent on acceptance by the host country, not solely on a decision of the Security Council. In any event, it would be unrealistic to maintain a peacekeeping force on a country's territory against its will. The host country is also consulted about the origin of troops contributing to the operation. It has a right to reject forces from particular countries if it believes they might not be impartial or sympathetic to the host country's policies and politics.[23] However, there have been exceptions to the principle of consent. For example, in 1978, the UN Interim Force in Lebanon (UNIFIL) was deployed without the prior agreement of the parties in the earlier conflict.[24]

The second key principle laid down by the League was that peacekeepers cannot use force except in self-defence, 'as an absolutely last resort'.[25] Before 1988, half of all PKOs had consisted only of unarmed military observers. Those operations that were armed were required to respect the principle that shooting is acceptable only in self-defence.[26] They could use a weapon only for protection of themselves, the lives of their fellows, or to protect UN positions and property—not to defend local people. Under no circumstances could peacekeepers initiate an attack.[27] Given this, there is a significant difference between PKOs and traditional military operations. While the goal of a classic military manoeuvre is to defeat the enemy

---

[20] Marrack Goulding, 'The Evolution of United Nations Peacekeeping' (1993) 3 *International Affairs* 451, 453.

[21] UNEF I, Completed Peacekeeping Operations <http://www.un.org/Depts/dpko/dpko/co_mission/unef1backgr1.html>.

[22] Zacarias, above n 19, 30.

[23] International Peace Academy, *Peacekeeper's Handbook* (Pergamon, 1984) 36; United Nations Department of Public Information, *The Blue Helmets: A Review of United Nations Peace-keeping* (United Nations Publications, 1996) 6.

[24] UNIFIL was deployed at the request of the Lebanese government. Israel, the party in the conflict with Lebanon did not agree on UNIFIL deployment. See UNIFIL <http://www.un.org/Depts/dpko/missions/unifil/background.html>.

[25] August Norton and Thomas G. Weiss, 'Rethinking Peacekeeping' in Indar Jit Rikhye and Kjell Skjelsbaek (eds), *The United Nations and Peacekeeping: Results, Limitations and Prospects: the Lessons of 40 Years Experience* (Macmillan and International Peace Academy, 1990) 26; International Peace Academy, above n 23, 38.

[26] Goulding, above n 20, 455.

[27] International Peace Academy, above n 23, 40.

by using 'enforcement and coercion with military troops',[28] PKOs have a very different purpose. They are defined by the UN as 'operations involving military personnel, but without enforcement powers. . .to help maintain or restore international peace and security'.[29] In addition, they are not conducted with the aim of bringing armed conflict between two warring parties to an end, but rather are deployed after ceasefire agreements have been signed by their leaders.[30]

The third and final principle requires peacekeepers to be impartial and independent. Peacekeepers must interpose themselves between former warring parties and therefore are expected to be neutral with respect to the conflict. They must not advance the interests of one party over the other, otherwise they would violate the terms on which the operation has been accepted by the parties.[31]

At the same time as these peacekeeping principles were being consolidated, the institutions which were to manage the operations were developing. In 1961, the Office for Special Political Affairs was created by the Secretary-General.[32] It provided the infrastructure for limited planning of the PKOs undertaken during the Cold War. In 1965, the Special Committee on Peacekeeping Operations was established by the General Assembly to conduct a comprehensive review of everything related to peacekeeping.[33] However, despite these developments, many Cold War-era PKOs were hastily organised responses to crises, rather than deliberately planned and suitably resourced operations. Consequently, they often lacked clear guidance, leadership and objectives.[34] In addition, financial shortfalls, high costs and the difficulties of obtaining consent from belligerents demonstrated to member states that peacekeeping could only effectively function if the three principles endorsed by UNEF I were in place.[35]

In this period, PKOs largely focused on securing an agreed ceasefire between warring parties and controlling the withdrawal of their forces. However, as early as the 1960s, peacekeepers in the Congo and Cyprus[36] began to undertake supplementary tasks. These extra duties included maintaining law and internal security, the training of national armed forces and securing the removal of all foreign military,

[28] Paul F. Diehl, *International Peacekeeping* (Johns Hopkins University Press, 1993) 5.

[29] UN Department of Public Information, above n 23, 4.

[30] Thomas R Mockaitis, *Peace Operations and Intrastate Conflict: the Sword or the Olive Branch?* (Praeger, 1999) 2.

[31] Goulding, above n 20, 454.

[32] UN Department of Public information, Dag Hammarskjöld United Nations Oral History Collection (1995–2007) Dag Hammarskjöld The UN Years (9 January 2011) <http://www.un.org/Depts/dhl/dag/oralhist.htm>.

[33] Secretary-General, *Comprehensive review of the whole question of peacekeeping operations in all their aspects*, GA Res 2006 (XIX), 19th sess,1330th plen mtg (18 February 1965).

[34] O'Neill and Rees, above n 16, 24.

[35] Bellamy et al, above n 4, 73.

[36] ONUC (the Congo 1960–1964), UNFICYP (Cyprus, 1964-).

paramilitary and advisory personnel not under UN command.[37] The peacekeeping operation in the Congo (ONUC) was the first operation to include substantial numbers of civilian personnel to assist in carrying out the mandate.[38] Developing a positive relationship with the local people in conducting these more complex tasks was important for the successful implementation of PKOs. Indeed, as former Secretary-General Hammarskjold said, without a positive relationship with the local people, it would not be possible for PKOs to be sustained.[39] Thus, the mandates and functions of PKOs gradually acquired some human rights-related activities, including the protection of civilians, the maintenance of law and order, and the provision of humanitarian assistance.[40]

The people deployed in PKOs during the Cold War were predominantly men. Between 1957 and 1989, only 0.1% of deployed military personnel were women, while between 5% and 23% of international civilian staff were females.[41] That women participated in such low numbers in peacekeeping operations seemed not to be questioned and there were no efforts to promote larger participation by women. As there was still limited interaction between peacekeepers and local populations, it is perhaps not surprising that the question of gender did not arise. In 1961, the UN troops to be deployed in the Congo were instructed officially that they 'should give protection against acts of violence to all the people, Africans and Europeans alike'.[42] Besides this brief reference to the duty to protect 'all people' and general references to protect civilians, documentation of actual experiences with local populations can not be found in the academic literature on the Cold War era. However, controversies concerning race emerged almost from the beginning of PKOs. For example, racial tensions between peacekeepers in Lebanon were recorded in 1978, when cultural differences led to hostility between 'white' and 'non white' troops in UNIFIL.[43]

---

[37] The UN Department of Public Information, United Nations Operation in the Congo, ONUC Mandate, Completed Peacekeeping Operations (2001) <http://www.un.org/Depts/DPKO/Missions/onucM.htmand> and The UN Department of Public Information, United Nations Peacekeeping Force in Cyprus, Cyprus-UNFICYP Mandate (2007) Department for Peacekeeping Operations (DPKO) 12 September 2007 <http://www.un.org/Depts/dpko/missions/unficyp/mandate.html>.

[38] Goulding, above n 20, 452.

[39] Secretary-General's Final Report on UNEF I, UN Doc A/6627 (12 July 1967) in Katarina Mansson, 'The Forgotten Agenda: Human Rights Protection and Promotion in Cold War Peacekeeping' (2005) 10(3) *Journal of Conflict and Security Law* 379,382.

[40] Ibid.

[41] Louise Olsson, 'Mainstreaming Gender in Multidimensional Peacekeeping: A Field Perspective' (2000) 7(3) *International Peacekeeping* 1, 2.

[42] UN Department of Public Information, above n 32.

[43] Marianne Heiberg, 'Observations of UN Peacekeeping in Lebanon' (Oslo, Norsk Utenrikspolitisk Institutt, 1994) 26.

The majority of PKOs during the Cold War took place in the Middle East.[44] As discussed earlier, troops deployed to these operations were primarily from Western European countries such as Italy, Belgium, Britain, the Netherlands and Sweden. These PKOs also received large public support, and the expectation was that all parties in the conflict would restrain from violence and respect the UN forces.[45] Although between 1948 and 1988 the UN undertook only 18 PKOs,[46] they had accumulated such a positive reputation that the Secretary-General was awarded the Nobel Peace Prize in 1988.[47]

In conclusion, all missions prior to 1990 reinforced the symbolic framework for understanding the UN and its actions confirming commitment to pacific action in response to international disputes. The PKOs launched during the Cold War confirmed three basic principles: the consent of the host state, the use of arms only in self-defence, and impartiality and neutrality. Additionally, peacekeeping mandates gradually shifted the role of peacekeepers from being unarmed military observers to military interposition between warring parties, engaged in monitoring cease fire agreements. These mandates also began to include extra tasks such as maintaining order and internal security, and conducting training for national armed forces. Although they had started to involve more civilian personnel, these operations had few interactions with local populations. While embryonic international institutions were established to manage PKOs, they were mostly organised in an ad hoc fashion and primarily involved military men. In addition, although the question of gender was not raised during this period, racial and cultural concerns emerged. However, these developments during the Cold War era did not adequately prepare the UN for the explosion of PKOs that followed the end of the Cold War.

2.3 The Multi-Dimensional Nature of UN Peacekeeping Operations After 1990: The Case of Bosnia and Herzegovina

At the end of the Cold War there was a proliferation of PKOs across the globe. PKOs rapidly expanded their mandates and started to use diplomatic, civil and military means, including conflict prevention, peace enforcement, peace building, peacemaking and humanitarian operations to restore or maintain peace.[48] The 1990s also marked a new era in international relations and led to an expansion of

---

[44] Bellamy et al, above n 4, 72.

[45] Larry Fisk and John Schellenberg (eds), *Patterns of Conflict, Paths to Peace* (University of Toronto Press, 2000) 81.

[46] O'Neill and Rees, above n 16, 30.

[47] Robert Rubinstein, 'Intervention and Culture: An Anthropological Approach to Peace Operations' (2005) 36(4) *Security Dialogue* 527, 535.

[48] UK Joint Doctrine and Concepts Centre (ed), *The Military Contributions to Peace Support Operations* (UK Ministry of Defence, 2004) 13.

local, intrastate conflicts that have posed greater problems for PKOs to manage than earlier more conventional wars. Many of these conflicts have taken place within state borders, and have targeted primarily civilian populations.[49] However, some scholars argue that 'these intrastate conflicts are not actually new', and that what is new is the extent of UN involvement in internal disputes and the adaptation of PKOs through their configuration and methods.[50] Thus, the UN framework that was established to respond to the interstate conflicts that prevailed before the 1990s faced a number of new challenges.

With the end of the Cold War not only have PKOs multiplied, but the geographic focus of operations has also shifted. The earlier focus on the Middle East has now extended towards Africa and Europe and, to a lesser degree, to Central America and Asia. As a result of the internal nature of many conflicts, peacekeeping has become more complex and broader in scope. Since 1990, more than 60 PKOs have been established, many of which were authorised in a very short period of time during the mid 1990s.[51] The Security Council broadened the traditional scope and mandate of peacekeepers' activities, aiming to adjust them to changes on the ground. As a result, peacekeeping forces since the end of the Cold War have been expected to perform a wide variety of tasks that had not been expected from them earlier. For example, the UN Observer Mission in El Salvador (ONUSAL) established in 1991 was the first mission that sought not only to stop conflict, but also to address the root causes of the civil war.[52] Thus, PKOs have evolved to be different from the traditional monitoring mandates carried out in the Cold War era when peacekeepers had 'no direct peace building responsibilities'.[53] The transformation of PKOs was recognised in 1992 by Secretary-General Boutros Boutros-Ghali who welcomed the 'increase and broadening of the tasks of peace-keeping operations'.[54]

Boutros-Ghali broke down peacekeepers' new tasks into four main components: preventive diplomacy, peacemaking, peacekeeping and post-conflict peace building.[55] Boutros-Ghali described peace building as 'action to identify and support

---

[49] Since the end of World War II, 16.5 million people have died in internal conflicts, compared with 3.3 million in interstate wars. Sandra Whitworth, *Men, Militarism and UN Peacekeeping: A Gendered Analysis* (Lynne Rienner Publishers, 2004) 38.

[50] Georges Abi-Saab, 'United Nations Peacekeeping Old and New: An Overview of the Issues' in Daniel Warner (ed), *New Dimensions of Peacekeeping* (Martinus Nijhoff Publishers, 1995) 8.

[51] While 18 peacekeeping operations were deployed between 1948 and 1988, UN troops were deployed 20 times between 1988 and 1993. For details on all peacekeeping operations since 1948, see: Department for Peacekeeping Operations, List of operations: 1948–2010 <http://www.un.org/en/peacekeeping/list.shtml>.

[52] Beatrice Pouligny, *Peace Operations Seen From Below: UN Missions and Local People* (Kumarian Press, 2006) 3.

[53] Lakhdar Brahimi et al, *Report of the Panel on the United Nations Peace Operations*, UN Doc A/55/305-S/2000/809 (21 August 2000), para 17.

[54] Boutros Boutros-Ghali, *An Agenda for Peace Preventive Diplomacy, Peacemaking and Peace-keeping*, UN Doc A/47/277-S/24111 (17 June 1992), para 49.

[55] Ibid para 5.

structures which will tend to strengthen and solidify peace in order to avoid a relapse into conflict'.[56] He outlined some of the actions that were involved, including: disarming the previously warring parties and the restoration of order, possible destruction of weapons, repatriating refugees, monitoring elections, reforming or strengthening governmental institutions, advisory and training support for security personnel, or promoting formal and informal processes of political participation.[57] PKOs have become complex and multidimensional, involving a large number of different stakeholders, including not only militaries but also international and local non-governmental organisations (NGOs) and state actors.

With the expansion of intrastate conflicts, the three basic peacekeeping principles have been challenged. Since 1990, PKOs have frequently been deployed in situations where peace has not yet been consolidated and where military contingents might consider it 'operationally justified', or find themselves 'morally compelled', to use force.[58] During the Cold War peacekeepers only had to deal with two parties to conflicts, but their successors are often confronted with several parties to a conflict. As a result, one of the core principles, the use of force only in self-defence, has come under scrutiny. Since peacekeepers can only use force in self-defence, they do not have the capacity to protect civilians from grave human rights violations. The cases of genocide in Rwanda and Bosnia and Herzegovina (BH) are clear examples where the withdrawal of peacekeepers in the midst of conflict left the civilian populations unprotected and in the hands of perpetrators. As a result, local people and many international commentators have criticised peacekeepers for abandoning thousands of civilians who were slaughtered by paramilitary armies in these two countries.[59] On the other hand, if peacekeepers intervene, they may be accused of promoting the interests of one party over those of others, as happened in the Congo.[60]

Consequently, the principle of impartiality has also been questioned. Acting as an interposing force between warring parties, peacekeepers cannot take one side in the conflict. Indeed, favouring one party over the other would contravene the core nature of the peacekeeping role. Yet, in 1994 during the war in BH, the North

[56] Ibid paras 20–21.

[57] Ibid para 55.

[58] Ibid 11.

[59] See for example, Christopher H. Smith et al, Hearing before the Subcommittee on International Operations and Human Rights: 'The Betrayal of Srebrenica: Why Did the Massacre Happen? Will it Happen Again?'105th congress, 2nd sess (31 March 1998) <http://commdocs.house.gov/committees/intlrel/hfa49268.000/hfa49268_0f.htm>, and Payne et al, 'Remembering the Victims of the Genocide that Occurred in 1994 in Rwanda and Pledging to Work to Ensure That Such an Atrocity Does Not Take Place Again', H.Con.Res.406, 108th congress, 2nd sess (22 July 2004) <http://thomas.loc.gov/home/gpoxmlc108/hc406_ih.xml>.

[60] Zacarias, above n 19, 18.

Atlantic Treaty Organisation (NATO), as a partner of the UN mission in BH, openly stood next to Bosnian Muslims in order to defend them from Serb attacks.[61]

Lastly, the principle of host state consent has often become difficult to achieve and may be subject to manipulation by local parties. A party may give consent and then withdraw it when the PKO no longer serves its interests.[62] The reliability of consent may depend on whether it is given freely, or reluctantly as a result of external pressure.[63]

These changes were followed by institutional developments as well. In 1992, the UN Secretariat was restructured and the Department for Peacekeeping Operations (DPKO) was established to develop greater institutional capacity for planning and managing peacekeeping.[64] In consultation with the Department of Humanitarian Affairs (DHA) and the Department of Political Affairs (DPA), the DPKO is involved in planning the operation and implementation of peacekeeping mandates once they have been determined by the Security Council.[65] After the Security Council passes a resolution, it is then submitted to the DPKO, which tries to secure offers of contingents from member states.[66] The increasing ambitions of PKOs have made it more difficult for the UN to manage operations and mandates more flexibly, and to adapt to rapid change. The Security Council has, on some occasions, deployed PKOs in dangerous circumstances, before the DPKO has been able to obtain commitments from member states for the forces necessary to conduct an operation.[67] These new changes also affected the cost of PKOs, which soared in the 1990s.[68]

Known also as 'the second generation'[69] of PKOs, post-Cold War operations not only include military contingents, but also an increasing number of civilians who are deployed on missions by the UN or by other international or regional agencies.[70] Civilians can play different roles in PKOs. They may be members of

---

61 Ibid 19–20.

62 Brahimi et al, above n 53, para 48.

63 Ibid.

64 Bellamy et al, above n 4, 49.

65 Peter Voetmann, 'The Structure, Planning and Execution of UN Peace Operations' (The Royal Norwegian Ministry of Foreign Affairs, 1997) in Monograph No 10 on Conflict Management, Peacekeeping and Peacebuilding <http://www.iss.co.za/pubs/monographs/No10/Contents.html>.

66 Zacarias, above n 19, 26–27.

67 Brahimi, above n 53, para 56.

68 For more information on costs of peacekeeping operations see, United Nations Peacekeeping Operations (January 2011) <http://www.un.org/depts/dpko/dpko/bnote.htm>.

69 After the end of the Cold War the proliferation of peacekeeping activities required new categorisation and they were divided into: traditional, or first-generation, or Cold War peacekeeping; and new, or second-generation, or multidimensional peacekeeping. See, Mari Katayanagi, *Human Rights Functions of United Nations Peacekeeping Operations* (Martinus Nijhoff Publishers, 2002) 42.

70 For example, in 1989 there were 11,121 military, police and civilian personnel deployed in peacekeeping operations and the annual budget was $230.4 million. In December 1994, 77,783 personnel were deployed, while in 2006 the number was 97,007. The estimated total cost of operations from 1948 to 30 June 2010 was about $69 billion. For more see: United Nations Peacekeeping Operations (January 2011) <http://www.un.org/Depts/dpko/dpko/bnote.htm>.

UN civilian police, civilian administrative personnel, and logistical or technical support staff. They may also play significant roles as human rights experts, working with refugees and minorities, or assisting local governments in rebuilding communities. They work on many different projects related to the reconstruction of post-conflict societies. As a result, PKOs have started to balance military functions with other major tasks, such as making provision for an election in Namibia or supervising human rights compliance in El Salvador.[71]

The UN Protection Force in the former Yugoslavia (UNPROFOR) was an early example of these new developments.[72] In 1992, UNPROFOR was the largest UN operation and deployed tens of thousands of UN peacekeepers who worked alongside various regional and international governmental agencies and NGOs.[73] UNPROFOR included peacekeepers from 32 countries.[74] Its mandate was stretched to cover the five republics of the former Yugoslavia: Croatia, BH, Macedonia, Montenegro and Serbia. Its mandate in BH was particularly complex since peacekeepers were deployed while hostilities were still raging. The dire situation in BH also prompted far more ambitious and expansive involvement of the UN than in any previous PKO. More than 100,000 foreigners, a dozen UN agencies and over 200 NGOs were estimated to be part of the humanitarian operation.[75] By the middle of 1995, almost two-thirds of all peacekeepers in the world were deployed in the region, with the number of troops peaking at about 22,500.[76]

In BH, the military component of peacekeeping forces played a vital role in providing both material assistance and security to local authorities to run elections.[77] They also assisted internally displaced persons (IDPs) and refugees to return home. The mission also included a strong civilian component, which undertook elements of civilian policing and humanitarian work.[78] The peace building activities in PKOs are mainly carried out by agencies within the UN system, such as the World Food Programme (WFP), the UN Development Programme (UNDP), and the UN Children's Fund (UNICEF), and specialised agencies, such as the World Health Organisation (WHO) and the UN Educational,

---

[71] UN Transitional Assistance Group in Namibia (UNTAG, April 1989–March 1990) and United Nations Observer Group in El Salvador (ONUSAL, July 1991–April 1995).

[72] UNPROFOR, U.N.Doc.S/RES/743 (1992).

[73] Goulding, above n 20, 456.

[74] United Nations Department of Public Information, Former Yugoslavia-UNPROFOR (31 August 1996) <http://www.un.org/Depts/dpko/dpko/co_mission/unprof_b.htm>.

[75] Peter Andreas, *Blue Helmets and Black Markets: The Business of Survival in the Siege of Sarajevo* (Cornell University Press, 2008) 1.

[76] William J. Durch and James A. Schear (eds), 'Faultlines: UN Operations in the Former Yugoslavia', in William J. Durch and James A. Schear (eds), *UN Peacekeeping, American Politics, and the Uncivil Wars of the 1990s* (New York, St. Martin's, 1996).

[77] Elizabeth M. Cousens, 'Building Peace in Bosnia' in Elizabeth M. Cousens and Chetan Kumar (eds), *Peacebuilding as Politics: Cultivating Peace in Fragile Societies* (Lynne Rienner, 2000) 121.

[78] Bellamy et al above n 4, 6.

Scientific and Cultural Organisation (UNESCO).[79] In order to conduct their activities, these agencies employ local people to assist in the implementation of their projects. As a result, local populations interact in many different ways with peacekeepers, including as their employees and as beneficiaries of the UN humanitarian projects. This development is in stark contrast to operations before 1990, when peacekeepers had very limited contact with host populations.

Chapter VI of the UN Charter anticipates a possible role for regional organisations to contribute to peace and security.[80] For example, NATO[81] was given a mandate to implement the military aspects of the Dayton Peace Agreement in BH after the Dayton Peace Agreement was signed in 1995. The NATO-led multinational force, called the Implementation Force (IFOR), launched the largest military operation ever authorised by the Security Council.[82] Initially, IFOR consisted of some 60,000 solders, predominantly men.[83] Regional organisations, such as NATO, employed a large number of civilians who assisted in the implementation of their mandates. In these cases, civilians had their own command, rules and codes of conduct while working alongside peacekeepers.

While the intrastate conflicts that prevailed after 1990 raised new concerns within the UN regarding effective responses, the high public expectations for the UN's successful management of post-conflict transitions did not change. However, more recently, perceived shortcomings in UN management have led to wide swings in public opinion about PKOs. High expectations have been replaced by deflated assessments of the capacity of the UN to cope successfully with post-conflict situations.[84] The extent of public concern may be explained by the euphoria that was associated with the relatively straight-forward peacekeeping management during the Cold War. Some scholars argue that expectations of people are often greater than what might be reasonably expected from the UN when deployed in field operations.[85] Yet the UN's ability to act is influenced by the international environment and political commitment on the part of member states, not only to

[79] A.B. Featherson, *Towards a Theory of United Nations Peacekeeping* (St. Martin's Press, Macmillan, 1994) 132.

[80] UN Charter, above n 10, article 33.

[81] North Atlantic Treaty Organisation established under the North Atlantic Treaty (1945).

[82] Operation Joint Endeavour (IFOR), Sec Res 1031, 3607th mtg, (1995). IFOR and its legal successor, Stabilization Force (SFOR), operated under Chapter VII of the Charter that gives robust rules of engagement for the use of force if necessary to accomplish its mission and protect itself. See, 'The situation in Bosnia and Herzegovina', Sec Re. 1088, 3723rd mtg, UN Doc S/RES/1088 (1996) and Chapter VII of the UN Charter on 'Action with respect to threats to the peace, breaches of the peace, and acts of aggression'.

[83] Bellamy et al, above n 4, 175.

[84] Yasushi Akashi, Special Representative of the Secretary-General of the United Nations Protection Force for the former Yugoslavia in Daniel Warner (ed), *New Dimensions of Peacekeeping* (Martinus Nijhoff Publishers, 1995) ix.

[85] O'Neill and Rees, above n 16, 192.

agree on action, but also to provide the resources for successful accomplishment of its missions.[86]

Kjell Skjelsbæk underlines how important it is to know what can be expected from peacekeeping before making judgments. He cautions that peacekeeping operations should not be seen as a sign of the end of a conflict, but rather 'the beginning of the opportunity to resolve it'.[87] The ambitious aims of the UN Charter may also create unrealistic expectations about the effectiveness of PKOs. As Kjell emphasises, peacekeeping cannot prevent conflict 'if…parties to a conflict are determined to use arms'.[88]

With respect to gender representation in PKOs, there has been an increase in women's participation since 1990. As early as 1993, 11 out of the 19 operations had a significant presence of women, with 33% of civilian staff being female.[89] In 1994, UN officials indicated for the first time that the UN would welcome more women soldiers.[90] However, even now very few women are in either military peacekeeping forces or civilian police contingents. In September 2010, of the 13,075 UN police officers, only 1,287 were women, and of 85,986 soldiers, only 2,068 were women.[91] Although, for example, almost 50% of peacekeepers in the mission in Guatemala (MINUGUA) in 1995 were women, they were largely concentrated in organising the election and in human rights monitoring.[92] Thus, while the percentage of women in PKOs is rising, women mainly serve in administrative, information, public relations and secretarial positions. Very few women occupy high-level professional and policy positions.[93]

In sum, since the Cold War, PKOs have expanded well beyond purely military endeavours and have become multidimensional interventions. As I have shown in the case of BH, the PKOs since the post-Cold War era have involved a large number of civilians to help carry out many aspects of the operations, including humanitarian assistance, minority return projects and other peace building activities. While women's participation in PKOs has increased, they are likely to occupy low level secretarial or administrative positions within the mission, and policymaking is still very much a male domain. In addition, while operations prior to the 1990s

---

[86] Ibid.

[87] Norton and Weiss, above n 24, 25.

[88] Ibid 53.

[89] UN Division for the Advancement of Women, 'Women 2000' (Department of Policy Coordination and Sustainable Development UN New York, 1995) 4.

[90] Janet Beilstein, 'The Expanding Role of Women in United Nations Peacekeeping' in Lois Ann Lorentzen and Jennifer Turpin (eds.), *The Women and War Reader* (New York University Press, 1998) 140, 143.

[91] UN Department for Peacekeeping Operations, 'Gender Statistics by Mission: For the month of September 2010' (14 October 2010) <http://www.un.org/en/peacekeeping/contributors/gender/2010gender/sept10.pdf>.

[92] Beilstein, above n 90, 140.

[93] Ibid 141.

performed largely military functions, post-Cold War operations have involved more direct interactions with local populations as a result of peace-building activities.

2.4 The Profile of Peacekeepers: Who Are They?

There has been a lack of research on the profiles of individuals who perform peacekeeping tasks. The following section provides an overview of peacekeepers: their backgrounds, training and gender.

The UN does not have its own army. National armies and state police forces are the sources of uniformed personnel required by the UN for the purpose of PKOs. The UN Charter provides for member states to enter into binding agreements with the Security Council under which they commit themselves to provide troops.[94] As a result, PKOs rely on member states to voluntarily provide the necessary personnel, types of forces, equipment and assistance.[95] Peacekeepers are therefore contributed by their nation states to keep or maintain the peace in conflict or post-conflict societies.

The idea initially was that the three main components of peacekeeping forces—military, police and civilian[96]—should represent nations from all around the world, and create one multiethnic and multiracial force by combining cultural, linguistic and educational knowledge.[97] It was thought that the larger the number of countries that participated in PKOs, the greater the range of experiences and cultural differences among peacekeepers would be. Although in the 1990s France and the United Kingdom had the highest number of peacekeepers, other countries such as Jordan, Nepal and Nigeria made sizable contributions as well.[98] Indeed, the multinational nature of UN forces had many advantages, especially when it came to language barriers. For example, in the Western Sahara, the South American contingent communicated easily with the local Shwari people who speak Spanish.[99]

Some analysts argue that in practice this principle of peacekeepers' diversity undermined the effectiveness of PKOs and raised racial tensions. For example,

---

94 UN Charter, art 43 (1).

95 Ibid art 43 (2).

96 Monica Blagescu and Schnabel Albrecht (eds), 'Reforming UN Peace Operations, New Challenges for Peacekeeping Training'. Proceedings of the 2001 Annual Meeting of the International Association of Peacekeeping Training Centres' (United Nations University, 2002) 2.

97 Frederick Fleitz, *Peacekeeping Fiascos of the 1990s: Causes, Solutions and US Interests* (Praeger, 2002) 61.

98 Rosalyn Higgins, 'The New United Nations and Former Yugoslavia' (1994) 69 *International Affairs* 465, 472.

99 Deborah Hart, *The Realism of Peace: George Gittoes* (Darwin, Museum & Art Gallery of the Northern Territory 1995) 35.

when soldiers of colour or an ethnic minority find themselves among white soldiers, they will often be chosen over white soldiers for the most difficult and life-threatening tasks.[100] As Whitworth argues, when it comes to actual danger, the tight-knit military unit often breaks down along racial lines.[101] In 1996, when Fijian and Ghanaian peacekeeping troops met at a sporting event, weapons had to be impounded to avoid the possibility of open warfare between them.[102] Further, the UN Peacekeeping Force in Cyprus (UNFICYP) excluded troops from African and Asian countries, with some sources alleging that Greek Cypriots vetoed Third World troops, especially Africans, for racial reasons.[103] This illustrates the lengths to which the UN has been forced to go to exclude contingents that are considered 'objectionable' by warring parties, pursuant to respecting one of the bedrock principles for deployment of contingents—consent of the host country.[104]

As a result of recent intractable conflicts associated with PKOs, developed countries are increasingly reluctant to volunteer their armies since the operations can be extended and unsafe, with the likelihood of loss of life. Increased peace-keeping deaths, hostage-taking, kidnapping, illegal arrests and detention have raised concerns in the UN system as a whole.[105] That peacekeeping has become a demanding and even dangerous activity is demonstrated by the fact that between 1990 and 1996, 1,500 peacekeepers died while serving on missions.[106] For this reason, countries which voluntarily contribute their personnel to serve within PKOs are reasonably concerned about the safety and the welfare of their soldiers.[107]

Despite these changes, developing countries are now more willing to contribute forces to PKOs than developed countries.[108] In contrast to the Cold War era, when developed countries provided the bulk of the troops, over the last few years 77% of the troops in military contingents have been contributed by developing nations. Attracted by money and the desire to play a more prominent role in international affairs, they have continued to contribute troops and participate in operations.[109]

---

[100] Janette Beals et al, 'The Prevalence of Posttraumaic Stress Disorder Among American Indian Vietnam veterans: Disparities and Context', (2002) 15(2) *Journal of Traumatic Stress* 89 in Sandra Whitworth, above n 59, 168.

[101] Ibid 168.

[102] O'Neill and Rees, above n 16, 25.

[103] Fleitz, above n 97, 61.

[104] Ibid.

[105] Report of the Secretary-General, *Safety and Security of United Nations Personnel*, GA, 55th sess, UN Doc A/55/494 (2000).

[106] UN Chronicle, Fifty Unforeseen Years (1998) 12 July 2007 <http://findarticles.com/p/articles/mi_m1309/is_3_35/ai_54259331>. As of 29 May 2010, the UN has recorded 2,700 peacekeeper fatalities since1948. See International Day of UN Peacekeepers (29 May 2010) <htp://www.un.org/en/events/peacekeepersday/2010/>.

[107] United Nations, *The Blue Helmets: A Review of United Nations Peacekeeping* (United Nations Publications, 1996) 8.

[108] O'Neill and s Rees, above n 16, 195.

[109] Brahimi, above n 54, 17.

For example, as of February 2010, the top five contributing countries were Bangladesh, Pakistan, India, Nigeria and Egypt.[110] However, because they lack financial resources, troops from developing countries can lack training and therefore be less prepared for the demands of multidimensional peacekeeping, which consequently has an impact on overall performance in peace operations.[111] Moreover, the low standard of training of some contingents can also affect operational efficiency and cause friction among peacekeepers.[112]

One of the challenges is to establish a basic peacekeepers' profile to clarify training requirements. For example, one of the on-going dilemmas is whether training should focus on infrequent traditional operations, or the more frequent asymmetrical armed conflicts.[113] Reflecting the lack of a standard profile, peacekeepers have self-identified variously as 'helpers in uniforms', 'leaders and educators', 'careerists', 'martial adventurers' or 'male warriors' with a strong masculine image oriented towards combat.[114]

The fact that the majority of peacekeepers are militarily trained men is likely to raise questions about the difference between military and peacekeeper masculinities.[115] For example, permission to use a weapon only in self-defence could be problematic for some soldiers and perceived as a serious limitation. Soldiers are required to adjust to the specific physical and psychological needs of peacekeeping, which 'calls for different response from the one he has been trained to make'.[116] Also, many soldiers have never been trained in anything but warfare and may therefore be wary and insecure about engaging with the non-military communities they need to protect.[117] Instead of facing 'the enemy', peacekeepers must deal with the local population and be comfortable with the different norms of indigenous behaviour.[118]

Although peacekeepers are encouraged to 'treat the inhabitant of the host country with respect, courtesy and consideration',[119] interactions with locals have

---

[110] United Nations Peacekeeping Fact Sheet, <http://www.un.org/en/peacekeeping/documents/factsheet.pdf>.

[111] O'Neill and Rees, above n 16, 2.

[112] O'Neill and Rees, above n 16, 25.

[113] Brent C. Bankus and William R. Flavin, 'Training US Army Peacekeepers' (2004) 15 (1) *Small Wars and Insurgencies* 129.

[114] Maren Tomfrorde, 'Motivation and Self-Image among German peacekeepers' (2005) 12 *International Peacekeeping* 576, 584.

[115] In 2010, only 2.42% of military peacekeepers were females. See, DPKO/OMA Statistical Report on Female Military and Police Personnel in UN Peacekeeping Operations Prepared for the 10th Anniversary of the SCR 1325 <http://www.un.org/en/peacekeeping/documents/gender_scres1325_chart.pdf>.

[116] International Peace Academy, above n 23, 38.

[117] Tomfrorde, above n 114, 578.

[118] Ibid.

[119] United Nations, *Ten Rules Code of Personal Conduct For Blue Helmets* (1997) para 3.

recently been strongly discouraged.[120] For example, Dutch peacekeepers reported that during their pre-deployment training they were warned by their trainer not to have contact with the local population in BH. When explaining the reasons for this, the trainer used negative stereotypes, describing Balkan people as 'barbaric and uncivilized'[121] and representing Balkan men as aggressive.[122] Thus, instead of being trained for daily tasks in the UN mission, according to the interviewed peacekeepers, they were prepared to encounter 'aggressive' locals.[123] Likewise, a Canadian soldier who served in Somalia reported that 'interactions with the population in Somalia were discouraged to the point of threats of fines and jail. If you were caught giving candy, a bottle of water, or anything to the Somali locals, you would be fined or jailed'.[124] It is notable that such messages are quite different from the earlier UN thinking that imagined the positive contributions that would be made through interactions of multiethnic peacekeepers and local people.

With respect to gender, peacekeepers bring attitudes, and cultural and moral ideas about gender from their home countries. Once deployed, these attitudes and norms may be challenged. The importance of ensuring respect for local women in peace building activities has become a concern and is now incorporated in pre-deployment training for peacekeepers. For example, the DPKO now includes an obligatory gender component in pre-deployment training for members of military contingents. Pre-deployment training tends to encourage peacekeepers to respect the cultural context of the country in which they will be serving, and to endeavour not to disrupt its norms.[125]

Female peacekeepers are under-represented in all PKO components.[126] The biggest discrepancy between male and female participation is in military contingents. Although article 8 of the Charter calls for equal participation of men and women in the work of the organisation, almost no women have served in the military contingents of peacekeeping operations.[127] The number of women in PKOs is, of course, conditional upon their status and representation in the armed forces in

---

[120] Evelyn Leopold, 'UN Bans Peacekeepers from Sex with Congolese', *Global Policy Forum* (10 February 2005) <http://globalpolicy.org/security/issues/congo/2005/0210nonfrat.htm>.

[121] J.C.H. Bloom et al, 'Srebrenica a 'safe' area: reconstruction, background, consequences and analyses of the fall of a safe area.' See Chapter 8 Peacekeeping and humanitarian action 'Stereotypes and Balkan Man' (Netherlands Institute of War Documentation, 2002).

[122] Ibid.

[123] Ibid.

[124] Rubinstein, above n 47, 541.

[125] Ibid 17.

[126] Judith Hick Stiehm, 'Peacekeeping and Peace Research: Men's and Women's Work' (1997) 18 *Women & Politics* 34.

[127] 'The United Nations shall place no restrictions on the eligibility of men and women to participate in any capacity and under conditions of equality in its principal and subsidiary organs'. Art 8 of UN Charter, above n 10.

their home countries.[128] In addition, the requirements that peacekeepers have to fulfil in order to participate in PKOs are often extensive and difficult to achieve for women, including the need to have senior job experience, to leave family members to go abroad and, in some cases, to gain approval from their husband or male family member.[129] A somewhat better situation applies in the case of civilian police secondments to PKOs, as the number of women participating is slightly higher than in the military. In fact, as Stiehm argues, there is a correlation between the type of mission and the number of women deployed: the larger the civilian component of the mission, the more women.[130]

Even though women comprise 30% of the international civilian staff of PKOs, they are mainly concentrated in junior posts such as administrative or service positions.[131] Despite the obstacles women face, there have been improvements which aim to establish policies that advance women in PKOs. Out of the 16 PKOs in progress in 2010, gender advisors or gender units were established in 10 missions, and the other 6 missions had gender focal points responsible for encouraging greater participation of women in all aspects of peacekeeping.[132] In 2010 the DPKO also developed guidelines that reiterate the necessity of increasing women's military roles in field missions.[133]

The previous discussion underlined the main characteristics of peacekeepers and the challenges they face in modern-day PKOs. With the evolution of multi-dimensional PKOs, peacekeepers from around the world gather and work in environments that are culturally and ethnically diverse. This has some advantages, but also weaknesses, such as the possibility of increased racial tensions and mistreatment of local women. In order to address the tensions that diversity can engender, various training packages have been developed which are of particular importance for peacekeepers from developing countries where training resources are scarce. Although there have been efforts to increase the participation of women in PKOs, female peacekeepers are still under-represented. Finally, despite the earlier recognition of the importance of developing positive relationships with local people ('beneficiaries'), peacekeepers have been gradually discouraged from having any contact with them.

---

[128] UN Department for Peacekeeping Operation Unit, above n 94, 3.

[129] Nadine Puechguirbal, 'The Feminine Face of United Nations CIVPOL in Haiti'. Paper disseminated during the course on Gender in Peacekeeping Operations at the UN University for Peace in 2004, 1, 4.

[130] Stiehm, above n 126, 34.

[131] Camille Pampell Conaway, 'United Nations Reform: Improving Peace Operations by Advancing the Role of Women'. Report from an expert group meetings in New York and Washington DC, November 14–16, 2006, 12.

[132] United Nations, Gender and Peacekeeping Operations. <http:www.un.org/Depts/dpko/gender/index.htm>.

[133] DPKO/DFS, 'Guidelines: Integrating a gender perspective into the work of the United Nations military in peacekeeping operations', March 2010 www.un.org/en/peacekeeping/.../dpko_dfs_gender_military_perspective.pdf.

2.5 The Profile of Beneficiaries and UN Peacekeeping Operations: Who Are Peacekeepers Protecting?

Unlike peacekeepers, who are predominantly trained military men, the beneficiaries of PKOs are mostly civilians. Intrastate conflicts are fought largely within local communities and thus have a severe impact on civilians. Those who are the intended beneficiaries of peacekeeping protection, namely local populations, refugees and IDPs, of which the majority are women and girls, endure severe social and economic hardships during conflicts. In the aftermath, these people regularly find themselves in extreme poverty while law and order continue to break down.

The post-conflict context is marked by weak economic structures, often coupled with sharp ethnic or religious tensions, particularly where the conflict has not resulted in a clear victory for any party.[134] There are often large numbers of weapons left behind from a war within local communities, and often these are in the possession of former combatants. High levels of corruption and organised crime, including trafficking in humans, are also common features of post-conflict societies.[135] Thus, the intended beneficiaries of peacekeeping are often still at high risk and may also be in physical as well as psychological need.

Some beneficiaries may be in the process of returning to their pre-war homes and reintegrating with groups that may include their former enemies.[136] Many civilians will have experienced severe human rights abuses such as ethnic cleansing, genocide, torture, or systematic rape. They may have been used as human shields by combatants, who may have forced them to leave their family members, community support networks, homes and assets.[137] Yet despite these adversities, local people do try to rebuild their lives. While some try to find ways to leave the country and search for better futures elsewhere, the majority remain where they are. Due to dire socio-economic circumstances, most women are jobless and ready to do any work on offer. Discrimination against women in the economy and labour market, coupled with restricted access of women to resources, increases their domestic burden of responsibilities and places a heavier workload upon them. They are especially vulnerable as they are more likely than men to lack livelihood options to generate an income.[138]

---

[134] Brahimi, above n 54, 5.

[135] Jan-Erik Lane, *Globalization and Politics: Promises and Dangers* (Ashgate Publishing, 2006) 73.

[136] Bellamy et al, above n 4, 236.

[137] Margaret Vogt, 'The Impact of Peacekeeping Operations on Local Populations'. Paper presented at the Conference on Building capacities for Peacekeeping and Women's Dimensions in Peace Processes, Santiago, 4–5 November 2002.

[138] Ibid 4.; Paul Higate, 'Gender and Peacekeeping Case Studies: The Democratic Republic of the Congo and Sierra Leone' (Institute for Security Studies, 2004) 91 Monograph Series 15; Paul Higate, 'Peacekeepers, Masculinities, and Sexual Exploitation' (2007) 10 (1) *Men and Masculinities* 99.

In such situations, the arrival of UN peacekeeping forces provides opportunities for income generation by employing local people in their aid projects.[139] Because of the poverty in post-conflict countries, socio-economic inequalities between local people and peacekeepers are readily apparent. Some women may be lucky enough to be employed with the PKO, which secures economic survival for themselves and their families. Frequently, local communities come to depend on the UN and humanitarian organisations for job opportunities, and on the spending of peacekeepers to sustain local economies.[140] Whitworth gives an example of Cambodian women who reported that many aspects of their lives had improved since the mission was established in their country, such as freedom of association and the emergence of an indigenous women's movement within the country.[141] Likewise, in the Congo, local people agreed that the presence of the UN Mission in the Democratic Republic of Congo (MONUC) was absolutely essential, not only for the peace process, but also for providing employment opportunities for locals and stimulating the presence and activism of civil society groups.[142]

Civil society organisations play a vital role in the reconstruction of post-conflict societies and are often directly involved in post-conflict rehabilitation. Often they are led by women who are particularly active and concerned with humanitarian work.[143] In many cases, women's organisations work together to build networks across the divides that led to the conflict and undertake projects aimed at establishing conditions necessary for justice and security, and national and regional peace.[144] Together with local and international NGOs, they are a powerful source of social capital for reconstruction and reconciliation. The benefit of working with women is demonstrated by the case of BH, where SFOR successfully recruited women's NGOs to mobilise local women to collect illegally held weapons from war veterans in their families and to educate children on how to avoid landmines.[145]

Violence towards women tends to escalate in both size and variety after conflicts. In particular, women living in the aftermath of conflict are likely to suffer from an increase in domestic violence. Men who return from battle frequently turn their aggression from the war zone to their families and communities. As Nikolic-Ristanovic argues, the majority of men are jobless after returning from war and they

[139] Paul Higate and Marsha Henry, 'Engendering (In)security in Peace Support Operations' (2004) 35 (4) *Security Dialogue* 482, 484.

[140] Ibid.

[141] Whitworth, above n 49, 66.

[142] Paul Higate, 'Gender and Peacekeeping Case Studies: The Democratic Republic of the Congo and Sierra Leone', above n 138, 15.

[143] Cynthia Cockburn and Dubravka Zarkov (eds), *The Postwar Moment: Militaries, Masculinities and International Peacekeeping* (2002) 105.

[144] Dyan Mazurana, Angela Raven-Roberts and Jane Parpart (eds), *Gender, Conflict and Peace-keeping* (Rowman and Littlefield Publishers, 2005) 2.

[145] Ibid 107.

may increase their consumption of alcohol, so domestic violence increases.[146] Men's dependence on women's income can also be a cause of frustration and perceived humiliation for men. Despite these difficulties, women are often the backbone of their communities in post-conflict societies. They bear a disproportionate burden of managing post-conflict relationships with war-traumatised family members and there is often a disproportionate number of households where the family heads are women.[147]

While shouldering the bulk of caring responsibilities, the conflict may also open new opportunities for women that did not previously exist.[148] Women often start building networks to work for peace during conflict, as women are drawn together by common experiences, needs and goals.[149] For example, BH 'saw an expansion of women's public roles and responsibilities during conflict' due to the challenge of surviving in the absence of men.[150] As Korac argues, the conflict in the former Yugoslavia contributed to the emergence of women's groups in the post-conflict environment.[151] Thus, it is important to consider women beneficiaries not only as victims of armed conflict, but also as actors. Focusing on their empowerment should be an integral part of post-conflict peace building.[152]

In conclusion, beneficiaries are local populations affected by the war. The majority of them are women who cope with the aftermath of conflict in a wide variety of ways. While they face a number of specific challenges, women often actively organise and build networks to share experiences and build bridges to peace and reconciliation. They are victims of conflict, but also agents of change.

2.6 The Problem of Sexual Exploitation in UN Peacekeeping Operations

As previously discussed, the increase in PKOs brought an increase in interaction between peacekeepers and local populations. It did not take long before reports expressing concerns about sexual activities between peacekeepers and local women and girls started to emerge from almost all countries where PKOs were being

---

146 Vesna Nikolic-Ristanovic (ed), *Women, Violence and War: Wartime Victimization of Refugees in the Balkans* (Central European University Press, 1999) 76.

147 Christine Chinkin and Hilary Charlesworth,'Building Women into Peace: the International Legal Framework' (2006) 27(5) *Third World Quarterly* 937, 941.

148 Ibid.

149 Joyce P. Kaufman and Kristen P. Williams, *Women War: Gender Identity and Activism in Times of Conflict* (Kumarian Press, 2010) 66.

150 Krishna Kumar, 'Civil Wars, Women, and Gender Relations: An Overview' in Krishna Kumar (ed) *Women and Civil War: Impact, Organizations, and Action* (Lynne Rienner, 2001), 5, 21.

151 Maja Korac, 'Women Organizing against Ethnic Nationalism and War in the Post-Yugoslav States' in Wenona Giles et al, *Feminists Under Fire: Exchanges Across War Zones* (Between the Lines, 2003) 25, 30.

152 Security Council Resolution, *Women, Peace and Security*, S/Res/1889 (5 October 2009), para 14.

conducted.[153] The first allegations were in 1992 concerning the PKO in Mozambique,[154] followed soon after by concerns about the sharp rise in prostitution, as well as trafficking for the purpose of forced prostitution, that accompanied UN missions in Cambodia, Somalia, and Bosnia and Herzegovina (BH).[155] These were followed by other reports describing peacekeepers' alleged involvement in sexual abuse and sexual exploitation in West Africa (Liberia, Sierra Leone and Guinea), the DRC,[156] Eritrea and East Timor.[157] Today, the links between the presence of peacekeepers and the 'sexual exploitation and abuse' of women and girls have been documented across the range of PKOs. However, the scope of the problem of sexual exploitation is difficult to determine due to a lack of reporting and the lack of clear distinction between sexual exploitation, sexual abuse and consensual forms of sexual interactions.[158]

There were allegations that peacekeepers in the UN mission in Mozambique (ONUMOZ) 'organised prostitution rackets' involving local women and children.[159] Among the reported factors that pushed girls into prostitution were

[153] Paul Higate, 'Revealing the Soldier: Peacekeeping and Prostitution' (2003) 1(5) *American Sexuality Magazine* 1.; Media, human rights organizations and the UN have documented involvement of peacekeepers in sexual exploitation and sexual abuse in peacekeeping operations ranging from those in Bosnia and Herzegovina and Kosovo in 1990s to Cambodia and East Timor in the early and late 1990s to West Africa 2002 and the Democratic Republic of Congo 2004. See Al-Hussein, Prince Zeid Ra'ad Zeid, 'A Comprehensive Strategy to Eliminate Future Sexual Exploitation and Abuse in the United Nations Peacekeeping Operations', study undertaken for the Secretary-General by the Permanent Representative of Jordan', UN Doc A/59/710, (2005) 7.

[154] Michael Fleshman, 'Tough UN Line on Peacekeeper Abuses: Action Initiated to End Sexual Misdeeds in Peacekeeping Missions' (2005) 19 *Africa Renewal* 1, 7.

[155] Kien Serey Phal, 'The Lessons of the UNTAC Experience and the Ongoing Responsibilities of the International Community in Cambodia' (1995) 2 (7) *Pacifica Review* 129, 133.; Natalia Lupi, 'Report by the Enquiry Commission on the Behavior of Italian Peacekeeping Troops in Somalia' (1998) 1(375-9) *Yearbook of International Humanitarian Law* 375; Human Rights Watch, Hopes Betrayed: Trafficking of Women and Girls to Post-Conflict Bosnia and Herzegovina for Forced Prostitution (2002); Sarah Martin, 'Must Boys be Boys? Ending Sexual Exploitation and Abuse in Peacekeeping Missions' (Refugee International, 2005).

[156] UNHCR and Save the Children UK, 'Sexual Violence and Exploitation: The Experience of Refugee Children in Liberia, Guinea and Sierra Leone' (2002); Higate, Paul, 'Gender and Peacekeeping Case Studies: The Democratic Republic of the Congo and Sierra Leone' (2004) 91 Monograph Series.

[157] Deutsche Presse Agentur, 'U.N. Investigates Alleged Sexual Abuse By Peacekeepers In Eritrea' (14 April 2005) ReliefWeb <http://www.reliefweb.int/rw/rwb.nsf/db900SID/ACIO-6BFN5E?OpenDocument> at 23 October 2007 and Ann Barker, 'UN Takes Steps to Prevent Sex Abuse in East Timor' (30 August 2006), *ABC News* (on line) <http://www.abc.net.au/pm/content/2006/s1728448.htm>.

[158] Report of the Secretary-General, *Special Measures for Protection from Sexual Exploitation and Sexual Abuse*, UN Doc A/59/782 (2005).

[159] Angela Mackay, 'Sex and the Peacekeeping Soldier: the New UN Resolution' (2001) *Peace News* (on line) <http://www.peacenews.info/issues/2443/mackay.html>.

poverty, lack of education, prior sexual abuse and the presence of peacekeepers in the country.[160] In December 1993, the commander of ONUMOZ, Aldo Ajello, received a complaint from the Save the Children Alliance regarding UN military personnel who had bought sex from hundreds of girls.[161]

With respect to the UN mission in Cambodia (UNTAC), a number of brothels and Thai massage parlours were established throughout the country soon after the arrival of UN peacekeeping personnel.[162] The number of prostitutes rose from about 6,000 in 1992 to more than 25,000 at the height of the mission, including an increased number of child prostitutes.[163] Although prostitution is not necessarily sexually exploitative and the presence of prostitutes was not new to Cambodia, Cambodians were troubled by the dramatic increase in prostitution and HIV/AIDS in their country. It was claimed that prior to the arrival of UNTAC, prostitution was generally hidden in Cambodian society, while after the arrival of UNTAC, it became something that was very open and prevalent.[164] More generally, it was reported by women's NGOs that UNTAC was believed to have caused a rise in 'sexual abuse and violence'.[165] A letter from a group of Cambodians that was sent to the mission's Special Representative to the Secretary-General alleged that harassment of women 'occur[red] regularly in public restaurants, hotels and bars, banks, markets, and shops'.[166]

During the UN mission in Bosnia and Herzegovina (UNMIBH) in 1995, there were also allegations of involvement of peacekeepers in sexual exploitation and abuse. However, while a rise in prostitution and HIV/AIDS was one of the main features of UNTAC, under UNMIBH there was a rise in the trafficking of women and young girls from Moldova, Ukraine and Romania for the purposes of forced prostitution. Trafficking in humans was a relatively unknown phenomenon in the region until the mid 1990s, but following the Dayton Peace Agreement, which was signed in 1995, the forced sex industry was driven by the arrival of tens of thousands of predominantly male peacekeepers.[167] Bars and brothels with women

---

[160] Viktoria Perschler-Desai, 'Childhood on the Market: Teenage Prostitution in Southern Africa,' 10 (4) (2001) *African Security Review* 111,117.

[161] Gayle Kirshenbaum, 'Who's Watching the Peacekeepers?' 12 Ms. Magazine (May/June 1994) in Ann Orford 'Politics of Collective Security' (1995–1996) 17 *Michigan Journal of International Law* 373.

[162] Martin, above n 155, 4.

[163] Angela MacKay, above n 159; Mang Channg, 'Sex Trade Flourishing in Capital', *Phnom Penh Post*, 12 February 1993, 6.

[164] Whitworth, above n 49, 5.

[165] Sandra Witworth, 'The Practice, and Praxis, of Feminist Research in International Relations' in Richard Wyn Jones (ed), *Critical Theory and World Politics* (Lynne Reinner, 2000) 149.

[166] Barbara Crossette, 'When Peacekeepers Turn into Troublemakers', *New York Times*, 7 January 1996,4, 9.

[167] Madeleine Rees, 'International Intervention in Bosnia-Herzegovina: the Cost of Ignoring Gender' in Cynthia Cockburn and Dubravka Zarkov (eds) *The Postwar Moment: Militaries, Masculinities and International Peacekeeping* (Lawrence and Wishart, 2002) 61.

trafficked from Central and Eastern Europe mushroomed near UN bases, while the number of females trafficked into the region increased with rises in the number of peacekeepers.[168]

In 2000, it emerged that some peacekeepers in the UN mission in Eritrea (UNMEE) were having sex with minors. Italian, Slovak and Danish peacekeepers were found in separate incidents to have been involved, while three Danish soldiers were found guilty of having sex with a 13-year-old Eritrean girl.[169] According to Louise Olsson et al, because the case involved a minor girl, it was a clearly grave sexual offence and the soldiers were sent home.[170]

In 2002, an Irish soldier was caught making an allegedly pornographic movie with his Eritrean girlfriend. Although both the Irish soldier and his girlfriend reported that they were having a consensual sexual relationship, nevertheless they were punished. The soldier was dismissed from the military, repatriated and served a jail sentence in his home country.[171] The woman in 'the movie' was charged for obscenity in her home country and sentenced to 2 years in jail.[172] It is unclear who can be considered the 'victim' of sexual exploitation in this case, since both parties were jailed The Eritrean case shows that even if peacekeepers and beneficiaries have consensual relationships, they have been accused of sexual exploitation. Thus, consent was seen as irrelevant in this case.

The UN presence in East Timor from 1999 until the present brought the issue of 'peacekeeper babies' to public attention. There were allegations that peacekeepers fathered babies with local Timorese women and then left them behind with their mothers without providing any ongoing support.[173] Likewise, by 2002 in Liberia, approximately 6,600 children were registered as being children of UN peacekeepers.[174] In response to these cases, the UN drafted a comprehensive strategy for assistance to victims of 'sexual exploitation and abuse', which would

---

168 Sarah Mendelson, *Barracks and Brothels: Peacekeepers and Human Trafficking in the Balkans* (Center for Strategic and International Studies, 2005) 10–12.

169 Martin, above n 155, 5.

170 Louise Olsson et al, 'Gender Aspects of Conflict Interventions: Intended and Unintended Consequences: Case Studies on the United Nations Mission in Eritrea/Ethiopia (UNMEE), the NATO Stabilization Force in Bosnia and Herzegovina (SFOR) and the Temporary International Presence in Hebron (TIPH)' Final report to the Norwegian Ministry of Foreign Affairs (international Peace Research Institute, Oslo, 2004) 13.

171 Declan Walsh and Nicola Byrne, 'Peacekeeper Jailed for Porn Films', (22 December 2002) *Scottish News* (on llne) <http://www.prisonplanet.com/peacekeeper_jailed_for_porn_films-retry.html>.

172 Martin, above n 155, 5.

173 Lindsay Murdoch, 'UN's Legacy of Shame in Timor', *The Age* (online), 22 July 2006 <http://www.theage.com.au/news/world/uns-legacy-of-shame-in-timor/2006/07/21/1153166587803.html?page=fullpage>.

174 Elisabeth Rehn and Ellen Johnson Sirleaf, *Women, War and Peace: The Independent Experts Assessment on the Impact of Armed Conflict on Women and Women's Role in Peacebuilding* (UNIFEM, 2002).

include some financial assistance for these mothers and their babies.[175] However, as Otto argues, the policy deems that children fathered by peacekeepers were conceived by an act of sexual exploitation, 'whether or not their parent(s) experienced the act in this way'.[176] In these cases sexual consent is not taken into account, and mothers and children may be portrayed as 'victims', while the fathers are portrayed as sexual predators. In either case, both parents and children are in danger of being stigmatised and ostracised by the UN or their communities. As a direct consequence of the alleged increase in cases of 'sexual exploitation and abuse' the DPKO has also created strict rules regarding non-fraternisation with local people.[177]

In sum, peacekeepers accused of sexual exploitation have been involved in sexual practices ranging from consensual sexual relationships with local women through to forced prostitution and sex work, exchanging sex for food, trafficking in women and the manufacture of 'pornographic films' involving local women.[178] Although sexual interactions between the local populations and peacekeepers are a feature of most, if not all, PKOs, the problematic dimensions of this activity are not clear. For example, the dramatic rise in the incidence of HIV/AIDS in Cambodia after peacekeepers were deployed may have been due to alleged sexual exploitation, but an alternative explanation may be that women who worked in the sex industry lacked information and the means of protection. Meanwhile, although the UN mission in BH became (in)famous for the involvement of peacekeepers in trafficking of women and girls, it is unknown how many women came into the country voluntarily to work in the sex industry. The UN mission in Eritrea became notorious for the involvement of a peacekeeper in making 'pornographic movies' with a local woman, while Liberia and East Timor are examples where the phenomenon of 'peace babies' became a central concern, yet there is no evidence to support the hypothesis that all 'peace babies' are necessarily a result of sexual exploitation.

2.7 Conclusions

This chapter outlined the context within which PKOs have developed and in which the problem of sexual exploitation has emerged. It traced the evolution of PKOs and described the mandates and tasks of peacekeepers, which gradually changed from

---

175 United Nations General Assembly, *United Nations Comprehensive Strategy on Assistance and Support to Victims of Sexual Exploitation and Abuse by United Nations Staff or Related Personnel*, A/Res/62/214 (7 March 2008).

176 Dianne, Otto, 'The Sexual Tensions of UN Peace Support Operations: A Plea for 'Sexual Positivity' (2007) XVIII *Finnish Yearbook of International Law* 42.

177 Secretary-General, *Seventeenth Report of the Secretary-General on the United Nations Organization Mission in the Democratic Republic of Congo*, UN Doc S/2005/167 (15 March 2005) 64.

178 Martin, above n 155, 5.

undertaking traditional peacekeeping to complex roles of peace builders working alongside humanitarian workers. The chapter outlined the profiles of peacekeepers and local populations and noted that until the 1990s interaction between them was sporadic and rare. The UN mission in Bosnia and Herzegovina (UNMIBH) was introduced as a case study of a multidimensional PKO involving the deployment of tens of thousands of predominantly male peacekeepers. While there was a clear recognition of the importance of developing good relationships with locals, non-fraternisation policies were developed and enforced in UNMIBH.

While peacekeepers are predominantly men and are culturally, educationally and linguistically diverse, the beneficiaries are local populations affected by the war. The majority of them are women and in the absence of men they often take prominent roles and responsibilities by building networks and becoming income providers for their families. After the 1990s, with the development of multidimensional PKOs, interactions between peacekeepers and local people increased, and allegations of sexual exploitation have been reported across the missions. Consequently, their interactions became subject to more regulation, although it was not clear which sexual practices between local women and peacekeepers were cases of sexual exploitation and which were non-exploitative. The majority of these cases were presented as sexually exploitative, although consent and the age of the parties involved was ignored. The next chapter will examine the policy developments that led to the promulgation of the SGB.

Chapter 3
The Secretary-General's Bulletin: Evolution and Reception

3.1 Introduction

This chapter aims to explore the policy and legal responses that followed the emergence of the problem of sexual exploitation in peacekeeping operations (PKOs). It will describe the official responses to the problem that led eventually to the promulgation of the Secretary-General's Bulletin (SGB) and will analyse the provisions of the SGB in relation to prostitution and sexual relationships. Furthermore, this chapter evaluates the reception of the SGB by researchers who undertook empirical studies into sexual exploitation in PKOs between 2003 and 2008. It begins by tracing the development of institutional responses to alleged sexual exploitation, and describes and analyses these developments in three stages. The first stage illustrates the unwillingness of UN officials to accept the emergence of a problem of sexual exploitation in PKOs, which resulted in a series of ad hoc responses at the level of individual missions. The second stage saw attempts at more coordinated actions through the efforts of the Department of Peacekeeping Operations (DPKO) and the Secretary-General (SG), as well as individual missions. As the allegations of sexual exploitation continued to mount and the problem was threatening the reputation of the UN itself, the third stage commenced with the adoption of a 'zero tolerance policy' on sex (ZTP), which was elaborated in the SGB. After examining these three phases, the chapter then examines the wording of the SGB in relation to prostitution and sexual relationships through the lenses of feminist scholarship and international human rights law. I argue that the SGB, rather than simply reiterating existing international legal norms and standards as it claims,[1] breaches them in many respects.

The final section of the chapter discusses the overwhelmingly positive response to the SGB from nongovernmental organisations (NGOs) and researchers.

[1] Secretary-General's Bulletin (SGB), *Special measures for protection from sexual exploitation and abuse*, ST/SGB/200313 (9 October 2002), para 3(2).

O. Simic, *Regulation of Sexual Conduct in UN Peacekeeping Operations*,
DOI 10.1007/978-3-642-28484-7_3, © Springer-Verlag Berlin Heidelberg 2012

It highlights the largely uncritical acceptance of the SGB's definition of sexual exploitation, which bans all forms of prostitution and, with minor and vague exceptions, adult sexual relationships between peacekeepers and 'beneficiaries of assistance', thus conflating prostitution and consensual sexual relationships with sexual exploitation. Drawing on feminist scholarship and the work of the few critics of the policy, the chapter concludes that the ZTP is an inappropriate response to the problem of sexual exploitation in PKOs, because it treats all sex between peacekeepers and beneficiaries as exploitative, which is inconsistent with international human rights law.

3.2 Phase 1: *Ad hoc* Mission-Level Responses to Allegations of Sexual Exploitation

This section describes and analyses the initial responses by various missions to the allegations of sexual exploitation in PKOs. As I explain below, the responses were not coordinated, but rather developed as *ad hoc* reactions to allegations made during specific PKOs. As a result, a few mission-specific codes of conduct were designed that addressed the particular problems occurring in those missions. The early mission responses in Mozambique, Cambodia, and Bosnia and Herzegovina (BH) are examined. They illustrate a lack of organisational capacity to deal with sexual exploitation in a coordinated manner, and a lack of willingness on behalf of the UN to take seriously the allegations of sexual exploitation that were occurring in PKOs. These initial responses did not aim to provide long-term solutions, but produced 'quick fixes' rather than coordinated action.

The first PKO in the post-cold-war period where allegations were made about peacekeepers sexually exploiting young girls was in Mozambique in 1992.[2] In 1993, the commander of the UN mission in Mozambique (ONUMOZ), Aldo Ajello, received a letter from the Save the Children Alliance who complained that UN military personnel had bought sex from hundreds of girls.[3] In 1996, the UN issued a report that concluded that 'soldiers of the United Nations Operation in Mozambique (ONUMOZ) recruited girls aged 12–18 years into prostitution'.[4] Besides a number of soldiers being sent home and a curfew being imposed on the rest of the troops, little action was taken as a result of the findings.[5] None of the soldiers faced investigations back home.

[2] United Nations Operation in Mozambique (ONUMOZ) 1992–1994.

[3] Gayle Kirshenbaum, 'Who's Watching the Peacekeepers?' Ms. Magazine (May/June 1994) 12. In Ann Orford 'Politics of Collective Security' (1995–1996) 17 *Michigan Journal of International Law* 373.

[4] United Nations, 'Promotion and Protection of the Rights of Children: Impact of Armed Conflict on Children.' Note by the Secretary-General, A/51/306 (26 August 1996), para 98.

[5] Kirshenbaum, above n 3.

Following Mozambique, the UN Advance Mission in Cambodia (UNAMIC) faced growing criticism because of the engagement of peacekeepers in prostitution with local women.[6] In response to this criticism, which largely assumed that sex with prostitutes was sexually exploitative, several actions were undertaken by mission staff. Peacekeepers were advised to be more discreet, for example, by not parking their white UN vehicles in front of massage parlours and by not frequenting brothels in their uniforms.[7] Also, an additional 800,000 condoms were shipped to Cambodia,[8] which seemed to be a reasonable response by the UN since there was a 'noticeable absence of condoms'[9] and high risk of contracting HIV/AIDS. The decision to ship condoms into the country could be understood as a concern for the well-being of both peacekeepers and prostitutes. Although local people did complain about UNAMIC personnel, the mission's Special Representative to the Secretary-General (SRSG) Yasushi Akashi reportedly took the view that 'boys will be boys' and no action was taken to inquire into complaints made by local people.[10] This decision may have been due to the fact that, at the time, the UN did not ban peacekeepers from using the services of prostitutes, so arguably the SRSG would not be expected to be concerned about peacekeepers' engagement in prostitution with local adult women.

While complaints about the mission in Cambodia were mainly concerned with allegations that seemed to treat the involvement of peacekeepers in (voluntary) prostitution as itself a form of sexual exploitation, in BH there was a rapid increase in trafficking in women for the purpose of forced prostitution after the arrival of peacekeepers in 1995.[11] Official efforts to stop the trafficking in women started in 1999 following numerous negative local and international media reports. Under pressure from the increased public attention and specific cases that emerged, UN officials eventually decided to take the problem of trafficking in women more seriously and to devise measures to address it. The Office of the High Commissioner for Human Rights (OHCHR) and the UN Mission in Bosnia and Herzegovina (UNMIBH) jointly launched the 'Trafficking Project' in 1999.[12] In the same year,

---

[6] Ibid 378; UNAMIC 1991–1992.

[7] Judy Ledgerwood, 'The Lessons from Cambodia,' Asian Recorder, April 16–22, 1993, 23060 in Sandra Whitworth, *Men, Militarism and UN Peacekeeping: A Gendered Analysis* (Lynne Rienner Publishers, 2004) 69.

[8] Ibid.

[9] 'Letters: An Open Letter to Yasushi Akashi (Head of the UN Operation in Cambodia in 1994)', *Phnom Penh Post*, 4 October 1994. In Cynthia Enloe, *Maneuvers: The International Politics of Militarizing Women's Lives* (University of California Press, 2000) 99.

[10] Sarah Martin, 'Must Boys be Boys? Ending Sexual Exploitation and Abuse in UN Peacekeeping Missions' (Refugee International, 2005) 4.

[11] Mara Radovanovic and Angelika Kartusch, 'Report on the Combat against Trafficking in Women for the Purpose of Forced Prostitution in Bosnia and Herzegovina' (Vienna, Ludwig Bolzmann Institute of Human Rights 2001).

[12] On 12 May 2000, UNMIBH and OHCHR released a joint report on 'Trafficking in Human Beings in Bosnia and Herzegovina: A Summary Report of the Joint Trafficking Project of the UN

UNMIBH issued its first legal guidance that provided a definition of human trafficking and banned it as a form of organised crime.[13] The mission also developed its first protocols for the treatment and repatriation of trafficked victims and, in 2001, established the Special Trafficking Operations Program (STOP) to handle trafficking cases.[14] At the same time, initial training resources to teach local Bosnian police officers to combat trafficking in humans were developed and delivered across the country.[15]

The BH example shows how UN officials at the mission level eventually decided to take the problem of sexual exploitation seriously and to devise measures to address it. However, while they acknowledged that trafficking in women occurred after the arrival of peacekeepers and devised measures to suppress it, there was a lack of willingness to recognise the direct and indirect involvement of peacekeepers in trafficking.[16] Although several peacekeepers were found to be directly involved in the organised crime of trafficking, none of them has ever been prosecuted, as they returned home before charges could be laid.[17] Thus, the UN did not follow through on its *ad hoc* responses and therefore failed to fully address the problem.

In sum, in the 1990s there was growing awareness of sexual exploitation allegations, but there was little clarity about which allegations were serious and problematic. Clearly, child prostitution in Mozambique and trafficking in women for forced prostitution in BH were cases of sexual exploitation that demanded a response from the UN. There was no official response to these allegations in Mozambique and in BH the response was only partial. There were no general guidelines about how to specifically address the alleged problem of sexual exploitation within the broader UN system of PKOs. It is notable that the UN already seemed to consider all peacekeeping sex as sexually exploitative, without making a distinction between, for example, the adult and child prostitution that took place in Mozambique.

Mission in Bosnia and Herzegovina and the Office of the High Commissioner for Human Rights'. The report explains the work of the international community to respond to the growing problem of trafficking in Bosnia and Herzegovina. See: <http://www.ohr.int/ohr-dept/hr-rol/thedept/hr-coord-cent/info-reps/hr-reports/default.asp?content_id=5099>.

[13] UNMIBH Legal Office, Guidance No. 21, 'Trafficking in Persons' May 1999.

[14] UNMIBH Special Press Conference, 'UNMIBH Trafficking project and Introduction to the New Special Trafficking Operations Program (STOP)', July 26 2001. See, Aida Cerkez-Robinson, 'New Special Police Units to Help Fighting Trafficking of Women,' *Associated Press*, July 26, 2001.

[15] Bosnia and Herzegovina-UNMIBH-Background, 12 August 2009 <http://www.un.org/en/peacekeeping/missions/past/unmibh/background.html>.

[16] Human Rights Watch, 'Hopes Betrayed: Trafficking of Women and Girls to Post-conflict Bosnia and Herzegovina for Forced Prostitution' (2002).

[17] Ibid 55.

3.3 Phase 2: Attempts at Coordinated Responses Within the UN System

The ineffectiveness of the *ad hoc* responses to allegations of sexual exploitation put pressure on the DPKO and raised public expectations for action. As a result, the DPKO and the SG moved towards developing a more coordinated and comprehensive response, which set in motion the second stage in the development of UN responses to these allegations. The DPKO and the SG began to jointly develop a number of guidelines and training materials that would be universally applied to all PKOs. The first guidelines were published by the DPKO in 1997 and outlined expected standards of behaviour for peacekeepers. The guidelines marked the start of a gradual change in how sexual exploitation was treated in training manuals and other materials. As a direct result of mounting reports about sexual exploitation by peacekeepers, between 1997 and 2002 the language used in DPKO materials became more directive about what kind of sex peacekeepers could engage in while on mission. Despite these efforts to address the problem more comprehensively, the flow of sexual exploitation allegations continued.

In 1997, the DPKO developed two sets of standards of conduct for uniformed peacekeepers. The first set was titled 'Ten Rules: Code of Personal Conduct for Blue Helmets' (Ten Rules), a pocket card that presented in plain language the standards of behaviour expected of every military person assigned to a peacekeeping mission.[18] Paragraph 4 of the Code prohibits sexual exploitation by giving the following instruction to peacekeepers: 'Do not indulge in immoral acts of sexual, physical or psychological abuse or exploitation of the local population or United Nations staff, especially women and children'. The second set of guidelines was promulgated under the title 'We Are United Nations Peacekeepers'.[19] Under the headline 'We will never', peacekeepers are required, among other commitments, never to 'commit any act that would result in physical, sexual or psychological harm or suffering to a member of the local population, especially women and children'.[20] In addition, they pledge to never 'become involved in sexual liaisons which could affect our impartiality or the well-being of others'.[21] Although the guidelines do not define 'others', it can be assumed that they refer to the local population since this commitment is listed among other commitments or duties towards local people. These two sets of guidelines prohibit 'immoral acts' and 'sexual harm or suffering', although they do not provide any definitions or explanations of these terms. While the troop-contributing countries are expected

[18] UN Department for Peacekeeping Operations, *Ten Rules: Code of Personal Conduct for Blue Helmets* (1997).

[19] Ibid.

[20] Ibid.

[21] Ibid.

to adopt the 'Ten Rules' and the commitments in 'We Are United Nations Peacekeepers', these documents are only guidelines, and thus non-binding.[22]

A year later, in 1998, the DPKO and the Joint UN Programme on HIV/AIDS (UNAIDS) developed a training manual on HIV/AIDS prevention for peacekeepers which stated that some 'men, women, or even children may have been forced into prostitution' and that the peacekeepers 'should consider carefully' whether to 'support and enforce that kind of circumstance by using their services'.[23] This manual acknowledges that women may be forced into prostitution, but leaves it to peacekeepers to decide whether to use the services of prostitutes who may have been forced into such work. It takes the view that as long as peacekeepers avoid engaging in forced prostitution, which is clearly banned, then the individual decision of a peacekeeper regarding prostitution should be respected.

In 1999, the DPKO established the first Office of Gender Affairs (OGA) as a part of the UN mission in Kosovo (UNMIK). The UNMIK OGA was requested to mainstream gender equality into the mission and to contribute to its promotion.[24] OGA's establishment in Kosovo was followed by the establishment of OGAs in the mission in East Timor (UNTAET) and other missions.[25] Among other tasks, the OGAs contributed to the development of in-mission Codes of Conduct that call for the prohibition of sexual exploitation in PKOs.[26]

In October 2001, the DPKO issued the training module 'Gender and Peacekeeping, In-Mission Training', developed specifically for military and civilian police peacekeepers.[27] The purpose of this module was to raise awareness about the importance of 'gender relations in the work they undertake' and improve understanding of how the relations between women and men are structured and how the presence of peacekeepers affects those relations.[28] In its section 'Gender and Human Rights' the module states that 'women may turn to prostitution to have money to feed their children' due to the impact of the conflict on livelihoods and the

[22] However, Prince Zeid suggested that these guidelines be included in each memorandum of understanding signed by the UN with each troop-contributing country and thus become legally binding. See, *A Comprehensive Strategy to Eliminate Future Sexual Exploitation and Abuse in United Nations Peacekeeping Operations*, UN GA, 59 sess, A/59/710 (24 March 2005) para 20.

[23] This training manual was developed in 1998, by DPKO and UNAIDS, and based on a booklet titled 'Protect Yourself and Those You Care About Against HIV/AIDS'.

[24] Maddalena Pezzotti, Chief, Office of Gender Affairs, 'UNMIK Office of Gender Affairs Places Gender Concerns at the Top of Peacekeeping Political Agenda in Kosovo' (United Nations Interim Administration Mission in Kosovo, UNMIK, October 2004) <http://www.peacewomen.org/assets/file/Resources/UN/dpko_unmikgenderaffairs_2004.pdf>.

[25] As of September 2005, 10 out of 18 peacekeeping missions have dedicated full-time gender advisors.

[26] Amy Smythe et al, 'Activities Report from the Office of Gender Affairs (OGA) of the United Nations Organization Mission in the Democratic Republic of Congo (MONUC)', 10 January 2003.

[27] DPKO Training and Evaluation Service Military Division, 'Gender and Peacekeeping Operations In-Mission Training' (2001).

[28] Ibid Introduction.

need to survive.[29] This is the only time that the DPKO uses the term 'prostitution'. The module does not take a position on prostitution, but reiterates its earlier position by alerting peacekeepers that some exploitation may be taking place and that they should be careful to avoid it.[30] The module does not make any reference to sexual relationships between peacekeepers and local women, which suggests that such relationships were not perceived as problematic at the time.

However, in 2002, the DPKO issued a second training module that gave some direction to peacekeepers about engaging in sexual relationships with local women. The 'Training Module on Gender and Peacekeeping', like the module from 2001, provides an overview and explanations of gender, sex and issues related to human rights and discrimination. However, the 2002 version expands on these topics and includes guided questions and answers about sexual relationships that might occur during a PKO, because such questions are 'often asked in relation to this [gender and sex] topic'.[31] Under the question 'Am I allowed to have sex in a peacekeeping mission?', the module says that peacekeepers are 'under obligation to uphold international human rights standards'.[32] This answer can be interpreted as suggesting that sex is allowed as long as it is not exploitative.

However, the 2002 training module also states that peacekeepers 'have power...and...must not allow themselves to abuse power by using prostitutes and thus encouraging prostitution'.[33] While previously only forced prostitution had been prohibited, at this stage the DPKO seems to have shifted its standpoint on prostitution to ban peacekeepers from using the services of prostitutes, regardless of whether it is forced or voluntary. This position seems to contradict the previous suggestion in the same module that sex is allowed as long as it is in accordance with international human rights standards. Despite these conflicting messages, there is no explanation of why the DPKO may have shifted its position on prostitution or about the apparent contradiction in its messages to peacekeepers.

The 2002 module further states that peacekeepers' 'actions' must be guided by 'international human rights standards, the UN peacekeeping code of conduct, [and] in the case of formed military units, the national laws of [their] country and [their] military disciplinary codes; the specific instructions in this regard from [their] supervisor; and the laws, culture, religion and values of the host country'.[34] This provision assumes that there will be no conflict between UN policies/guidelines and local laws, suggesting that peacekeepers must obey both while keeping factors such as culture and religion in mind. Although this may be challenging in practice, the module does not provide any guidance about what to do if these laws do conflict and

---

[29] Ibid 20.

[30] Ibid.

[31] DPKO, The Standard Generic Training Module on 'Gender and Peacekeeping' (2002) 12.

[32] Ibid 13.

[33] Ibid.

[34] Ibid.

which would have precedence. While it is understandable that the UN would want peacekeepers to respect local laws and acknowledge the particular cultural and religious contexts within which PKOs operate, it may be confusing to have so many potentially conflicting rules to follow and there is a need to discuss what this might mean in a particular local context.

In sum, the DPKO gradually coordinated its response to mounting reports of alleged sexual exploitation in PKOs between 1997 and 2002. As outlined, during this period explicit guidelines restricting sex between peacekeepers and local women were developed. While the initial guidelines and manuals did not explicitly ban voluntary adult prostitution and sexual relationships with locals, they did broaden the range of sexual conduct, such as forced prostitution, that was prohibited. By 2002 there was a mixed message about whether voluntary prostitution was also banned. However, in many respects phase two made attempts to distinguish between sexually exploitative and non-exploitative sex, while portraying peacekeepers as people who can make informed decisions and take personal responsibility for their sexual conduct. Finally, this phase also showed respect for the sexual agency of local women by not limiting their sexual choices

3.4 Phase 3: The Adoption of a Comprehensive 'Zero Tolerance Policy'

Despite increased efforts to address sexual exploitation, allegations continued and eventually the ZTP on almost all sex between peacekeepers and local people was adopted in 2003. This section examines this third phase of the DPKO's responses to sexual exploitation allegations. It outlines the context within which the SGB was developed and examines the policy's definition of sexual exploitation and the approach it takes to sexual relationships and to prostitution between peacekeepers and local women, drawing on radical and 'sex positive' feminist theories.

3.4.1 The Adoption of the SGB

In 2002, the UNHCHR and Save the Children UK[35] (UNHCR/SC-UK) published a report on the sexual exploitation of children by peacekeepers in Liberia, Sierra Leone and Guinea which eventually led to the promulgation of the SGB. The report found that 'survival sex' between local children and humanitarian workers in

[35] UNHCR and Save the Children UK, 'Sexual Violence and Exploitation: The Experience of Refugee Children in Liberia, Guinea and Sierra Leone, Report of Assessment Mission Carried Out from 22 October to 30 November 2001' (2002).

exchange for aid was prevalent.[36] It was found that the offenders were employees from local and international NGOs, as well as from UN agencies, who allegedly exchanged humanitarian aid for sexual services, mostly with girls aged from 13 to 18.[37] In November 2002, a UN investigation into these allegations was conducted by the UN Office of Internal Oversight Service (OIOS).[38] Although OIOS was unable to confirm the allegations contained in the UNHCR/SC-UK report, it nevertheless indicated that the problem of sexual exploitation of children was real.[39] The OIOS observed that conditions in the camps and in refugee communities in the three countries made refugees vulnerable to sexual and other forms of exploitation.[40]

In the same year, the Inter-Agency Standing Committee (IASC)[41] established the Task Force on Protection from Sexual Exploitation and Abuse in Humanitarian Crises (Task Force). It was made up of a number of UN and nongovernmental entities and aimed to develop specific measures to counter sexual exploitation and provide definitions of sexual exploitation and sexual abuse.[42] Initially the IASC had the overall objective of strengthening and enhancing the protection and care of 'women and children' during humanitarian crises and conflicts, and making recommendations that specifically aimed to eliminate sexual exploitation and sexual abuse by humanitarian personnel.[43] Based on the Task Force's recommendations, the IASC adopted agreed definitions of sexual exploitation and sexual abuse[44] and all agency members committed to incorporate a set of six core principles into their codes of conduct as well as staff rules and regulations. The six core principles ban prostitution and 'strongly discourage' sexual relationships between humanitarian

---

[36] Ibid.

[37] Ibid 43.

[38] The Office of Internal Oversight Services (OIOS) was established by the UN in 1994 to investigate internal affairs.

[39] Secretary-General, *Report of the Secretary-General on the Activities of the Office of Internal Oversight Services, Delivered to the General Assembly*, UN Doc A/57/451 (4 October 2002).

[40] Ibid 29.

[41] The Inter-Agency Standing Committee is comprised of both members (FAO, OCHA, UNDP, UNFPA, UNICEF, UNHCR, WFP, WHO) and standing invitees (ICRC, ICVA, IFRC, InterAction, IOM, SCHR, RSG/IDPs, UNHCHR, and the World Bank).

[42] United Nations Office for Coordination for Humanitarian Affairs (OCHA), 'Protection from Sexual Exploitation and Abuse' <http://ochaonline.un.org/HumanitarianIssues/ProtectionfromSexualExploitationandAbuse/tabid/1204/language/en-US/Default.aspx>.

[43] The Inter-Agency Standing Committee, 'Report of the Task Force on Protection from Sexual Exploitation and Abuse in Humanitarian Crises' (13 June 2002).

[44] Sexual exploitation is any abuse of a position of vulnerability, differential power, or trust for sexual purposes; this includes profiting monetarily, socially or politically from the sexual exploitation of another. Sexual abuse is actual or threatened physical intrusion of a sexual nature, including inappropriate touching, by force or under unequal or coercive conditions. The Secretary General's Bulletin, definitions, above n 1.

workers and local populations.[45] It should be noted that the IASC definitions and principles were initially drafted and agreed to in relation to humanitarian workers, not peacekeepers.

In May 2003, the OIOS report and IASC recommendations led the UN General Assembly (UN GA) to condemn the problem of sexual exploitation and abuse, and request the SG to ensure that remedial and preventive measures be implemented in all PKOs.[46] UN GA also requested the SG to maintain data on investigations into sexual exploitation by humanitarian and peacekeeping personnel in PKOs.[47] These actions led to the promulgation of the SGB on Special Measures for Protection from Sexual Exploitation and Abuse in October 2003, which contains the IASC-agreed definitions and six standards of behaviour. In its prohibition of sexual exploitation, the SGB includes prostitution and most sexual relationships between peacekeepers and local populations. Although it explicitly bans prostitution and, in contrast, 'strongly discourages' sexual relationships, both are treated as manifestations of sexual exploitation.

The SGB describes its approach as aimed at 'preventing and addressing the cases of sexual exploitation and abuse' and refers to the fact that sexual exploitation is already prohibited by international legal norms and by UN Staff Regulations and Rules.[48] The SGB also states that sexual exploitation has always been 'unacceptable behaviour and prohibited conduct' for UN staff.[49] While UN Staff Regulations and Rules do not specifically prohibit sexual exploitation, they do outline the 'basic rights and obligations of staff' that oblige them not to 'abuse the power and authority vested in them'.[50]

---

[45] 1) Sexual exploitation and abuse by humanitarian workers constitute acts of gross misconduct and are therefore grounds for termination of employment. 2) Sexual activity with children (persons under the age of 18) is prohibited regardless of the age of majority or age of consent locally. Mistaken belief in the age of a child is not a defence. 3) Exchange of money, employment, goods, or services for sex, including sexual favours or other forms of humiliating, degrading or exploitative behaviour is prohibited. This includes exchange of assistance that is due to beneficiaries. 4) Sexual relationships between humanitarian workers and beneficiaries are strongly discouraged since they are based on inherently unequal power dynamics. Such relationships undermine the credibility and integrity of humanitarian aid work. 5) Where a humanitarian worker develops concerns or suspicions regarding sexual abuse or exploitation by a fellow worker, whether in the same agency or not, s/he must report such concerns via established agency reporting mechanisms. 6) Humanitarian workers' agencies are obliged to create and maintain an environment which prevents sexual exploitation and abuse and promotes the implementation of their code of conduct. Managers at all levels have particular responsibilities to support and develop systems which maintain this environment.

[46] UN General Assembly, *Investigation into sexual exploitation of refugees by aid workers in West Africa*, 57th sess, A/Res/57/306 (22 May 2003).

[47] Ibid.

[48] Secretary-General's Bulletin, above n 1, Preamble.

[49] Ibid sec 3.

[50] *Staff Regulations*, ST/SGB/2003/5 (7 February 2003).Regulation 1.2: Core values (a).

Section 2 of the SGB prohibits UN forces from committing acts of 'sexual exploitation and sexual abuse' and requires troops to observe a particular duty of care towards women and children and to respect international humanitarian law.[51] It further states that 'sexual exploitation and sexual abuse violate universally recognised international legal norms and standards and have always been unacceptable behaviour and prohibited conduct for the UN staff'.[52] In order to 'protect the most vulnerable populations, especially women and children', the SGB outlines specific standards which 'reiterate existing general obligations under the United Nations Staff Regulations and Rules'.[53] Cases of 'sexual exploitation and sexual abuse' are to be considered as 'serious misconduct' meriting disciplinary measures, including summary dismissal.[54] All UN staff members are required to report any 'concerns or suspicions' regarding sexual exploitation and sexual abuse by their fellows.[55] The Task Force instituted Focal Points on Protection from Sexual Exploitation and Abuse to coordinate the implementation of the SGB and actively promote protection from sexual exploitation and abuse.[56]

The SGB applies to all UN staff, including staff of its separately administered organs and programmes.[57] It defines sexual exploitation as 'any actual or attempted abuse of a position of vulnerability, differential power, or trust, for sexual purposes, including, but not limited to, profiting monetarily, socially or politically from the sexual exploitation of another'.[58] Although the SGB was promulgated as a response to the UNHCR/SC-UK report, the SGB expanded its protection to include sexual exploitation of adult women as well. It is not clear what the rationale was behind the SG decision to stretch the protection to adults and, as a consequence, deem irrelevant the age and consent of individuals. So although the UNHCR/SC-UK report recommended the prohibition of sex between humanitarian workers and 'beneficiaries' who are under 18,[59] the SGB goes further and includes adults. There are only two cases in which the SGB legitimises sex between peacekeepers and local women: where a peacekeeper is legally married to the local person[60] and where the 'beneficiaries of assistance' are over the age of 18 and 'the circumstances

[51] Ibid sec 2.2.

[52] Ibid.

[53] Ibid sec 3.2.

[54] Ibid sec 3.2 (a).

[55] Ibid sec 3.2 (e).

[56] The Executive Committees on Humanitarian Affairs and Peace and Security (ECHA/ECPS) UN and NGO Task Force on Protection from Sexual Exploitation and Abuse, 'Terms of Reference for In-country Focal Points on Protection from Sexual Exploitation and Abuse by UN/NGO/IGO Personnel' (November 2008).

[57] Secretary-General's Bulletin, above n 1, sec 2.1.

[58] Ibid sec 1, definitions. Sexual abuse is defined 'as the actual or threatened physical intrusion of a sexual nature, whether by force or under unequal or coercive conditions.'

[59] UNHCR and Save the Children UK, above n. 35, 22.

[60] Secretary-General's Bulletin, above n 1, sec 4.4.

of the case justify an exception' which would be at the discretion of the Head of Mission to decide.[61]

In sum, the third phase that came with the SGB was a more extreme response to alleged cases of sexual exploitation than the first two phases. The SGB not only bans prostitution, but also 'strongly discourages' sexual relationships between peacekeepers and local people. While it invokes international law to justify its prohibition of almost all sex between local women and peacekeepers, as I will explain in the following two sub-sections, the SGB breaches these norms. I will now critically examine the SGB's provisions on sexual relationships and prostitution more closely, since these two themes are a focus of my empirical research. I will draw on feminist perspectives and international human rights law to develop my analysis.

3.4.2 Sexual Relationships

'Sexual relationships between UN staff and beneficiaries of assistance, since they are based on inherently unequal power dynamics, undermine the credibility and integrity of the work of the UN and are strongly discouraged'.[62]

While prostitution is explicitly banned in the context of PKOs, sexual relationships are 'strongly discouraged'. However, the SGB makes an exemption from this provision by allowing that:

> The Head of Department, Office or Mission may use his or her discretion in applying the standard prescribed in section 3.2 (d), where beneficiaries of assistance are over the age of eighteen and the circumstances of the case justify an exception.[63]

Requiring adults to ask for permission to have a sexual relationship is incompatible with both sexual freedoms and privacy rights. It also seems unrealistic to expect peacekeepers to ask for such permission from the Head of Mission, given that the potential repercussions of such a request are not clear. Would asking permission be treated as sexually exploitative and mean the peacekeeper involved faced repatriation? Where disciplinary repercussions are a possible outcome, it seems unlikely that staff would approach the Head of Mission to discuss their sexual lives. Therefore, this exemption from the 'strong discouragement' provision seems deliberately unworkable in practice, designed to have the effect of prohibiting sexual relationships. Sexual relationships between peacekeepers and local women should not be a concern of the Head of Mission, unless there is a legitimate reason to suspect that sexual exploitation is taking place.

[61] Ibid sec 4.5.

[62] Secretary-General's Bulletin, above n 1, sec 3.2 (d).

[63] Ibid sec 4.4.

The main justification for the 'strong discouragement' approach is described in the SGB as the 'inherently unequal power dynamics' between locals and UN staff which 'undermines the credibility and integrity of the work of the UN'. Although the SGB does not define 'unequal power', the internal guidelines on sexual exploitation developed in 2005 for the PKO in the Democratic Republic of Congo (DRC) state that 'international personnel are in a position of considerable power over the local population'.[64] The guidelines explain that because international personnel enjoy shelter, money and food during the mission, while local populations are often 'very vulnerable', there is 'a high risk that relationships between international personnel and the local population will be exploitative'.[65] In addition, the training module for the Focal Points on Protection from Sexual Exploitation and Abuse by UN personnel and partners states that 'peacekeepers virtually always have more power over those we are there to serve'.[66]

By constructing 'us' (peacekeepers) and 'them' (local population) dichotomies, the UN helps to legitimate what some scholars regard as either a form of international control or the latest form of imperialism.[67] Peacekeepers often see themselves as citizens of 'civilised' nations whose values of peace and democracy are not shared by others.[68] So, in the 'moral universe of imperialism', as in the moral universe of peacekeeping mythologies, there are those who must be saved and those who must do the saving.[69] Zisk Marten argues that there are many differences between peacekeeping and colonialism, but also important similarities. She suggests that the idea of 'forceful intervention' to create political and social change is common to both. Also, the belief that such change would benefit the targeted population and the powerful liberal democracies who led the interventions is present in both.[70] They also share the requirement to use outside military force to create desirable changes in a society that would not move in that direction on its own.[71] Martin believes that there is no doubt that outsiders have attempted to control the political destiny of BH by force.[72] Although some scholars argue that peacekeeping is a form of imperialism, for the purpose of this book I use the term

---

[64] MONUC Conduct Unit, 'Issues to know: Sexual Exploitation', 27 November 2005 <http://monusco.unmissions.org/news.aspx>.

[65] Ibid.

[66] UNICEF, 'Inter-Agency Training for Focal Points on Protection from Sexual Exploitation and Abuse by UN personnel and partners: Facilitator's Manual' 2007 <http://www.unitarpoci.org/media/course_extras/vaw_focal_point_manual.pdf> 32.

[67] Constanze Schellhaas and Annette Seegers, 'Peacebuilding: imperialism's new disguise?' (2009) 18 (2) *African Security Review* 11.

[68] Ibid16.

[69] Ibid157.

[70] Kimberly Zisk Marten, *Enforcing the Peace: Learning from the Imperial Past* (Columbia University Press, 2004) 7.

[71] Ibid 38.

[72] Ibid 52.

'imperial' to stress peacekeepers' immunity, the lawlessness that exemption from local laws encourages, and the superior attitude of peacekeepers towards local populations.

The power of peacekeepers seems generally understood as economic since, according to the United Nations Junior Ranks Handbook, it is based on 'disparity of wealth between UN personnel and inhabitants of mission areas, who often live in conditions of dire poverty'.[73] Therefore, the economic power that UN staff enjoy over the local population seems to be the main reason for the 'strong discouragement' of sexual relationships, presenting an obstacle to the achievement of mutual consensual relationships between local women and peacekeepers. Due to the 'unequal power' in a peacekeeping context, the SGB suggests that it is highly likely that exploitative dynamics will be present in any relationship between a peacekeeper and a local woman. This approach makes assumptions about the complexities of power in sexual relationships. The result of such an approach is that basically all sexual relationships between peacekeepers and 'beneficiaries' are deemed to be unequal and exploitative.

I place my discussion about sexual relationships in peacekeeping operations within two feminist camps: 'radical' and 'sex-positive'. Although, there are many views in these two camps, in this book I draw on one end of the spectrum of radical feminism which represents the heart of radical feminist thinking. Radical feminists would accept the view that the power of men over women in (hetero)sexual relationships is inherently negative, an indicator of domination 'over' and a potential danger for women. As MacKinnon puts it 'men/women is a distinction not just of difference, but of power and powerlessness'.[74] By protecting 'the most vulnerable populations, especially women' from sexual exploitation, the SGB draws a distinction between vulnerable, powerless women and powerful male peacekeepers. Dworkin argues that male domination is pervasive and that all men are in the position of dominance over women simply because they are men. She suggests, similarly to the SGB, that relationships between men and women are asymmetrical, and men are in a position of domination.[75] In the context of peacekeeping, Defeis believes that peacekeepers, the majority of them men, exercise 'enormous power over the local population' in a 'hypermasculine culture that encourages sexual exploitation and abuse'.[76]

The SGB takes the same approach, assuming that local women cannot give meaningful consent to sexual relationships with peacekeepers. While the line between consensual and forced sexual relationships is contested, taking an overly

[73] DPKO, *UN Peacekeeping Handbook for Junior Ranks* (1997) 35.

[74] Catharine MacKinnon, *Feminism Unmodified: Discourses on Life and Law* (Harvard University Press, 1987) 123.

[75] Andrea Dworkin, *Pornography: Men Possessing Women* (Perigee Books, 1981).

[76] Elisabeth Defeis, 'U.N. Peacekeeping and Sexual Abuse and Exploitation: An End to Impunity' (2008) 7 (2) *Washington University Global Studies Law Review* 185, 191.

protective approach, as the SGB does, is inconsistent with women's equality.[77] This view denies women the sexual agency that is critical to their humanity and dignity. Although, the idea of consent in a post-conflict society is complex, I use the idea of consent in the sense of women's agency. While I acknowledge that it may be 'reasonable to be skeptical about people's choices'[78] which are 'socially constructed and constrained',[79] I believe that it is possible to give meaningful consent in times of war and in post-conflict periods.

In contrast to radical feminists, 'sex-positive' feminists such as Hartsock suggest that it is necessary to reconceptualise power from a feminist standpoint, one that is rooted in women's life experiences. Hartsock refers to power 'as energy and competence rather than dominance', which can 'point beyond understandings of power as power over others'.[80] Likewise, Young argues that power 'can be possessed by individuals in greater or lesser amounts'.[81] Many other feminists have also argued for a reconceptualisation of power as a capacity to transform or empower oneself, and understand power as power-to rather than power-over.[82] As Carmichael points out, the SGB conceptualisation of power raises the question of whether any sexual relationship can be said to be 'inherently equal', since power in 'human relationships can be exercised in multiple and subtle ways'.[83]

There are number of post-colonial scholars whose views are consistent with 'sex-positive' perspectives. To post-colonial feminists such as Kapur, the contexts in which women live matters. Her research is focused on India and how the colonial heritage of international law reinforces Western imperial ideas. She expands this view of women as 'victim subjects' by connecting 'cultural and gender essentialism', whereby women are portrayed as victims of their own culture.[84] She asserts that the exclusive focus on victim subjects has taken feminists back to a protectionist and conservative discourse.[85] While this discourse did invite feminist scholars to

[77] Dianne Otto, 'The Sexual Tensions of UN Peace Support Operations: A Plea for 'Sexual Positivity' (2007) XVIII *Finnish Yearbook of International Law* 40, 41.

[78] Anne Phillips, 'Feminism and Liberalism Revisited: Has Martha Nussbaum Got It Right?' (2001) 8(2) *Constellations* 262.

[79] Martha C. Nussbaum, *Sex and Social Justice* (Oxford University Press, 2000).

[80] Nancy Hartsock, *Money, Sex and Power: Towards a Feminist Historical Materialism* (Longman, 1983) 12, 224.

[81] Iris Marion Young, *Justice and the Politics of Difference* (Princeton University Press, 1990) 31.

[82] Sarah Hoagland, *Lesbian Ethics: Toward a New Value* (Institute of Lesbian Studies, 1988), Starhawk, *Truth or Dare: Encounters with Power, Authority, and Mystery* (Harper, 1987), Wartenberg, Thomas, *The Forms of Power: From Domination to Transformation* (Temple University Press, 1990).

[83] Jennine Carmichael, *First, Do No Harm: Addressing the Problem of Sexual Exploitation and Abuse by International Aid Workers and Peacekeepers* (MA Thesis, The University of Melbourne, 2006) 30.

[84] Ratna Kapur, 'The Tragedy of Victimization Rhetoric: Resurrecting the "Native" Subject in International/Post-Colonial Feminist Legal Politics' (2002) 15 *Harvard Human Rights Journal* 6.

[85] Ibid 5.

analyse the lives of women as unemancipated and universal subjects, it also at times resulted in imperialist views of women in the developing world, with the result that they are often presented as 'authentic victim subjects'.[86] Kapur is concerned that international feminist legal politics have reinforced the representation of Third World women as disempowered, victimised and brutalized, which recreates the imperialist image of native subjects as backward, ignorant, illiterate and different. She is concerned that this view prolongs the colonial rationale for intervening in the lives of native subjects and justifies the rescue operations advocated by Barry and other radical feminists.[87] The work of radical feminists has been influential in the debate on victim subjects and has recreated a colonial image of them. However, although post-colonial scholars are attentive to context, their work is not situated in a peacekeeping context.

Scully also argues that the rhetoric of the sexual vulnerability of women and girls has serious implications for women's leadership in post-conflict societies. She raises important questions such as what are the implications of defining a female subject as requiring sexual protection in the context of building a post-conflict society?[88] Zarkov is also concerned that classical feminist studies of women and war shifted from the promotion of agency and empowerment to a theoretically and politically much more problematic conceptualisation of sexual victimisation and victimhood of civilian women.[89] She argues that Eurocentrism, racism, and Orientalism have ensured that there have always been women and regions that have been seen as more empowered and emancipated than others. Thus, it has also been very easy to perceive some of them entirely through the prism of victimisation. Not surprisingly, women in the Balkans and African wars have been seen as belonging to the latter group and their sexual victimisation has been seen as the ultimate destiny of women in war.[90]

The ambiguous positioning of BH, both within and outside of the 'symbolic continent' of Europe, resulted in the exclusion of BH and the rest of the former Yugoslavia from Europe, which in turn affected the way relationships between women, gender and war in the region were theorised.[91] This ultimately created a shift in Western feminist theories on war. Studies on sexual violence against women in wars have contributed hugely to our understanding of the intersections between gender, sexuality, collective identities and violence. However, feminist studies of Yugoslavia, followed by the Rwandan war, largely focused on studies of

[86] Ibid 11.

[87] Ibid 11,12.

[88] Pamela Scully. 'Vulnerable women: A critical reflection on human rights discourse and sexual violence' (2009) 23 *Emory International Law Review* 113.

[89] Dubravka Zarkov, 'Towards a new theorizing of women, gender and war' in Evans M, Davis K and Lorber, J (eds) *Handbook of Gender and Women's Studies* (SAGE, 2006) 230.

[90] Ibid.

[91] Milica Bakic-Hayden and Robert M. Hayden, 'Orientalist Variations on the Theme "Balkans": Symbolic geography in recent Yugoslav Cultural Politics' (1992) 51(1) *Slavic Review* 9.

war rape.[92] Zarkov also suggests that agency and victimisation should be only two of the many possible narratives of the positioning of women within a violent conflict. Instead of assuming the presence of either agency or victimisation, a feminist studying of a violent conflict should rather ask when and how agency and victimisation are prioritised in the experiences and representations of war, what other narratives of women's and men's positioning within the war there are, and how they are obscured or denied.[93] Because of such positioning of BH, there has been no scholarly discussion about sexual relationships in war and peacekeeping contexts. The former Yugoslav feminists have focused almost exclusively on rape and sexual violence instead.

The SGB's understanding of power assumes the radical feminist view, denying women's sexual agency and depicting women as inherently sexually vulnerable, which is incompatible with women's autonomy and human rights. As Otto argues, the SGB reinforces gender inequality and relies on protective representations of women that locate sexual power and agency with men.[94] Consequently, the SGB reinforces gender stereotypes by portraying all local women as powerless and all peacekeepers as powerful.

Alternatively, 'sex-positive' feminists would suggest that power should be viewed as ability, choice of engagement and potentially transformational.[95] Such an approach to power would be consistent with the promotion of gender equality and women's empowerment. The UN has been instrumental in setting norms on gender equality, making reference to the equal rights of women in the UN Charter,[96] which has been developed in international human rights law in treaties like the International Covenant on Civil and Political Rights (ICCPR)[97] and the International Covenant on Economic, Social and Cultural Rights (ICESCR),[98] well as CEDAW.[99] Together, these guarantee non-discrimination between men and

---

[92] Zarkov, above n 89, 231.

[93] Ibid 233.

[94] Dianne Otto, 'Making Sense of Zero Tolerance Policies in Peacekeeping Sexual Economies' in Vanessa Munro and Carl F. Stychin (eds.), *Sexuality and the Law: Feminist Engagements* (Routledge-Cavendish, 2007) 259, 278.

[95] Sarah Hoagland, above n 82.

[96] Preamble of the UN Charter, 'We the peoples of the United Nations determine, to...reaffirm faith in fundamental human rights, in dignity and worth of the human person, in the equal rights of men and women'. See also, 'The United Nations shall promote: universal respect for, and observance of, human rights and fundamental freedoms for all without distinction as to race, sex, language, or religion', art. 55 (c).

[97] The States Parties to the present Covenant undertake to ensure the equal right of men and women to the enjoyment of all civil and political rights set forth in the present Covenant (art. 3).

[98] The States Parties to the present Covenant undertake to ensure the equal right of men and women to the enjoyment of all economic, social and cultural rights set forth in the present Covenant (art. 3).

[99] States Parties shall take in all fields, in particular in the political, social, economic and cultural fields, all appropriate measures, including legislation, to ensure the full development and advancement of women, for the purpose of guaranteeing them the exercise and enjoyment of human rights and freedoms on a basis of equality with men (art. 3).

women, as well as women's right to exercise and enjoy all human rights and fundamental freedoms equally with men. Also CEDAW, Article 2, requires States Parties to (d) 'refrain from engaging in any act or practice of discrimination against women and to ensure that public authorities and institutions shall act in conformity with this obligation' and (f) to 'take all appropriate measures, including legislation, to abolish or modify existing laws, regulations, customs and practices which constitute discrimination against women.' Thus, rather than abolishing laws that discriminate against women, the UN adopted a policy which directly discriminates against them. The UDHR Article 29 (2) declares that the law may limit the individual's rights and freedoms 'solely for the purpose of securing due recognition and respect for the rights and freedoms of others and of meeting the just requirements of morality, public order and the general welfare in a democratic society.' It is not clear how sexual relationships between peacekeepers and local women may jeopardise 'the rights and freedoms of others' or are against morality, public order and welfare.

The Beijing Platform for Action most explicitly recognises women's sexual rights:

> The human rights of women include their right to have control over and decide freely and responsibly on matters related to their sexuality... Equal relationships between men and women in matters of sexual relations and reproduction, including full respect for the integrity of the person, require mutual respect, consent and shared responsibility for sexual behaviour and its consequences.[100]

The SGB also observes that sexual relationships between peacekeepers and local women undermine the credibility and integrity of the UN. Of course UN staff have a duty to conduct themselves professionally and since integrity is a core value of the UN, staff are obliged to act and work in accordance with established guidelines and ethical behaviour.[101] The individual and professional conduct of UN staff should demonstrate the highest professional standards and mirror the organisational structure. While it is reasonable for the UN to be concerned that cases of sexual exploitation harm its image, it is not clear how consensual sexual relationships could endanger the credibility of the UN and the professionalism of its staff members. As Otto argues, the reasons given by the UN for discouraging sexual relationships seem to have little to do with concerns for the human rights of local populations or UN staff, and more to do with the global image of the UN.[102] However, upholding the image of the UN by effectively banning consensual sexual relationships may be at the expense of the local women's and peacekeepers' rights to privacy, liberty, autonomy and bodily integrity, as well as sexual rights as an indivisible part of human rights.

---

[100] The United Nations Fourth World Conference on Women, Platform for Action (Beijing, China, September 1995), para 96.

[101] Henri Fourcault, 'United Nations Organizational Integrity Initiative', 25 March 2004 <http://unpan1.un.org/intradoc/groups/public/documents/UN/UNPAN021339.pdf>.

[102] Otto, above n 94, 260.

The 'strong discouragement' of sexual relationships between peacekeepers and local women seems to interfere with the right to privacy, to which all human beings are entitled. Article 17 of the ICCPR protects the right to privacy from arbitrary or unlawful interference. Also, Article 12 of the UDHR protects against arbitrary interference with privacy, family and home. The right to privacy is central to the exercise of sexual autonomy and allows everyone to make decisions about their own sexuality without arbitrary interference. In the case *Toonen v. Australia,*[103] the ICCPR Committee found that adult consensual sexual activity in private was protected by article 17, and that criminalisation constitutes arbitrary interference. It stated that 'it is undisputed that adult sexual activity in private is covered by the concept of 'privacy'...'[104] This aspect of decision follows the European Court of Human Rights' judgements in *Norris v Ireland,*[105] *Modinos v Cyprus,*[106] and *Dudgeon v UK,*[107] where laws banning consensual sex between adult males were held to violate the right to privacy, Article 8, in the European Conventions of Human Rights. The HRC also found a violation of Article 17(1) in conjunction with Article 2(1). It found that *Toonen* had suffered discrimination on prohibited grounds in the enjoyment of his right to privacy. In his dissenting opinion in the US Supreme Court case of *Bowers v. Hardwick,*[108] Justice Blackmun suggests that:

> Only the most wilful blindness could obscure the fact that sexual intimacy is a sensitive, key relationship of human existence, central to family life, community welfare, and the development of human personality....The fact that individuals define themselves in a significant way through their intimate sexual relationships with others suggests...that there may be many 'right' ways of conducting those relationships, and that much of the richness of a relationship will come from the freedom an individual has to choose the form and nature of these intensely personal bonds.

In the view of the Committee on ICCPR, this right is required to be guaranteed against 'all interference and attacks whether they emanate from State authorities or from natural or legal persons'.[109] It seems that this right has not been respected from 'arbitrary' and 'unlawful' interference in peacekeeping contexts. Although Committee acknowledges that 'protection of privacy is necessary relative', the public authorities should only be able to call for 'information relating to an

[103] *Toonen v. Australia*, CCPR/C/50/D/488/1992, UN Human Rights Committee (HRC), 4 April 1994.

[104] Ibid, para 8.2.

[105] *Norris v Ireland* (Application no. 10581/83) European Court of Human Rights, Judgment 26 October 1988.

[106] *Modinos v Cyprus* (Application no. 15070/89) European Court of Human Rights, Judgment 22 April 1993.

[107] *Dudgeon v The United Kingdom*, (Application no. 7525/76) European Court of Human Rights Judgment 22 October 1981.

[108] *Bowers v. Hardwick*, 478 U.S. 186, 196 (1986), overruled by *Lawrence v. Texas*, 539 U.S. 558 (2003).

[109] General Comment No 16: The right to respect of privacy, family, home and correspondence, and protection of honour and reputation (Art 17) 08/04/1988 para 1.

individual's private life' if the knowledge of such information is 'essential in the interests of society as understood under the Convention'.[110] Even in such cases, 'relevant legislations must specify in detail the precise circumstances in which such interferences may be permitted.'[111] Thus, while the right to privacy and other human rights are not absolute, any limitation must be necessary, proportionate and not arbitrary. It is important to note that the cases that cover the right to privacy in international law concern homosexual rights. There are no cases that concern heterosexual sexual relationships and the breaches of the right to privacy. In the peacekeeping context, both peacekeepers and local women have the right to engage in consensual sexual relationships, which are a private matter between adults. The SGB's 'strong discouragement' of such relationships is therefore contrary to international human rights law.

3.4.3 *Prostitution*

'Exchange of money, employment, goods or services for sex, including sexual favours or other forms of humiliating, degrading or exploitative behaviour, is prohibited. This includes any exchange of assistance that is due to beneficiaries of assistance.'[112]

To avoid any doubt about whether the preceding paragraph includes prostitution, in its guidance on the SGB the DPKO states that 'UN staff are prohibited from soliciting or engaging in prostitution'.[113] While there is no internationally recognised definition of prostitution, the definition that I adopt in this research is that it refers to adult, voluntary and adequately renumerated sex work which is non-exploitative sexual conduct. On the contrary, the exchange of money for sex with children, forced and unfairly renumerated sexual activity are all sexually exploitative.

Similarly to the 1949 Convention for the Suppression of the Traffic in Persons and of the Exploitation of the Prostitution of Others, the SGB includes prostitution as a form of 'humiliating, degrading or exploitative behaviour' and implies that all sex, whether consensual or not and whether adequately paid or not, is a 'harmful experience'.[114] Thus, the approach of the SGB is similar to the approach of the 1949 Convention which states in its preamble that 'prostitution [is] incompatible with the dignity and worth of the human person and endangers the welfare of the individual, family and the community'. The Convention was primarily directed at addressing international organised crime and was not driven by a concern for the human rights

[110] Ibid, para 7.

[111] Ibid, para 8.

[112] Secretary-General's Bulletin, above n 1, sec 3.2 (c).

[113] DPKO, 'Standard Operating Procedure: Public Information Activities on Sexual Exploitation and Abuse' (3 April 2006).

[114] Carmichael, above n 83, 29.

of those involved. It denied 'victims' the capacity to consent to prostitution and urged states to take measures to abolish prostitution and to rehabilitate its 'victims'. Likewise, the SGB treats prostitution as a form of sexual exploitation that should be banned, regardless of the consent of a woman who offers sex in exchange for adequate remuneration.

The 1979 Convention on the Elimination of All Forms of Discrimination against Women (CEDAW) echoes the 1949 Convention in calling on all state parties 'to take all appropriate measures to suppress all forms of traffic in women'.[115] However, CEDAW does not call for the suppression of prostitution, but for the suppression of 'the exploitation of prostitution' (pimping).[116] General Recommendation 19 of the CEDAW Committee on violence against women makes it clear that CEDAW requires State Parties to suppress trafficking and the exploitation of the prostitution of women, but that they also must acknowledge that prostitutes 'are specially vulnerable to violence because their status, which may be unlawful, tends to marginalize them'.[117] Thus, the CEDAW Committee interprets CEDAW obligations to require State Parties to protect prostitutes from violence and exploitation.[118] The CEDAW Committee also recognises that due to their marginal status, prostitutes should enjoy the equal protection of laws against rape and other forms of violence.[119] It does not consider prostitution to be inherently exploitative, but exhorts States to actively address the stigma that is associated with prostitutes' marginality. Likewise, the 1993 Declaration on Elimination of Violence against Women condemns 'trafficking in women and forced prostitution',[120] making an important distinction between forced and consensual prostitution. This use of language credits adult women with the agency to consent to prostitution and treats only forced prostitution as a human rights violation.

The 2000 Protocol to Prevent, Suppress and Punish Trafficking in Persons, Especially Women and Children, Supplementing the UN Convention against Transnational Organised Crime, bans trafficking in persons for the purpose of exploitation, including 'exploitation of prostitution of others' or 'other forms of sexual exploitation'.[121] However, the latter was left undefined in the 2000 Protocol since states could not agree on the key question of whether prostitution is inherently

[115] *Convention on the Elimination of All Forms of Discrimination against Women* (CEDAW), opened for signature 18 December 1979, UNTS 13 (entered into force 3 September 1981) art.6.

[116] Committee on the Elimination of Discrimination Against Women, 'Violence Against Women', General Recommendation 19 (1992), para 15.

[117] Ibid art 6, para 15.

[118] Ibid.

[119] Ibid.

[120] *Declaration on Elimination of Violence against Women* (1994), art 2 (b).

[121] *The Protocol to Prevent, Suppress and Punish Trafficking in Persons, Especially Women and Children, Supplementing the United Nations Convention against Transnational Organized Crime*, GA Res 25, annex II, 55th sess, UN Doc A/45/49 (entered into force 9 September 2003) art 3 (a).

exploitative or not.[122] While one group of states claimed that any distinction between forced and voluntary prostitution is morally unacceptable, the majority of governments rejected the idea that voluntary prostitution is sexually exploitative and constitutes trafficking.[123] They therefore rejected the idea that voluntary prostitution should be included in the definition of trafficking. This was supported later by the Office of the United Nations High Commissioner for Human Rights (OHCHR), United Nations Children's Fund (UNICEF) and the International Organisation for Migration (IOM).[124] Thus, the 2000 Protocol affectively leaves it to State Parties to decide whether voluntary prostitution is exploitative.

Although international human rights law has yet to provide for comprehensive protection specific to the enforcement of the rights of sex workers, there is a legal basis for it in treaties which promulgate the right to free choice of work. The right to free choice of work and to just and favourable work conditions are fundamental economic rights that are embodied in international human rights law and listed in Article 23(1) of the UDHR. Article 6(1) of the ICESCR also includes the right to free choice of work, while Article 11(1) of the CEDAW recognises 'the right to work as an inalienable right to all human beings.' CEDAW Article 11, in particular sections 1(d) and 1(f), calls upon States Parties to ensure equal protection for women from poor working conditions. Since sex work is primarily female, a ban on it constitutes a restriction on the right to work on the grounds of sex, which is discriminatory.[125] Therefore, it also breaches the gender equality provisions found in the UDHR Article 2, ICCPR Article 3, ICESCR Article 3 and CEDAW Article 2 (g) which calls on state parties '[t]o repeal all national penal provisions which constitute discrimination against women.'

The debate among states about whether prostitution is inherently exploitative is reflected in feminist scholarship. The argument that prostitution is inherently exploitative and degrading is presented in the work of radical feminist Catherine MacKinnon, who asserts that prostitution 'subordinates and exploits women in social life'.[126] Sheila Jeffreys also argues that prostitution is a 'harmful traditional practice' which creates stereotyped sex roles and is for the benefit of men.[127] Similarly, Laurie Shrage maintains that the sex industry should not be supported

---

[122] Joyce Outshoorn, 'The Political Debates on Prostitution and Trafficking of Women' (2005) 12 (1) *Social Politics: International Studies in Gender, State and Society* 150.

[123] Anne Gallagher, 'Human Rights and the New UN Protocols on Trafficking and Migrant Smuggling: A Preliminary Analysis' (2001) 23(4) *Human Rights Quarterly* 975, 984.

[124] Justice Sujata V Manohar et al, 'Preliminary Report on Women and Migration', International Law Association: New Delhi Conference (2002), on file with author.

[125] Jo Bindman, 'Redefining Prostitution as Sex Work on the International Agenda' (Antislavery International, unpublished report, 1997) <http://www.walnet.org/csis/papers/redefining.html>.

[126] Catharine A MacKinnon, 'Prostitution and Civil Rights' (1993) 1 *Michigan Journal of Gender & Law* 15.

[127] Sheila Jeffreys, 'The Legalization of Prostitution: A Failed Social Experiment (2003) United Nations'. Speech delivered at the Swedish mission side event at the Commission on the Status of Women, United Nations, New York, 5 March, 2003.

because 'feminists find the prostitute's work morally and politically objectionable'.[128] She argues that the sex industry is structured by values and attitudes that are oppressive to women, since it depends upon the normalisation of certain principles that marginalise women politically and socially.[129] Thus, from her perspective, a sex industry is incompatible with the equality of women.[130] Kathleen Barry argues that states should be closing down brothels and criminalising their customers, and that economic resources invested in prostitution could be used to 'provide gainful employment for women'.[131] Radical feminists argue that no woman would prostitute herself by free will or choice, and they deem irrelevant any discussion of either the conditions under which prostitution might be performed or women's consent. They regard all prostitution, and in particular prostitution in PKOs, as oppression of women and as an act of violence against women. While they perceive women as inherently vulnerable, they portray peacekeepers as sexual perpetrators.

There are a number of post-colonial scholars whose views are consistent with radical feminism. Post-colonial feminist scholar Fareda Banda uses the sex industry as an example of jobs that are 'often unregulated, poorly paid and expose women to violence and being trafficked'.[132] Fayemi also argues that prostitution and female trafficking are not only exploitation of 'feminine sexuality by profiteers, but also the objectification of women's dignity'.[133] She does not differentiate between these two industries and claims that both are 'immoral and illegal'.[134] Fayemi further claims that prostitution 'markets the violence, the practices of subordination, and objectification of women, as sex machines that can be controlled and customized'.[135] It is 'a brutal sexual desire by a person (usually male) and a reluctant and loathing submission, purchased by money on the other (usually female)'.[136]

Although Balkans feminist scholars have been preoccupied with rape, sexual violence and sex trafficking, a few have published short papers or articles about prostitution as exploitation. Boric, a leading Croatian feminist activist and academic, reportedly stated that the women's movement in Croatia condemns legalisation of prostitution and asked the government 'to shift its focus from the

[128] Laurie Shrage, 'Should Feminists Oppose Prostitution?' (1989) 99 (2) *Ethics* 347.

[129] Ibid.

[130] Laurie Shrage, 'Comment on Overall's "What's Wrong with Prostitution? Evaluating Sex Work" (1994) 19(2) *Signs: Journal of Women in Culture and Society* 564.

[131] Kathleen Barry, *The Prostitution of Sexuality* (New York University Press, 1995) 33.

[132] Fareda Banda and Christine Chinkin, 'Gender, Minorities and Indigenous Peoples' (Minority Rights Group International, 2004) 11.

[133] Ademola Kazeem Fayemi, 'The Challenges of Prositution and Female Trafficking in Africa: An African Ethico-Feminist Perspective' (2009) 3(1) *The Journal of Pan African Studies* 200.

[134] Ibid 210.

[135] Ibid 201.

[136] Ibid.

woman's body to clients'.[137] She expressed the concern that Croatia has become a very attractive place for the booming sex industry and that it is of concern that some people support legalisation of prostitution.[138] Kesic similarly argues that prostitution, the sex industry and pornography are 'a commercial attraction for violence' and the 'the selling of women's bodies'.[139] Such ideas reflect the views of radical feminists such as Raymond and MacKinnon, who have been influential in the region's sexual politics. Overall, there has been little discussion among feminists about prostitution in the post-conflict Balkans. Since trafficking was the major problem, all discussions about prostitution and trafficking are conflated, which mirrors the SGB's position.

In the context of peacekeeping, several scholars have adopted the radical feminist perspective when discussing the SGB approach to prostitution. Kanetake, for example, argues that the UN needs to condemn all forms of prostitution in PKOs in order to regain its image and public confidence in peacekeeping.[140] For this reason, Kanetake argues that it is 'understandable' that the SGB bans all forms of prostitution.[141] Similarly, Defeis believes that prostitution must be prohibited in PKOs because of its 'inherently coercive character'.[142] She urges that prostitution should be criminalised in the peacekeeping context and that troop-contributing countries should be obliged to recognise the 'inherently coercive nature of peacekeeper prostitution', regardless of any domestic laws that may make distinctions between voluntary and forced prostitution.[143] Grady also does not draw any distinction between voluntary and forced prostitution in the peacekeeping context. She supports the SGB approach to prostitution since sex trafficking and 'prostituting of women and children' become a facet of illegal economies.[144]

Peacekeepers are deployed to places where the social fabric has been destroyed and where the local population endures severe psychological and economic hardship.[145] The factors that contribute to the view that prostitution is a form of sexual exploitation, which are often mentioned by these scholars, are poverty and the

---

137 Ured za ljudska prava, 'Okrugli stol pod nazivom: Argumenti pro & contra legalizacije prostitucije' 30 May 2005 <http://www.ljudskaprava-vladarh.hr/Default.aspx?art=93&sec=59>.

138 Ibid.

139 Vesna Kesic, 'Odgovor Ogurlicu: Diskriminacija ocigledna vec iz naslova i opreme teksta koji zene ('lijepe djevojke') i jeftino pivo nude u paketu kao mamac za svjetsko prvenstvo u nogometu' 25 April 2007 <http://www.ured-ravnopravnost.hr/page.php?id=237&type=article>.

140 Machiko Kanetake, 'Whose Zero Tolerance Counts? Reassessing a Zero Tolerance Policy against Sexual Exploitation and Abuse by UN Peacekeepers' (2010) 17(2) *International Peacekeeping*, 202–203.

141 Ibid 202.

142 Defeis, above n 76, 205.

143 Ibid.

144 Kate Grady, 'Sexual Exploitation and Abuse by UN Peacekeepers: A Threat to Impartiality', (2010) 17(2) *International Peacekeeping* 215, 217.

145 Anna Shotton, 'A Strategy to Address Sexual Exploitation by U.N. Peacekeeping Personnel', (2006) 39 *Cornell Law Review* 97,103.

vulnerability of women in post-conflict societies, and the fact that the bulk of peacekeepers are men who are wealthier than the local population, and who exercise and may abuse the economic power they have over the locals.[146] This radical feminist position is echoed in the ZTP, which views prostitution as an entirely negative activity that is a source of harm and humiliation, and therefore should be banned. It treats prostitution as a form of sexual exploitation which degrades, objectifies and exploits women.

One of the major criticisms of radical feminist theory is its inability to acknowledge any difference between voluntary and involuntary prostitution.[147] An alternative view is based on liberal feminism which frames prostitution as a viable employment option that, when chosen by women, should be treated as work, not exploitation.[148] Nussbaum, for example, argues that although prostitution is usually a lowly paid job, prostitutes have a degree of choice about which clients they accept and what activities they perform, and thus 'should be allowed to pursue their trade'.[149] She asserts that women have the ability to choose the type of work and sexual relationships they engage in.[150] Phillips critiques Nussbaum's understanding of choice and women's autonomy. She cautions that it is difficult to say what does 'count as an authentic choice or preference', and how we are to view the 'choices' of women in cultures that attach less value to autonomy.[151] She gives an example of the fact that women living in a society where girls who freely enjoy their sexuality are considered unmarriageable. These women will insist on the genital mutilation of their own daughters, but that does not mean that this is practice that women 'choose'.[152] Phillips argues for a different understanding of the relationship between equality and autonomy that reinstates equality as a central feminist concern. It is not just whether individuals have the minimum necessary for choice, but whether their positioning in social hierarchies shapes their choices in unequal ways.[153]

Pateman argues that prostitution is a form of work where a prostitute sells 'sexual services' and should be treated in the same way as any other wage-earning

---

[146] Defeis, above n 76,108; Machiko Kanetake, above n 140, 209.

[147] Jody Freeman, 'The Feminist Debate over Prostitution Reform: Prostitutes' Rights Groups, Radical Feminists, and the (Im)possibility of Consent' (1990) 5 *Berkeley Women's Law Journal* 94.

[148] Shannon Bell, *Reading, Writing and Rewriting the Prostituted Body* (Indiana University Press, 1994); Wendy Chapkis, Performing Erotic Labor (Routledge, 1997); Gail Pheterson, *A Vindication of the Rights of Whores* (The Seal Press, 1989) and *The Prostitution Prism* (Amsterdam University Press, 1996).

[149] Martha C.Nussbaum, *Sex and Social Justice* (Oxford University Press, 1999) 281.

[150] Ibid.

[151] Anne Phillips, above n 78, 'Feminism and Liberalism Revisited: Has Martha Nussbaum Got It Right?' (2001) 8(2) *Constellations* 262,254.

[152] Ibid 262.

[153] Ibid 264.

labour.[154] Liberal feminists are generally concerned with the economic conditions under which prostitution takes place. Excluded from high-income employment, they argue that women often enter into prostitution as a means of economic survival.[155] The sex industry can thus become an important component of local economies, for example, in communities adjacent to military bases, in PKOs and where transnational corporations attract a largely male workforce.[156]

'Sex positive' feminists take this analysis a step further by questioning the underlying 'sexual negativity' of radical feminists. Kempadoo, for example, defends prostitution and claims that 'the global sex trade cannot be simply reduced to one monolithic explanation of violence to women', suggesting that the diverse cultural contexts and conditions under which prostitution is performed need to be considered. Murray and Doezema argue that when they are pictured as naïve, poor Third World women are perceived as unable to act as agents in their own lives, or to make uncoerced decisions to work in the sex industry.[157] Kempadoo says: 'It is not always clear that it is due to abject poverty, or lack of their skills and possibilities that women turn to this particular income-generating activity', but rather that sex work is one of a number of 'sources of livelihood' utilised by women.[158] Sex workers have to be treated in the same way as 'any other set of migrant workers who need improved conditions, safety, access to health services, and freedom from harassment and abuse'.[159] She argues that the representation of Third World women by radical feminists such as Barry characterises them as not yet 'whole or developed', resembling minors who are in need of assistance and guidance. In striking contrast to this image stands the image of the emancipated Western woman who has 'control over her income, her body and her sexuality'.[160] Such imagery is structured within the framework of colonial thought which assumes that women in the Third World are infantile, incapable of self-determination or autonomy, and from backward civilizations.[161] The notion of 'the suffering third world prostitute' has often been invoked to justify Western interventionist programs.[162] Rescue work attempts to force sex workers to leave prostitution without providing real solutions

---

[154] Carole Pateman, *The Sexual Contract* (1988) 202.

[155] Holly B. Fetcher, 'Three Stories of Prostitution in the West: Prostitutes 'Groups, Law and Feminist "Truth"', (1994) 4 *Columbia Journal of Gender and Law* 26.

[156] Alison Jaggar, 'Is Globalization Good for Women?' (2001) 53(4) *Comparative Literature* 306.

[157] Jo Doezema, 'Choice in Prostitution' in Conference Book: Changing Faces of Prostitution, Helsinki 3–5 May, 1995 (Helsinki: Unioni, The League of Finnish Feminists); Alison Murray, 'Debt Bondage and Trafficking: Don't Believe the Hype' in K. Kampadoo and J. Doezema, *Global Sex Worker's Rights: Rights, Resistance and, Redefinition (*Routledge, 1998).

[158] Kempadoo and Doezema, Ibid 1,11.

[159] Ibid128.

[160] Ibid 11.

[161] Kapur, above n 84, 11.

[162] Jo Doezema,'Ouch! Western Feminists' 'Wounded Attachment' to the 'Third World Prostitute' 67 (2001) *Feminist Review* 16.

to the larger problems of unemployment, poverty, female subordination and violence.[163]

In the Balkans, prostitution was empirically investigated in 2009 when Simic and Rhodes undertook a qualitative study of sex work in Serbia, interviewing street sex workers about their experiences in the industry. This recent study asked sex workers about their views and experiences, and their perceptions of the risk of HIV. According to Simic and Rhodes, the sex workers understood sex work 'as a consensual sexual exchange for money according to agreements made in advance with clients'. They also emphasise the importance of 'being in control in sex work transactions', which protects them against violence to both their dignity and their bodies.[164] Sex workers reported that the various authorities were against them, but the police in particular were waging an 'undeclared war' against sex workers in Serbia. Some of them even said that while they could manage their clients, their 'greatest enemy' was the police.[165] Simic and Rhodes argue that sex workers are active in the search for respect and preservation of dignity.[166] Community-organised interventions, criminal justice and welfare institutions in Serbia reproduce rather than resist the cycle of violence that sex workers face.[167] It is of concern, but not surprising, that the police are often perceived as 'an enemy' rather than as a source of assistance and help. However, radical feminists endorse 'rescue' operations, which seek to 'save' sex workers from the industry. Throughout the last century, radical feminists and an alliance of the Christian right waged a so called 'moral crusade' against prostitution, and police raided sex establishments to detain and arrest prostitutes.[168] According to SANGRAM, it is ironic that these raids, led by police and which often led to abuse of sex workers, have been supported by some feminists in the women's rights movement.[169]

Although they acknowledge that prostitutes are likely to have limited options, 'sex-positive' feminists argue that a woman's choice to work in the sex industry and her right to sexual self-determination should be respected.[170] From this position, prostitution is not inherently exploitative, but the conditions under which the work is done may be problematic. Hence, 'sex-positive' feminists focus their attention on

---

[163] Taimur Khan et al, 'Sex Workers Project at the Urban Justice Center, Critique of the Anti-Prostitution Pledge and its Global Impact' (2007) <http://www.sexworkersproject.org/media-toolkit/downloads/20070330-BriefingPaperOnAnti-ProstitutionPledge.pdf>.

[164] Milena Simic and Tim Rhodes, 'Violence, Dignity and HIV Vulnerability: Street Sex Work in Serbia', (2009) 31(1) *Sociology of Health and Illness* 5.

[165] Ibid 6.

[166] Ibid13.

[167] Ibid14.

[168] Ronald Weitzer, 'Moral Crusade against Prostitution' (2006) 43 (3) *Society* 33.

[169] SANGRAM, 'Are we not Women? Women in Prostitution, Feminist Activists, and Sex Worker's Rights Groups in Dialogue' (2008) 14 *Point of View* 12.

[170] Kamala Kempadoo, 'Women of Color and the Global Sex Trade: Transnational Feminist Perspectives' (2001) 1(3) *Meridians* 28.

combating forced prostitution and improving wages and working conditions for those who choose to work as prostitutes.[171]

Thus far, few 'sex-positive' feminists have been critical of the ZTP. One critique, developed by Otto, addresses the over-inclusiveness of the definition of sexual exploitation in the context of PKOs, which includes consensual sex between local people and peacekeepers.[172] She argues that the SGB treats almost all sex as coercion and completely ignores the environment that frames both agency and survival.[173] Similarly, Ndulo, while acknowledging that prostitution becomes a source of income for some girls and women in the peacekeeping context, believes that they still 'willingly engage in prostitution' so 'one should not totally disregard the[ir] agency'.[174] Carmichael is also critical of the SGB approach and argues that grouping sex with 'humiliating or exploitative behaviour'[175] implies that all sex, 'or at least sex between foreign men and local women', is a harmful experience, 'particularly when a transactional exchange is involved'.[176] While there is no doubt that, as explored in Chap. 2, the post-conflict environment heightens potential sexual exploitation, these scholars argue that women should be seen as active agents and not victims who need protection from male sexual power.[177] Therefore, by conflating consensual and enforced sex, the SGB denies women's sexual agency and is inconsistent with women's equality, privacy and sexuality rights.[178] It also strips peacekeepers of sexual agency and depicts them as sexual predators, which supports patriarchal ideologies that absolve men from personal responsibility for their sexual conduct.[179] The SGB also portrays peacekeepers as inherently powerful, ignoring the complexities and diversity of masculinities that may exist in PKOs. As Connell argues, in multicultural settings there are likely to be multiple definitions of masculinity that exist in hierarchical relationships.[180] Thus, masculinities, like femininities, are not homogeneous, and to treat them as such is a deeply troubling denial of human dignity.

---

[171] Outshoorn, above n. 122, 146.

[172] Otto, above n 77, 260.

[173] Ibid.

[174] Muna Ndulo, 'The United Nations Responses To The Sexual Abuse And Exploitation Of Women And Girls By Peacekeeping Missions' (2008) 27(1) *Berkeley Journal of International Law* 143.

[175] 'Exchange of money, employment, goods or services for sex, including sexual favors or other forms of humiliating, degrading or exploitative behaviour, is prohibited.' Secretary-General Bulletin, above n 4, section 3.2 (c).

[176] Carmichael, above n 83, 29.

[177] Otto, above n 77.

[178] Ibid 41.

[179] Ibid 53.

[180] Bob Connell, 'Masculinities, violence and Peacemaking' *Peace News* (online), 2001 <http://www.peacenews.info/issues/2443/connell.html>.

In recent feminist scholarship, there is growing recognition of the need to transcend the victim/agent dichotomy in anti-prostitution and pro-sex-worker feminist theorising. O'Neill argues that sex workers do not simply exist as agents or victims, labourers or criminals, products of liberation or products of exploitation.[181] Depicting and using sex workers solely as a symbol of exploitation clouds the complexity of their lives. Mgbako and Smith also argue that there is a need to move beyond the polarised debate in which both sides too often present agency and victimhood as mutually exclusive realities. Acknowledging that prostitution is work does not mean denying that sex workers can be victims of physical and sexual exploitation, and health degradation.[182] However, as Schultz argues, if 'we insist that prostitution and other forms of commercial sex are not work, we perpetuate the myth that work is always uplifting and freely chosen'.[183] Rather than continuing this polarised debate, feminists should work towards eradication of the underlying societal conditions of gender, poverty and abusive working conditions that often drive people into prostitution.[184]

In sum, the treatment of prostitution in international law has undergone significant changes over the last 50 years. As demonstrated, there has been a significant shift from the 1949 Convention and its call for the abolition of all forms of prostitution, to the 2000 Protocol, which explicitly prohibits only forced prostitution. However, the SGB reiterates the provisions and language of the 1949 Convention, rather than following the developments in international human rights law since then. The SGB's approach to prostitution echoes the radical feminist view that prostitution is inherently degrading and exploitative and must therefore be prohibited in all circumstances. Accordingly, it portrays all prostitutes as exploited and all peacekeepers who engage the services of prostitutes as sexual predators. While there is a legitimate concern that the conditions under which women prostitutes work in PKOs may put them at increased risk of exploitation, as 'sex-positive' feminists argue, this should not justify the denial of women's agency and choice to work in the sex industry. Rather, the economic and patriarchal inequalities that are present need to be addressed. Likewise, the agency and choice to engage in sex with prostitutes should not be denied to peacekeepers.

---

[181] Maggie O'Neill, *Prostitution and Feminism: Towards a Policy of Feeling* (Wiley-Blackwell, 2001) 18.

[182] Chi Mgbako and Laura Smith, 'Sex Work and Human Rights in Africa' (2011) 33(4) *Fordham International Law Journal* 1179.

[183] Vicki Schultz, 'Sex and Work' (2006) 18 *The Yale Journal of Law and Feminism* 233.

[184] Ibid 227.

3.4.4 Conclusions

Since the adoption of the SGB, some UN strategies have been developed to strengthen the ZTP approach. In 2004, the SG appointed Prince Zeid, Jordan's Ambassador to the UN and the Permanent Representative of a major troop- and police-contributing country, as well as a former civilian peacekeeper. Prince Zeid was appointed as the SG adviser on addressing the problem of sexual exploitation and sexual abuse by peacekeepers. He was instructed to travel to the eastern Congo to investigate the allegations of sexual exploitation and sexual abuse by peacekeepers, and to advise how to deal with the problem.[185] Prince Zeid's 'Comprehensive strategy to eliminate future sexual exploitation' recommended to the General Assembly that the SGB should apply not only to UN staff members, but to all categories of peacekeepers, including civilian police, military observers, members of national contingents, UN volunteers, consultants and individual contractors.[186] In April 2005, the Special Committee on Peacekeeping Operations (comprising troop- and police-contributing Member States and others) agreed, recommending that the SGB standards should apply to all peacekeeping personnel.[187] In the same year, Conduct and Discipline teams that specifically deal with allegations of sexual exploitation were established. The SGB also served as a foundation for elaborating the SG's rules on non-fraternisation with local people, which at present tend to exclude any socialising with locals as one of the measures to prevent sexual exploitation.[188] These rules not only prohibit sex between peacekeepers and local people, but all social contact.

In sum, the SGB regards almost all sex between peacekeepers and local women as sexual exploitation, including sexual relationships and adult voluntary prostitution, regardless of consent, age and fair remuneration. The SGB claims that by banning prostitution and 'strongly discouraging' sexual relationships, it merely reiterates international legal norms and standards. However, as I have outlined in these sections, the SGB is in many respects inconsistent with international human rights norms and standards. Driven by radical feminist thinking, the SGB relies on gender stereotypes, takes an overly protective approach and limits the full exercise of women's and peacekeepers' human rights and freedoms. It denies their sexual rights and their agency, and depicts women as powerless, or as victims who lack responsibility and have no control over their lives and bodies, meaning they are inevitably sexually exploitable. The SGB also portrays male peacekeepers as predators who cannot treat women as equals. Finally, although the SGB uses the

---

[185] United Nations General Assembly, *Comprehensive review of the whole question of peacekeeping operations in all their aspects*, GA Res A/59/710 (24 March 2005).

[186] Ibid.

[187] *Report of the Special Committee on Peacekeeping Operations and its Working Group on the 2005 resumed session*, GA A/59/19/Add.1, 59th session (New York, 4–8 April 2005).

[188] *Seventeenth report of the Secretary-General on the United Nations Organization Mission in the Democratic Republic of Congo*, UN Doc S/2005/167 (15 March 2005) para 68.

word 'discouragement' in relation to sexual relationships, this can be interpreted as a prohibition unless the narrow conditions stated in the exception are made more workable. Thus, the SGB conflates sexual exploitation with consensual sexual relationships and prostitution.

3.5 Responses to the 'Zero Tolerance Policy' by Researchers

This section outlines the overwhelmingly positive response to the SGB from researchers who have examined sexual exploitation in PKOs. It looks at four studies into sexual exploitation of adult women in the context of PKOs published between 2003 and 2008, focusing on the methodology used by the researchers and their approach to the SGB, in particular whether they accept the conflation of sexual exploitation with consensual sexual relationships and prostitution.

The first empirical study on sexual exploitation in PKOs undertaken in the wake of the SGB was conducted by Paul Higate, who has published several scholarly papers on this theme.[189] Higate's main study was carried out in the DRC and Sierra Leone in 2003 and his other research builds upon this work. In his ethnographic observations and informal discussions, as well as face-to-face and semi-structured individual and group interviews in Freetown and Kinshasa, he interviewed 45 peacekeepers, including military observers, UN civilians and NGO staff. The main aim of his study was to understand the 'exploitative aspects of gender relations...with a focus on the dynamic between privileged and powerful peacekeepers and local women and girls'.[190] Higate takes as a starting point for his study the SGB position on 'inherently unequal power' held by peacekeepers in relation to local women.

The focus of his study was on the factors 'driving prostitution and allied forms of exploitation in PKOs'.[191] Similarly to the SGB, Higate considers the practice of prostitution 'by its very definition exploitative in nature'[192] and the power dynamic between local women and peacekeepers unequal. Higate suggests that the low capacity of women to generate income in the aftermath of conflict may lead to

---

[189] Paul Higate, 'Revealing the Soldier: Peacekeeping and Prostitution' (2003) 1(5) *American Sexuality Magazine*; Paul Higate, 'Gender and Peacekeeping Case Studies: The Democratic Republic of the Congo and Sierra Leone' (Pretoria: Gender and Peacekeeping, Institute for Secuity Studies, 2004) 91 Monograph; Paul Higate and Marsha Henry, 'Engendering (In)security in Peace Support Operations', *Security Dialogue* (2004) 35 (4); P. Higate, 'Peacekeepers and Gender: DRC and Sierra Leone', *Pambazuka News* (online) 7 August 2004 <http://www.pambazuka.org/en/category/features/23056>; Paul Higate, 'Peacekeepers, masculinities, and sexual exploitation', (2007) 10 (1) *Men and Masculinities* 99.

[190] Ibid Higate, 'Gender and Peacekeeping Case Studies: The Democratic Republic of the Congo and Sierra Leone' 5.

[191] Ibid.

[192] Ibid 21.

commercial sex work, which is sometimes the only way to earn money for themselves or their families. He describes those peacekeepers who exchange sex for money as 'perpetrators'[193] and observes that the 'sharp financial disparity between peacekeepers and host populations provides peacekeepers with an opportunity to exert power and authority over those weakened by conflict and thus vulnerable to exploitation and abuse'.[194]

Although Higate treats prostitution as a sexually exploitative activity, it is notable that his interviewees, male and female peacekeepers, recognised 'the importance of the income generated by sexual contact with male peacekeepers for the families of these women'.[195] For example, one male military observer expressed the view that 'by having sex with prostitutes, they [peacekeepers] are helping them by giving them money so they can feed their family'.[196] This response acknowledges the agency of local women and respects their decision-making to engage in prostitution in order to secure survival for themselves and their families. However, Higate discredits such views, suggesting that they represent 'male misperceptions and misunderstandings of the gender/power dynamic' in PKOs.[197]

By taking the same approach as the SGB, Higate depicts peacekeepers as predisposed to perpetrating sexual exploitation due to the 'financial disparity' between them and 'vulnerable and perhaps previously exploited women and girls'.[198] He portrays all peacekeepers as powerful and all local women as 'weakened', 'vulnerable' and 'exploited'. Higate argues that 'activities of this kind [prostitution] almost always [involve] peacekeepers abusing their positions of trust [and] power',[199] stating that women are 'vulnerable and part of a socially subordinate group'[200] who consequently suffer from 'long term impacts...of such abuse'.[201] Higate does not consider the possibility that women have the right to freely decide to exchange money for sex, or that they have the capacity to make self-interested decisions about the best options for their survival, and to take responsibility for such decision-making, even if their choices are severely constrained. Yet he finds that local women in the DRC were seen by some peacekeepers as 'actively choosing prostitution and other types of sexual exchange'.[202] Some peacekeepers even described themselves as 'helpless victims of the predatory advances of local women' with 'a powerful sex drive that

[193] Ibid.
[194] Ibid 6.
[195] Ibid 15.
[196] Ibid 32.
[197] Ibid 37.
[198] Ibid 13.
[199] Higate, 'Revealing the Soldier: Peacekeeping and Prostitution', above n 189,1.
[200] Higate and Henry, above n 189, 481.
[201] Ibid 483.
[202] Ibid 490.

prostitutes exploit',[203] and not the other way around as the SGB suggests. According to these views, peacekeepers are the 'victims of exploitation', rather than the local women.

While a number of Higate's interviewees suggested that 'occasionally the relationships between peacekeepers and local women could have a genuine 'romantic' dimension', he argues that because of 'the stark inequalities between the parties', such relationships 'should make us sceptical'.[204] Although he acknowledges 'the possibility that emotional feelings might develop [between peacekeepers and local women]', he comments that these 'could be born out of false hope that the longer-term prospects of a relationship may lead them out of their current conditions of poverty'.[205] Moreover, Higate says that 'it is difficult to imagine that they [local women] are able to exercise any real "choice" about the ways in which their bodies can become units of sexual exchange'.[206] Similarly to the SGB, he does not perceive local women as capable of consenting to sexual relationships in the context of PKOs and, as a result, deems their consent irrelevant.

Although Higate uses terms such as 'gender relations', 'sexual activities', 'sexual liaisons' and 'sexual contacts' interchangeably throughout his study, it is clear that he considers all of these interactions to be sexually exploitative. He even suggests 'a sharpening of the various Codes of Conduct in order that ambiguities and tensions between the notions of "prostitution" and "bona fide relationship" be removed'.[207] Thus, Higate denies any agency to local women and would go even further than the SGB by banning all sex in PKOs between peacekeepers and local women as sexually exploitative.

A second study on sexual exploitation in PKOs was undertaken by Sarah Martin, who conducted a qualitative study in Liberia and Haiti for Refugees International. The report, published in 2005, looks at the causes of 'sexual exploitation and sexual abuse' and the efforts made by the UN to address the problem. It explores the question of prostitution in PKOs as well as peacekeepers' views on the ZTP. Since the study does not outline its methodology, it is not clear how many peacekeepers and representatives of local women's organisations were interviewed by Martin. Like Higate, she fully supports the ZTP and 'urges the major troop-contributing countries to adopt them [ZTP] immediately'.[208] Although Martin does not explicitly state that prostitution is sexual exploitation, she suggests that in Haiti sexual exploitation 'has been a way of life...[and that] the poverty stricken population has

---

[203] Paul Higate, 'Revealing the Soldier: Peacekeeping and Prostitution', above n 189,1.

[204] Paul Higate, 'Gender and Peacekeeping Case Studies: The Democratic Republic of the Congo and Sierra Leone', above n 189, 22.

[205] Ibid.

[206] Ibid.

[207] Ibid.

[208] Sarah Martin, 'Must Boys be Boys? Ending Sexual Exploitation & Abuse in UN Peacekeeping Missions' (Refugees International, 2005) iv.

long been forced to turn to commercial sex work to support itself'.[209] She observes that prostitution, despite being illegal in Haiti, is a reality and that the 'women line the streets of Petionville…to sell themselves to wealthy Haitians and foreign men who visit the restaurants and clubs'.[210] Thus, Martin acknowledges that many women turn to prostitution in order to support themselves and underscores that prostitution is a fact of life in Haiti, despite being illegal.

Martin reports that male peacekeepers 'laughed' and 'clearly did not take this issue seriously' when she asked them how they felt about the ZTP.[211] One of the interviewees, a Brazilian peacekeeper explained: 'We are men. It is very difficult. But I am able to go across the border to the Dominican Republic on the weekends'.[212] This peacekeeper was referring to employing the services of prostitutes legally in a neighbouring country. This implies that at least some peacekeepers see nothing morally wrong with prostitution. This view is confirmed by an international NGO worker who complained to Martin: 'I've had UNMIL [UN Mission in Liberia] people tell me that *some prostitution* [my emphasis] is not exploitative and that the Liberian women choose to be prostitutes. This attitude is unacceptable.'[213] While some peacekeepers make a distinction between voluntary and forced prostitution, the international NGO worker and Martin, like the SGB, do not. Some peacekeepers interviewed by Martin suggested that although 'military peacekeepers are kept in walled compounds, they are still pursued by local women,'[214] implying, like some of Higate's interviewees, that peacekeepers need the protection of the SGB rather than local women.

Although 'a number of peacekeepers' told Martin that their relationships with local women 'have a genuine romantic dimension to them',[215] Martin is sceptical and concludes that 'the stark inequalities between the parties ensure that such cases are rare'.[216] She explains that, because of the economic imbalance of power between peacekeepers and local women, it is unlikely that there is any 'real choice' possible for the women involved in such relationships.[217] This perspective is in line with the SGB view that 'inherently unequal' power imbalances make genuine sexual relationships in PKOs impossible and hence they should always be placed under scrutiny.

Thus, Martin, like Higate, supports the ZTP and does not question its inclusion of prostitution and sexual relationships in its definition of sexual exploitation.

---

[209] Ibid 3.

[210] Ibid.

[211] Ibid 6.

[212] Ibid.

[213] Ibid 15.

[214] Ibid 16.

[215] Ibid 24.

[216] Ibid.

[217] Ibid.

While she encourages the UN to empower women in 'social, political and economic activities'[218] and recognises that for some women prostitution is a survival tactic, she still supports the ban on prostitution enforced by the SGB. She also believes, in line with the SGB, that genuine sexual relationships between peacekeepers and local women are not possible because of the unequal economic power between the two. Similarly to Higate, Martin depicts local women as powerless and vulnerable, and in need of protection from predatory male peacekeepers.

The third study was undertaken in 2005 by Daniel Gustafsson and directly addressed peacekeeping and prostitution.[219] Gustafsson's aim was to analyse peacekeepers' demands for prostitution in light of the Swedish Armed Forces' preventative strategy on sexual misconduct, including prostitution. He conducted interviews with six Swedish peacekeepers who had served in BH and Kosovo. The interviews were not in the form of direct questions, but rather open discussions on peacekeeping and prostitution.[220] While Gustafsson does not explicitly use the term 'sexual exploitation' in his study, he refers to prostitution as a 'problem' and as an 'unfortunate pattern of behaviour' in PKOs.[221] Similarly to Higate, Gustafson describes peacekeepers engaged in prostitution as 'perpetrators'.[222] Although he aims to discuss prostitution in his study, he conflates prostitution with trafficking in women. The section in his study titled 'Link between peacekeeping and prostitution in Bosnia and Kosovo' describes the problem of trafficking in women that emerged in these two countries after the peacekeepers' arrival, without distinguishing trafficking from prostitution.

The peacekeepers that Gustafson interviewed confirmed that prostitution flourished in BH and Kosovo and that brothels were located around military bases. As one of the interviewees said, 'Kosovo is full of bordellos…not only peacekeepers go there…everyone does'.[223] Another interviewee added that 'every town I have visited had their own bordello…you did not have to drive many meters before you came across one'.[224] These interviewees suggest that brothels are a fact of life in these missions and that soldiers visit them on a regular basis, as do locals. Since none of his interviewees openly admitted to paying money for sex, but rather 'only [to] visiting sex clubs' while on short leave in neighbouring countries, such as Greece,[225] Gustafsson concludes that the Swedish Armed Forces have been successful in preventing Swedish soldiers from buying sex while on the mission.[226]

[218] Ibid vi.

[219] Daniel Gustafsson, *Peacekeeping and Prostitution: A Case Study of the Swedish Experience from Kosovo and Bosnia* (MA Thesis, University of Lund, 2005).

[220] Ibid 8.

[221] Ibid 6.

[222] Ibid.

[223] Ibid 42.

[224] Ibid.

[225] Ibid 44.

[226] Ibid 53.

While Gustafsson does not analyse the SGB's zero tolerance approach to prostitution, it is clear that he supports the policy since he considers prostitution, as well as trafficking, sexually exploitative. One of his recommendations is to re-emphasise the prohibition of 'purchas[ing] of sexual services as well as visits to sex and strip clubs', and another is to extend this ban to all peacekeepers when on leave from the mission.[227]

The fourth study was undertaken in 2008 by Kathleen Jennings. She undertook a study into the SGB, interviewing peacekeepers in the same PKOs as Martin, namely Haiti and Liberia.[228] This was the first study that specifically examined the institutional ramifications and impact of the ZTP through the eyes of peacekeepers affected by the policy. It was also the first study that questioned the broad definition of sexual exploitation promulgated by the SGB. Jennings conducted 49 interviews and 12 focus groups, and used other qualitative methods, such as participation in a UN-sponsored anti-prostitution workshop, observation of nightlife settings and informal conversations with informants. Jennings explores the ways in which the ZTP is perceived, understood and interpreted by peacekeepers. She argues that while the ZTP aims to protect local women from sexual exploitation, it does this by encouraging demeaning racial and gender based stereotyping of the local population.[229] She asserts that, as a result of the SGB, local women and girls are portrayed as highly sexualised in their advances towards 'innocent' peacekeepers in both of the missions that she analysed.[230] She compares these findings with Higate's interviewees' construction of the African women as 'sexual predators'.[231] Thus, Jennings is concerned about the SGB implications and the stereotypes it promotes.

Although Jennings does not explicitly condone or approve of prostitution, she raises the issue of loss of livelihood as a result of enforcing the ZTP for women who work as prostitutes. While the ZTP aims to abolish the demand side of prostitution by prohibiting peacekeepers from exchanging money for sex, such an approach, according to Jennings' research, is unlikely to change the underlying structures of peacekeeping economies, which are characterised by extreme income inequality. She argues that the ZTP may make 'some people's lives more precarious, by removing a source of income upon which they depend', and wonders to what extent the UN should recognise its responsibility towards prostitutes whose livelihoods are endangered by the ZTP.[232] She concludes that these questions have not received adequate attention within the UN and suggests some measures that should be taken by the UN, such as providing grants or vocational training to prostitutes.[233]

[227] Ibid 50.

[228] Kathleen M. Jennings, 'Protecting Whom?: Approaches to Sexual Exploitation and Abuse in UN Peacekeeping Operations' (Fafo, 2008).

[229] Ibid 10.

[230] Ibid 62.

[231] Higate and Henry, above n 189, 491.

[232] Jennings, above n 228, 64.

[233] Ibid.

However, Jennings also sees such measures as a problem, since local people might raise the question of why prostitutes, who are typically a stigmatised group, 'deserve' such rewards.[234]

Jennings is also concerned about the SGB's 'strong discouragement' of sexual relationships and argues that the provision should either be better clarified or discarded since it 'complicates attempts to explain or fairly enforce the zero tolerance policy'.[235] She found it problematic that the SGB does not adequately distinguish between various forms of sexual behaviour,[236] and that the ambiguity about what constitutes a 'real' relationship or an exploitative one is left unresolved.[237] Interviewees told her that it is impossible to deal with the 'strong discouragement' clause and that sexual relationships should either be explicitly banned or allowed, except if they involve minors or physical abuse.[238] Also, the military personnel that Jennings interviewed informed her that they are not 'strongly discouraged' from having sexual relationships with locals, but in fact they are banned.[239] This indicates that the SGB provision of 'strong discouragement' is interpreted in the field as a total ban.

Jennings considers that the SGB assumption that sexual relationships between peacekeepers and local women are based on power differentials disregards the views of all locals and all peacekeepers, regardless of their socioeconomic, educational and racial diversity, and as such is 'arguable'. However, despite these drawbacks, she still believes that the SGB is 'progressive and laudable'.[240] Although it seems contradictory to, on the one hand, acknowledge that the SGB stereotypes local women and peacekeepers, and on the other hand to conclude by praising the SGB, Jennings' study makes an important contribution towards critical analysis of the SGB.

There are three main points to note about the preceding studies. Firstly, except for Jennings, the researchers do not question the definition of sexual exploitation adopted by the SGB which conflates all forms of consensual sexual conduct with sexual abuse, human trafficking and other forms of sexual violence. Secondly, other than Jennings, the researchers do not have a problem with the fact that consensual sexual relationships between local women and peacekeepers are 'strongly discouraged' by the SGB. Instead Higate even proposes that such relationships should be totally banned. Thirdly, none of the studies seeks the perceptions of local women engaged in sexual relationships with peacekeepers or in prostitution in PKOs.

---

[234] Ibid 47.

[235] Ibid 8.

[236] Ibid 65.

[237] Ibid 23.

[238] Ibid 23.

[239] Ibid 58.

[240] Ibid 70.

My main point in discussing these studies is to illustrate that, despite attracting the attention of researchers for almost a decade, what has been lacking in studies of sexual interactions between peacekeepers and local women is clear differentiation between voluntary and coerced sexual relationships, between forced and voluntary prostitution, and between sexual relationships and sexual exploitation.[241] The overwhelming attention to protection from sexual exploitation in the SGB, which calls for a ban of nearly all sex, has, as Franke would argue, 'almost eliminated the legal existence of any kind of sex' in which women may want to engage.[242]

3.6 Conclusions

This chapter has canvassed a range of responses to the allegations of sexual exploitation in PKOs, by individual missions, the DPKO and the SG. These responses were initially developed in an *ad hoc* manner at the individual mission level, aiming to provide a 'quick fix' for the alleged problems. As the allegations continued to mount, more coordinated responses were developed by the DPKO and the SG, which were also supplemented by the policies of individual missions. From 1997 onwards, numerous codes of conduct, guidelines and training materials were produced that aimed to prevent alleged sexual exploitation. Much of this work was consistent with international human rights law and respected the sexual autonomy of both peacekeepers and local women. However, after the 2002 UNHCHR/SC-UK report, the SGB adopted a zero tolerance approach to almost all sex in PKOs as a comprehensive solution to sexual exploitation. The SGB approach bans prostitution and 'strongly discourages' sexual relationships between peacekeepers and local women.

I explored the SGB provisions on prostitution and 'strong discouragement' of sexual relationships and concluded that the SGB takes a radical feminist standpoint that considers almost all sex exploitative. I argued that a ban on prostitution and 'strong discouragement' of sexual relationships are inconsistent with international human rights norms, such as the right to privacy.

The SGB is problematic for two reasons. First, its definition of sexual exploitation is over-inclusive because it encompasses adult voluntary prostitution and sexual relationships. Second, the SGB assumption that there are universally agreed international standards that regard prostitution and sexual relationships as sexually exploitative practices is wrong. The SGB has almost eliminated the legal existence of any kind of sex that local women and peacekeepers may wish to pursue.

Despite these shortcomings, the SGB approach has largely been endorsed by researchers. Only Jennings questions the SGB provision of 'strong discouragement'

---

[241] Otto, above n 94, 262.

[242] Katherine M. Franke, 'Theorizing Yes: An Essay on Feminism, Law, and Desire' (2001) 101 (1) *Columbia Law Review* 199.

of sexual relationships, which she, based on the interviews she conducted with peacekeepers, finds an impossible provision to deal with because of its ambiguity. In relation to prostitution, she suggests that the UN should take some responsibility for ensuring the livelihoods of prostitutes which became threatened by the ZTP. In sum, the ZTP is widely accepted, despite the hardship it causes to many local women and peacekeepers, and despite its inconsistency with international human rights law. I turn now to the methodology of my own empirical research which explores these questions further.

Chapter 4
Research Background, Aims and Methods

4.1 Introduction

Chapter 3 outlined various responses to the Secretary General's Bulletin (SGB) from feminists and researchers who had undertaken empirical studies into sexual exploitation in peacekeeping operations (PKOs). It highlighted that the SGB's definition of sexual exploitation, which covers prostitution and sexual relationships, has been largely driven by radical feminist thinking. While some empirical research seeking the views of peacekeepers affected by the SGB has been undertaken, no research has sought the views of those most affected by the zero tolerance policy (ZTP), local women in PKOs. My research makes a contribution to filling this gap. This chapter outlines the context, aims and research methods for the original contribution of this book, namely the empirical study which aims to make the personal experiences of those affected by the SGB visible.[1] To this end, the research involved interviewing three groups of participants: women from Bosnia and Herzegovina (BH) who had been in sexual relationships with peacekeepers during the mission in BH (Group A), local women who were working within the PKO in BH (Group B), and UN peacekeeping personnel and policy makers in general (Group C). The main purpose of the research was to ask local women and peacekeepers for their responses to the SGB, in the belief that their views would inform further legal and policy development.

As a self-reflective researcher and a feminist, I acknowledge my own position and experience within this research and the particular perspective I bring to it. Such acknowledgments are a key aspect of standpoint feminist theory,[2] which informs this research. As a BH woman, I believe that I am especially well placed to research my 'own people' and, in particular, BH women. While BH is a specific context, and women in BH are a specific cultural group whose experiences can not necessarily

[1] Stevi Jackson, *Heterosexuality in Question* (Sage, 1999) 94.

[2] Alessandra Tanesini, *An Introduction to Feminist Epistemologies* (Wiley-Blackwell, 1999) 138.

O. Simic, *Regulation of Sexual Conduct in UN Peacekeeping Operations*,
DOI 10.1007/978-3-642-28484-7_4, © Springer-Verlag Berlin Heidelberg 2012

be equated to the experiences of other women who live under the protection of UN missions, it can nevertheless be expected that women will share some similar views as a result of their common experience of war and post-conflict societies in which PKOs are present. At the very least, it suggests that a blanket policy for all missions might not be appropriate.

This chapter is organised into two main parts. The first part explores gender politics in BH by describing the local context of my study and providing a general overview of the BH socio-political and cultural milieu prior to the war, during the war and in the post-conflict transitional period. This part has five sub-sections. The first provides a very brief general historical overview of BH. The second outlines the gender and sexual norms prevailing in the country prior to the civil war, which were generally favourable to women. The third examines gender norms during the war and the escalation of sexual violence, directed in particular towards Bosnian Muslim women. In the fourth sub-section I discuss gender norms in the post-conflict transitional period during which there was a revival of conservative religious mores, and the creation of new languages and identities. During this period tens of thousands of predominantly male peacekeepers arrived in BH. In the fifth and final sub-section I position myself in relation to the case study.

The second part of the chapter describes the aims and methodology of the empirical case study. This part is divided into six sub-sections. The first discusses the research aims and methods. The second describes the process of designing the interview questions for all three groups of interviewees. The third looks at the ethical considerations raised by the research. The fourth sub-section describes the process of finding the interviewees for the research project, and the fifth describes how the interviews were conducted with each of the three groups. Finally, the sixth sub-section identifies the challenges and limitations of the research. The data collected in the course of the empirical study will be analysed in Chaps. 5 and 6.

4.2 Gender Politics in Bosnia and Herzegovina (BH)

4.2.1 Brief History of the Creation of the State of BH

The Socialistic Republic of BH came into being after WWII with the creation of the Socialistic Federal Republic of Yugoslavia. Along with five other republics[3] and two provinces,[4] BH was incorporated into a federal system, which gave each republic equal representation in all major governance bodies. Mihailo Crnobrnja describes it as a country 'of condensed diversity' where three religions, four

[3] Serbia, Croatia, Montenegro, Macedonia, Slovenia and BiH.

[4] Vojvodina and Kosovo.

languages and two different alphabets were in use.[5] In many respects, BH became a symbol of multi-ethnic Yugoslavia, and the crossroads of all its differences: cultural, economic, religious and ethnic. Yugoslavian people often called BH 'little Yugoslavia' where Bosnian Serbs, Croats and Muslims lived peacefully together embracing all their cultural and religious differences.[6] Bosnian people thought of themselves as sharing a common language, lifestyle and ethnic origin while at the same time following three religious traditions, namely Orthodox Christian (Serbs), Catholic Christian (Croats) and Islam (Bosniacs). BH also had the highest number of inter-ethnic marriages in the former Yugoslavia, which were mainly concentrated in urban areas.[7]

Although all the people in BH shared the same language, Serbo-Croatian, and learned both alphabets (Cyrillic and Roman) in school, one indicator of ethno-religious background that remained was their first names. While Bosniacs use given names of Turkish or Arabic origin, Serbs and Croats use given names of Slavic origin.[8] However, although some names are used by both Serbs and Croats, there were many names used specifically by Serbs and specifically by Croats. Despite differences in tradition and religion, the main divisions within Yugoslavian society after WWII were not between the ethnic groups, but were increasingly between working and middle class people, and between rural and urban communities.[9] The larger urban cities, such as Sarajevo and Banjaluka, were more ethnically mixed than elsewhere in BH.[10]

Following the death of President Tito in 1980, the dissolution of the Yugoslav Federation began with a severe economic and social crisis, exacerbated by rising ethnic nationalism and a more forceful articulation of the ethnic, political and economic interests of its constituent republics, which resulted in the breaking apart of Yugoslavia.[11] The first multi-party elections in Yugoslavia in 1990 resulted in a victory for the nationalistic parties, leading to Slovenia and Croatia proclaiming independence, followed by BH in 1992. In the same year the newly independent state of BH was plunged into 4 years of internal conflict, during which thousands of

[5] Mihailo Crnobrnja, *The Yugoslav Drama* (McGill-Queen's University Press, 1996) 15.

[6] Ibid 174.

[7] Steven Burg, *The War in Bosnia and Herzegovina: Ethnic Conflict and International Intervention* (M.E. Sharpe, 2000) 16; Robert Donia, *Bosnia and Herzegovina: A Tradition Betrayed* (Columbia University Press, 1995) 9.

[8] Tone Bringa, *Being Muslim the Bosnian Way* (Princeton University Press, 1995) 19.

[9] Christopher Bennett, *Yugoslavia's Bloody Collapse: Causes, Course and Consequences* (NYU Press, 1997) 63; Susan Woodward, *Balkan Tragedy: Chaos and Dissolution After the Cold War* (Brookings Institution Press, 1995) 238, 241.

[10] Martina Fischer, *Peacebuilding and Civil Society in Bosnia-Herzegovina. Ten Years after Dayton* (Münster Lit Verlag, 2006) 132.

[11] See, Bogdan Denitch, *Ethnic Nationalism: The Tragic Death of Yugoslavia* (University of Minnesota Press, 1996).

women were raped and around 300,000 people were killed or disappeared.[12] The war ended with the Dayton Peace Agreement (DPA) in December 1995,[13] but many of its effects, like poverty and ethnic hostility, remain.

4.2.2 Gender Politics and Sexual Norms Before the Conflict in BH

Although women in the former Yugoslavia, including BH, lived in a patriarchal society, they also shared a socialist culture which granted them some important human rights and freedoms. After WWII, women were granted rights of divorce, employment, abortion, contraception and education.[14] The protection of marriage and family relations was also recognised as a particular concern of the state.[15] The post WWII laws promoted secularism, banned Muslim women from wearing the veil and prohibited polygamy, which was widespread among the Muslim population before WWII.[16] The new laws also prohibited prostitution, which was legal in the Kingdom of Yugoslavia until 1939.[17] One of the main concerns of the women's movement in the early years of the socialist republic was working to 'rehabilitate' prostitutes, since prostitution represented a clear 'symbol of women's oppression in history and contemporary society'.[18] Following the socialist feminism tradition, feminists in the former Yugoslavia focused on the economic oppression of women, and understood prostitution as injurious to women because it was caused by both patriarchy and capitalism.[19]

By the late 1960s, almost one quarter of the masters degrees and 17% of the doctorates awarded in Yugoslavia were conferred on women.[20] However, while in the 1980s Yugoslavia had one of the highest rates of university-educated women in the world, the gap between urban and rural women widened, with 17% of rural

[12] Kvinna Till Kvinna, *Engendering the Peace Process, A Gender Approach to Dayton-and Beyond* (Kvinna Till Kvinna Foundation, 2000) 17.

[13] The General Framework Agreement for Peace in Bosnia and Herzegovina (Dayton Peace Accords) was formally signed in Paris on December 14, 1995.

[14] Vida Tomsic, *Women in the Development of Socialist Self-Managing Yugoslavia* (Jugoslovenska stvarnost, 1980) 127.

[15] Ibid.

[16] Ibid 105.

[17] Salko Saric, 'Prostitution in Mostar' [Prostitution in Mostar] (1999) 114 *Journal of Education, Science and Culture* 3.

[18] Sabrina Ramet, *Gender Politics in the Western Balkans: Women, Society, and Politics in Yugoslavia and the Yugoslav Successor States* (Pennsylvania State University Press, 1999) 47.

[19] Laurie Shrage, 'Comment on Overall's "What's Wrong With Prostitution? Evaluating Sex Work"'(1994) 19(2) *Signs: Journal of Women in Culture and* Society 564, 566.

[20] Ramet, above n 18, 47.

women remaining illiterate.[21] This high concentration of educated urban women meant that many of them were in a good position to gain employment with the UN mission when it arrived following the DPA. As I argued in Chap. 2, as beneficiaries of UN protection, women use the opportunities to generate income which arise with the influx of peacekeepers. In the case of BH, the fact that many women were educated and spoke English assisted them in gaining work within UNMIBH.

Before the outbreak of the war, more than 40% of women in Yugoslavia worked full time, which gave them economic independence.[22] Although women enjoyed significant labour rights, they dominated in feminised occupations, such as services, administration, education, health care and cultural institutions.[23] Despite this, household tasks and family responsibilities in BH continued to be considered women's work, not men's. The burden of family obligations remained a significant obstacle for women in the workplace and in the political sphere.[24] Thus, the 'socialist value of gender equality' was oriented towards maintaining the central role of women in the household, assisting working mothers, for example, by providing for long maternity leave.[25] Therefore, even urban women in the former Yugoslavia remained the primary caregivers, and their social status was derived from marriage and reproduction, rather than their workforce participation.[26]

Sexual freedom, including the freedom to choose a partner of a different ethnic or religious background, was enjoyed in urban centres.[27] Cities offered more anonymity and confidentiality than villages where it was not possible to hide a date or commence a relationship with privacy. In the rural parts of BH, marriage was considered the most important aspect of women's lives, and channelled sexuality into reproduction.[28] However, while women kept to tradition in the villages under pressure from the elders, if they moved away they were more likely to adopt the urban and Western standards of lifestyle that were prevailing in the cities.[29] Unlike the other Eastern European countries under communism, Yugoslavia's borders were open, 'allowing communication and exchange of

[21] Bette Denich, 'Women, Work, and Power in Modern Yugoslavia' in Alice Schlegel (ed) *Sexual Stratification* (Columbia University Press, 1977) 215.

[22] Kvinna Till Kvinna, above n, 12.

[23] Andjelka Milic, 'Women and Work in Former Yugoslavia and Their Present Situation' in Barbara Lobodzinska (ed), *Family, Women, and Employment in Central-Eastern Europe* (Praeger, 1995) 240.

[24] Denich, above n 21, 222.

[25] Milic, above n 23, 238.

[26] Andrei Simic, 'Machismo and Cryptomatriarchy: Power, Affect, and Authority in the Contemporary Yugoslav Family' (1983) 11(1/2) *Ethos* 68.

[27] Ibid 74.

[28] Bringa, above n 8, 119.

[29] Ibid 61.

ideas'.[30] Thus, in many respects Yugoslavia was open to the West and western ideas of liberty, including sexual liberation.

While socialism did not allow other political groups to be formed apart from the Communist Party, feminist groups in the capital cities of Serbia, Croatia and Slovenia were established in the 1980s[31] and became an urban phenomenon.[32] Although feminist ideas were unpopular under socialist rule, feminists were not completely silenced or made illegal.[33] They organised themselves into groups and became '...actively involved in advocacy and support work on women's issues...including rape and domestic violence, pornography and women's "right to employment" as well as working to "rehabilitate prostitutes"'.[34] The first National Feminist Conference in Yugoslavia was held in Ljubljana, Slovenia, in 1987. Faced with the emergence of nationalism in their republics, conference participants proclaimed in one of the resolutions that 'women were united in sisterhood, and their common experiences as women [should] over-ride male concerns for territorial rights and geographical boundaries'.[35] This marked the start of the establishment of women's civil organisations across Yugoslavia, which laid the groundwork for the expansion of the feminist movement a few years later in the wake of the civil war in BH.

With respect to the sex industry in pre-war BH, there was little research because prostitution was illegal and therefore had been driven underground. Although brothels continued to operate, they were mostly hidden from public view.[36] As Kesic argues, 'everybody knew of their existence, but most could not say where or who worked in these houses'.[37] Despite the lack of research, some data show that in the mid 1970s and late 1980s, the number of prostitutes increased due to the economic crisis that affected Yugoslavia.[38] Yet there was little feminist engagement with prostitution at that time. Only in 1989, with the establishment of the first SOS hotlines, did feminists start to work on problems surrounding male violence,

---

[30] Donna Hughes, Lepa Mladjenovic and Zorica Mrsevic 'Feminist Resistance in Serbia' (1994) 2(4) *The European Journal of Women's Studies* 512.

[31] Jelena Batinic, 'Feminism, Nationalism, and War: The 'Yugoslav Case' in Feminist Texts' (2001) 3(1) *Journal of International Women's Studies* 4.

[32] Sabrina Ramet, *Social Currents in Eastern Europe: The Sources and Consequences of the Great Transformation* (Duke University Press Books, 1994) 226.

[33] Batinic, above n 31, 5.

[34] Jovanka Stojsavljevic, 'Women, Conflict, and Culture in Former Yugoslavia' (1994) 3(1) *Gender and Development* 37.

[35] Ibid 36. See also, Jill Benderly, 'Rape, Feminism, and Nationalism in the War in Yugoslav Successor States' in Lois West (ed), *Feminist Nationalism* (Routledge, 1997) 59-72.

[36] Obrad Kesic, 'Women and Gender Imagery in Bosnia: Amazons, Sluts, Victims, Witches, and Wombs' in Ramet, above n 18, 187, 191.

[37] Ibid.

[38] Dragan Radulovic, *Prostitucija u Jugoslaviji* [Prostitution in Yugoslavia] (Filip Višnjić, 1986) 11.

predominantly in domestic circumstances.[39] Forced prostitution as a form of sexual exploitation and sexual violence became the focus of feminist research in BH only after the war broke out.

In summary, before the civil war in BH, although women enjoyed significant labour rights, their main roles continued to be those of housewives and mothers. There were also significant differences between the education and sexual freedoms of rural and urban women. Whilst a feminist movement existed before the war, it was mainly based on theoretical discussions among feminists rather than activism.[40] This period before the war was also characterised by a lack of empirical data about the sex industry, which was driven underground as a result of being made illegal in 1945. There are also no pre-war data about specific sexual violence between ethnic groups, which would become one of the major features of the war in BH.

4.2.3 Gender and Sexual Violence in BH During the Conflict

One of the main features of the BH conflict was the highly organised and calculated systemic rape of Bosnian Muslim women by the Bosnian Serb army. It has been estimated that in 1993 approximately 20,000 Bosnian Muslim women were raped by Bosnian Serb men in what were known as 'rape camps'.[41] The rape of women was used as a weapon of war and a deliberate military strategy to spread terror, destabilise the civilian population and reward soldiers.[42] It was a tool of ethnic cleansing where sexual violence against women, in particular Muslim women, was used to humiliate their ethnic group.[43] In the *Kunarac* case, the ICTY found, for the first time in judicial history, that rape was 'used by members of the Bosnian Serb armed forces as an instrument of terror'.[44]

The international community and the media quickly picked up the news of rape in BH, spreading it around the world. In BH, and more generally in the former

[39] Autonomus Women's Center, 'The History of Feminist Movement in Yugoslavia' <http://www.womenngo.org.rs/content/blogcategory/28/61/>.

[40] Svetlana Slapsak, 'Zene i rat u bivsoj Jugoslaviji' [Women and War in ex-Yugoslavia], *Republika* (online), 31 August 1996 www.yurope.com/zines/republika/arhiva/96/145/145-16.html.

[41] Dorothy Thomas and Regan Ralph, 'Rape in War: The Case of Bosnia' in Ramet, above n 18, 203, 214. See also, The European Community Investigative Mission into the Treatment of Muslim Women in the Former Yugoslavia: Report to European Community Foreign Ministers. UN Doc S/25240, annex I, 3 February 1993.

[42] Rhonda Copelon, 'Surfacing Gender: Reconceptualizing Crimes against Women in Time of War' in Lois Ann Lorentzen and Jennifer Turpin (eds), *The Women and War Reader* (New York University Press, 1999) 64.

[43] Ibid Turpin, 'Many Faces: Women Confronting War' 1, 5; Copelon, 63, 69.

[44] *Prosecutor v Kunarac et al*, Case No IT-96-23, Judgment, 12 June 2002.

Yugoslavia, rape was made a national issue by the major nationalistic parties who used the rape of a woman as a metaphor for the rape of a country.[45] Kesic argues that 'a raped Croat or Bosniac woman stands for a raped Croatia or Bosnia'.[46] Thus, in BH women's bodies became part of male nationalist politics. Rape was never a 'simple rape' of a woman by a man; it was given a national context: it was rape of a Muslim woman by a Serb man, or a Serb woman by a Croat man.[47] This led to divisions among women who were divided along ethnic lines as they had never been before.

At the same time women started to organise against militarism and war. Across the former Yugoslavia, women gathered in civil associations,[48] organising across different political, language, sexual and religious orientations to work towards building peace. From the beginning of the war until the present, women's groups in different parts of Yugoslavia organised protests calling for demilitarisation and peace.[49] It was through these associations that I sought interviewees for my research. Thus, while BH women were victims of the war, they were also survivors and agents of change, as I discussed in Chap. 2 when outlining the profile of beneficiaries of UN protection.

In summary, inter-ethnic sexual violence was prevalent during the war in BH. The earlier multi-culturalism of BH was replaced by a strong nationalistic rhetoric which worked to divide women along ethnic lines and undo the solidarity that women had felt before the war. Yet, in the wake of the war, women created organisations that sought to re-establish relationships and tolerance across ethnic differences.

4.2.4 Gender Politics During the Post-conflict Transitional Period

The sexual violence during the war created a particular context that was followed by the arrival of tens of thousands of predominantly male peacekeepers. The post-conflict transitional period in BH was marked by changes at all levels—socio-cultural, political and economic. Although one country, the DPA divided BH into two federal entities: the Republika Srpska and the Muslim-Croat Federation. As Jones argues, the DPA reinforced and institutionalised ethnic divisions and caused a huge internal

---

[45] Vesna Kesic, 'Muslim women, Croatian women Serbian women, Albanian women', *Eurozine* (online), 5 September 2003 <http://www.eurozine.com/articles/2003-05-09-kesic-en.html>.

[46] Ibid.

[47] Ramet, above n 18, 262.

[48] Dubravka Zarkov, *The Body of War: Media, Ethnicity, and Gender in the Break-up of Yugoslavia* (Duke University Press, 2007) 44.

[49] Lepa Mladjenovic and Donna M. Hughes,'Feminist Resistance to War and Violence in Serbia' in Marquerite Waller and Jennifer Rycenga (eds), *Frontline Feminisms, Women, War and Resistance* (Routledge, 2001) 247, 259.

movement of ethnic groups who wanted to find final refuge within their own ethnic communities.[50] Women were particularly affected by displacement, and many of these were heads of households as a result of the war.[51] This migration of the population, and the strict separation of ethnic enclaves, resulted in the creation of almost 'pure' ethnic communities who hardly interact with each other. The lack of interaction between ethnic groups consequently made sexual relations among women and men from different ethnic groups very difficult. The large-scale rape that occurred during the war had driven women away from men and 'a significant number of [them] felt unable to consider relationships with men'.[52] This breakdown in communications between different ethnic groups and between women and men continues today, 17 years after the DPA. The number of inter-ethnic marriages in BH has drastically decreased with official statistics recording the registration of mixed marriages as 5.1% of marriages in BH in 2005.[53]

New identities and languages also emerged in the wake of the new nation state, which created further divisions between ethnic groups. While 'Bosnian' refers to any person from BH, whether Serb, Croat or Muslim, 'Bosniac' refers specifically to a Bosnian of Muslim nationality. Also, Serbo-Croatian, which had been the official language in BH, ceased to exist in the new federation. Serbo-Croatian was broken down into three official languages, spoken by the three ethnic groups. Serbian is now spoken by Serbs, Croatian spoken by Croatians, and Bosnian spoken by Bosniacs. Language has become an important indicator of belonging to a particular ethnic group.

Today, due to the poor economic situation, almost 70% of young people cannot see any future for themselves in an ethnically divided BH, one of the poorest countries in Europe.[54] The majority of them want to leave the country and take advantage of educational or economic prospects in the countries of Western Europe or the USA. The dire economic situation affects women in particular, who, in the absence of men, have assumed an increased economic burden, but have less access to resources and benefits.[55] Especially in rural areas, women had earlier relied on

[50] Victoria Ingrid Einagel, 'Lasting Peace in Bosnia? Politics of Territory and Identity' in Pavel Baev Ola Tunander, Victoria Ingrid Einagel (ed), *Geopolitics in Post-Wall Europe: Security, Territory and Identity* (International Peace Research Institute, 1997) 248.

[51] Martha Walsh, 'Postconflict Bosnia and Herzegovina: Integrating Women's Special Situation and Gender Perspectives in Skills Training and Employment Promotion Programs' (International Labour Organization, 1997) 9.

[52] Cynthia Cockburn, *The Space Between Us: Negotiating Gender and National Identities in Conflict* (Zed Books, 1999) 207.

[53] T. Sikanic, A. Tipura, 'Ljubav pobjeđuje podjele' [Love wins divisions], *Nezavisne novine* (Banjaluka), 26 November 2006, 7.

[54] Branko Todorovic, 'Ways of Reconciliation in Bosnia and Herzegovina'. Paper presented at Stockholm International Forum on Truth, Justice and Reconciliation', 23 April 2002 <http://www.dccam.org/Projects/Affinity/SIF/DATA/2002/page1685.html>.

[55] Walsh, above n 51,13.

male labour for the more physically demanding agricultural tasks.[56] Without male support, the economic capacity of women has been reduced to producing foodstuffs and handmade traditional items for home consumption and market sale.[57] The economy in the post-conflict era is limited because of the general lack of purchasing power and the ready availability of inexpensive handmade items.[58]

During the post-conflict transitional period in BH tens of thousands of predominantly male peacekeepers arrived and they created the demand which led to the rapid growth of the sex industry.[59] In response to the market created by peacekeepers, bars and brothels mushroomed near UN bases.[60] Unemployment, poverty and a lack of economic prospects in the countries of Central and Eastern Europe led women from these countries to seek better lives abroad. According to Vandenberg, the majority of these women ended up in BH's illegal sex market, being sold and treated by the pimps as cattle, while being exposed to high levels of sexual and physical violence.[61] The Arizona Market, established by peacekeeping forces to foster trade between Serbs, Croats and Bosniacs, was a place where 'women from the former Soviet Union and elsewhere in Eastern Europe are sold to the highest bidder'.[62] Since this trafficking in women was illegal during the mission, any data on sexual relationships that occurred between peacekeepers and local BH women during UNMIBH is incomplete.

This section analysed gender politics during the post-conflict period and emphasised the changes that occurred in gender relations. During this period women struggled to survive in the dire economic situation and strict ethnic divisions were reinforced. Also, traditional and conservative politics that particularly affected women were revived. In the research that has been undertaken, peacekeepers who served in UNMIBH have only been mentioned in the context of the sex industry and trafficking in women.

4.2.5 Positioning Myself Within the Research

A key tenet of standpoint feminism is that the self-reflective researcher acknowledges their position and experiences within society that frame a particular

---

[56] Bringa, above n 8, 53.

[57] Walsh, above n 51.

[58] Ibid 22.

[59] Madeleine Rees, 'International Intervention in Bosnia-Herzegovina: The Cost of Ignoring Gender' in Cynthia Cockburn and Dubravka Zarkov (ed), *The Postwar Moment: Militaries, Masculinities and International Peacekeeping* (Zed Books, 2002) 51, 61.

[60] Ibid.

[61] Martina Vandenberg, 'Hopes Betrayed: Trafficking of Women and Girls to Post-Conflict Bosnia and Herzegovina for Forced Prostitution' (Human Rights Watch, 2002).

[62] Vesna Nikolic Ristanovic, *Social Change, Gender and Violence: Post-Communist and War Affected Societies* (Springer, 2002) 131.

perspective on the chosen topic.[63] It requires the researcher to be open about their position and experiences, both in order to be aware of the impact of their own perspective on their research and to systematically and consciously view data from different angles.[64] Standpoint feminism does this in order to enhance the validity of the research. It also takes an approach that gives particular weight to women's perspectives and experiences as being more insightful when compared to men's, which are seen to be distorted by their interests in maintaining their position of power.[65] Following the approach of standpoint feminism, it is important to identify myself and the particular context I come from.

I was born in the Socialist Federative Republic of Yugoslavia in the 1970s in Banjaluka, the second biggest city in Bosnia and Herzegovina. My parents are both Orthodox Serbs and were members of the Communist Party before the 1990s. I was raised in a middle-class family and educated in my hometown where I lived my whole my life before the war started. I was proud to be a 'Yugoslav girl' and belong to what I had regarded as a heterogeneous multi-cultural, multi-religious, multi-lingual community of people.

Until I was 13 years old, I was not aware of the ethnicity of my family and thus of myself. One day in the mid 1980s, I came home from school and asked my father who I was. He did not understand my question. I explained that I could not give an answer to my teacher about my ethnic origin, since I did not know. My father said, 'We are Serbs'. As a 13-year-old I did not give a second thought to what my father told me that day. The fact that I did not know my ethnic origins and religious background was not unusual then, since it was not discussed in my family or outside of it. However, not long after that I became fully aware of what 'ethnic' belonging means. When the civil war began in BH, I was 19 years old and my parents decided that it would be the best for me to go to Serbia. Since my mother was originally from Serbia and had lots of friends who offered to help me out, they decided that it was in my best interest to go there. I wanted to go to Western Europe, but my parents were too afraid to send me somewhere 'unknown' to them. During the war I was a refugee in Serbia and spent all those years travelling back and forth to see my parents and, if possible, my brother who was drafted into the war effort. This was the first time in my life that I had been separated from my parents and family. I went to Nis, a city in the southern part of Serbia, and enrolled in law school. In 2000 I decided to go back to BH and worked for a few years in various international organisations in different capacities, including in ethnic minority return assistance projects and projects related to combating trafficking.

In some respects my background meant I was well placed to undertake this research, but it also presented many challenges. As a woman who was born in the former Yugoslavia, I am familiar with the region, traditions and culture of my

[63] Tanesini, above n 2, 139.

[64] Mats Alvesson, *Postmodernism and Social Research* (Open University Press, 2002) 171.

[65] Tanesini, above n 2, 139.

country. I also speak the Serbian, Croatian and Bosnian languages and have a wide social network of friends and former colleagues, many of whom are active in civil organisations established by women, as I mentioned earlier, in their efforts to foster peace and help people recover from war-time sexual and other violence. This helped me to identify and find the BH women who comprised two of my interviewee groups. My background and these connections also helped to build an atmosphere of trust, familiarity and friendliness with my interviewees. However, the familiarity and other advantages I may have enjoyed because of my background also created challenges and even disadvantages. In post-conflict BH I am no longer simply a BH woman. I am a Serb woman. Therefore my attempts to cross ethnic-national borders and work with women from various cultural and ethnic backgrounds could be seen as 'betrayal of my own ethnic group' and as 'anti-Serb'.

As I have explained, in post war BH, ethnic identity has become people's most important attribute, one that can open a door or close it for good as I found out when I was seeking interviewees. Reduced to my ethnic identity and perceived first as a Serb, which outweighs even my gender identity, I found that some BH women from other ethnic groups refused to participate in interviews because of my ethnic origin. As a BH woman, I also brought my own experiences to interviews, and therefore needed to be careful about objectivity and my ability to hear and respect views that may not accord with my own. Ultimately, ethnic identity was not a significant factor in the research because I ended up interviewing a range of women from various social and ethnic backgrounds.

4.3 Aims and Methods

This empirical project aims to explore the distinction between voluntary and coerced sexual relationships, and between prostitution and sexual exploitation. By analysing women's experience of sexual relationships with peacekeepers, the research explores the problematic conflation of consensual sex with sexual exploitation by the SGB. It aims to ask women and peacekeepers whether they would draw a line between sexual relationships and prostitution in PKOs on the one hand, and sexual exploitation on the other. It also aims to explore how the interviewees view the policies set out in the SGB. While there has been an empirical study on sexual exploitation in UNMIBH,[66] which I discussed in Chap. 3, it did not examine the sexual relationships between local women and peacekeepers. Indeed, none of the existing empirical research undertaken on sexual conduct in PKOs have explored such relationships. Further, none of these studies have sought the views of local women about prostitution or sexual relationships with peacekeepers.

[66] Vandenberg, above n 61.

This section explains the aims and methodology of the empirical research project. It is organised into six sections. First, I discuss the case study method used for the research and the reasons I decided to do in-depth interviews. Second, I describe the process of designing the interview questions for each group of interviewees. The third explains ethical considerations I had to take into account for each of my interviewees. The fourth illustrates the process of finding the interviewees and the fifth how the interviews were conducted. Finally, the sixth section identifies the challenges and limitations of the research.

4.3.1 Aims and Methodology

The empirical research has two aims related to my broader research question. The first aim is to shed light on the SGB's approach to sexual exploitation from the perspective of three groups of people: BH women who were involved in sexual relationships with peacekeepers during the BH mission (Group A), BH women who were working within the PKO in BH in an administrative capacity (Group B) and peacekeepers in general (Group C). In particular, it seeks the views of all interviewees on sexual relationships and prostitution in PKOs and asks under what circumstances these might be considered exploitative. The second aim is to seek the views of interviewees about future policy guidelines on sexual relationships and prostitution in the context of PKOs.

The selection of interviewees was not to achieve a representative sample. Rather, it was to produce in-depth qualitative data about the experience of sexual relationships from Group A and their views on prostitution and sexual exploitation in the context of UNMIBH. The project also sought insights from Group B about their perspectives on policies relating to both sexual relationships and prostitution at the time of UNMIBH. From Group C, the interviews sought views about the institutional and practical application of the SGB, also with respect to sexual relationships and prostitution. Although the research findings are based on a modest sample, the in-depth interviews paid attention to detail and context, and thus produced rich material.

The case study method was adopted in this research. As Stake argues, case study is the study of the complexity and distinctiveness of a single case, by understanding its activity within important circumstances.[67] It allows the in-depth examination of a single instance of a social phenomenon, such as a cultural group, a village, or a family.[68] Berg defines the case study as a methodology that involves systematically gathering enough information about a particular social setting, person, event, or group to allow the researcher to effectively understand how they operate or

[67] Robert E Stake, *The Art of Case Study Research* (Sage, 1995) xi.

[68] Earl Babbie, *The Practice of Social Research* (Thomson Wadsworth, 2004) 309.

function.[69] Information which is gathered in a case study has the potential to be rich and detailed.[70] Seuring defines a case study as a holistic empirical inquiry used to gain an in-depth understanding of a contemporary phenomenon in its real life context, using multiple sources of evidence.[71]

It is sometimes argued that case studies are likely to reflect the bias of the researcher, however Yin notes that bias is not restricted only to this method, but can enter into any research.[72] Although the case study method can help the researcher gain a deep perspective to enhance a specific study, the limitation of this method is that it includes the potential biases of those being interviewed and/or the interviewer. Bias may come from one's own institutional, historical, class and cultural position.[73] In qualitative research in the interviewers' own culture, the risk of bias is always present, which I have been aware of since the beginning of my project. With this problem in mind, I have been careful to translate accurately and precisely the views expressed by the interviewees. As I have argued elsewhere in this chapter, bias is not necessarily 'negative', as the personal contextual knowledge and experience of a researcher can also enrich the research.

Interviewing three different groups of interviewees (Groups A, B and C) enabled me to gain perspectives from people who were differently situated in PKOs. While Group A were all involved in sexual relationships with peacekeepers during UNMIBH, Group B were employed by the mission and were living through the same post-conflict transition. Group C came from different countries and had served in various PKOs around the world at the time of the interviews, and had not necessarily served as peacekeepers in BH. These interviewees all had some institutional experience in administering or implementing the SGB. Whether or not sexual relationships and prostitution constituted sexual exploitation was discussed with all three groups of interviewees.

I have used qualitative interviews as the main source of evidence for this research. Qualitative interviewing helps us understand and make sense of the lives of people at either the informal or formal level.[74] As Yin emphasises, well-informed respondents can provide valuable insights into a case study.[75] Some of the main advantages of qualitative interviews are that information on motivations and opinions can be explored that are not easily obtained through quantitative techniques; information not previously thought about can be uncovered; issues

[69] B. L. Berg, *Qualitative Research Methods for the Social Sciences* (Allyn and Bacon, 2001) 225.

[70] Ibid.

[71] Robert Yin, *Case Study Research-Design and Methods* (Sage, 2003) 13.

[72] Robert Yin, *Case Study Research: Design and Methods* (Sage, 4th ed, 2009) 14.

[73] Dean MacCannell, 'Introduction to Special Issues on Semiotics of Tourism' (1989) 16 (1) *Annals of Tourism Research* 1, 3.

[74] Gayle Jennings, 'Interviewing: a Focus on Qualitative Techniques' in Peter M. Burns et al (ed), *Tourism Research Methods: Integrating Theory with Practice* (CABI, 2005) 99.

[75] Yin, above n 72, 13.

can be explored deeply and can be more clearly defined; and personal or sensitive information can be more easily tackled.[76]

Qualitative interviewing is a means of gathering rich, detailed answers to questions that give insight into what interviewees see as relevant and important.[77] Since I was inquiring into issues that are personal and sensitive, the use of qualitative interviews was most appropriate. As Glesne states, qualitative studies contribute to a greater understanding of perceptions, attitudes, and processes.[78] Qualitative research enables insights into how people think and act, and emphasises the meanings people associate with events in their lives.[79] This is precisely what the aim of my project was: to gain insights of people who were directly (Group A) or indirectly affected by the UN's policies on sexual interactions between peacekeepers and local women (Groups B and C).

The primary method for all three groups was through semi-structured interviews to gather detailed personal data to address the research question.[80] As Burgess argues, this format has the advantage of balancing the requirement that the responses address particular themes to be explored, while at the same time allowing interviewees to speak about their experiences in their own terms.[81] Semi-structured interviews also provided flexibility, which allowed me to be responsive to issues raised by the interviewees.

The qualitative data collection phase took place over a 6-month period in the second half of 2008 in BH, Australia and New York City. There were 45 participants involved in this study and their age range was 25–60. Group A consisted of 11 women from BH who had sexual relationships with peacekeepers during UNMIBH and Group B consisted of 13 women who worked for UNMIBH between 1992 and 2002. Group C consisted of 21 peacekeepers, 13 males and 8 females, who were employed in various peacekeeping missions around the world at the time of their interviews. While I conducted the majority of interviews with women from Groups A and B face-to-face, in the case of Group C I relied on telephone interviews as the primary mode of data collection.

---

[76] Bennett, M.M., 'Marketing Research in Tourism' in A. V. Seaton and M. M. Bennett (ed), *The Marketing Of Tourism Products: Concepts, Issues And Cases* (International Thomson Business Press, 1996) 8.

[77] Herbert Rubin and Irene Rubin, *Qualitative Interviewing: the Art of Hearing Data* (Sage, 2005) 14.

[78] C. Glesne, *Becoming Qualitative Researchers: An Introduction* (Longman, 1999) 24.

[79] Steven Taylor and Robert Bogdan, *Introduction to Qualitative Research Methods: A Guidebook and Resource* (John Wiley and Sons, 3rd ed, 1998) 7.

[80] Belinda Fehlberg, *Sexually Transmitted Debt: Surety Experience and English Law* (Oxford University, 1997) 91.

[81] Robert Burgess, *Field research: a Sourcebook and Field Manual* (Routledge, 1986) 107.

4.3.2 Designing the Interview Questions

Interview questions were designed to collect data to answer the research questions and thereby to fulfil the research purposes. However, as a feminist researcher, I attempted to overcome the traditional hierarchical relations between interviewer and the interviewee and make it possible for those interviewed to become the subject, and not the object of research.[82] The women from Groups A and B were encouraged to talk about their own experiences of the BH mission and give their own definitions and understanding of sexual relationships and prostitution, whether or not they might constitute sexual exploitation. Therefore, I did not provide any definition of what constitutes a sexual relationship, but left it to Group A, for example, to self identify as being involved in a sexual relationship. The interview method allowed me to interact and talk with interviewees from all three groups about their views and to gather information about the social interactions between local women and peacekeepers in PKOs.

Interview questions for all three groups consisted of both closed and open-ended questions about the two main themes of my research: sexual relationships and prostitution in PKOs. Since I was exploring sensitive subjects, I designed three different sets of questions because the three groups I planned to interview were differently situated and would draw on different experiences in relation to the research themes. I was also aware that they were likely to have different degrees of sensitivity towards the themes I was exploring. However, the introductory background questions and concluding questions were the same for all three groups. The background questions related to the general circumstances of the interviewees at the time of the interview. Interviewees were asked to briefly introduce themselves, their age, occupation and their experience with PKOs in a broad sense. These questions served as ice-breakers into the topic which was, for the majority of my interviewees, fairly sensitive and private. Following the background questions, I moved to specific questions tailored for each of the groups. The concluding questions were aimed at eliciting perspectives from all three groups about future UN regulations with respect to sexual relationships and prostitution.

The most challenging questions to design were for Group A because I was aware that I was exploring very personal matters and asking questions that some women may not have reflected on prior to the interview. The questions were designed to explore each interviewee's motivations, expectations and experiences of being involved in a sexual relationship with a peacekeeper, including the social impacts of these relationships. The interview ultimately sought to explore whether these relationships were 'sexually exploitative' in the opinion of women who personally experienced them. It also aimed to explore women's views about prostitution in the context of UNMIBH. The research was not about the specific sexual activities the

---

[82] Lorain Gelsthorpe and Allison Morris, *Feminist Perspectives in Criminology* (Open University Press, 1990) 91.

women engaged in, and in the event that an interviewee wanted to speak about such details, I planned to refer her to someone with professional expertise and/or to support services. I also discussed relevant support services with the interviewees at the conclusion of the interview, if their experiences were traumatic in any way.

Because of the particular vulnerability that distinguishes Group A from the other two groups, I designed questions in a way that would enable interviewees to gradually move from a general overview of their lives during the mission to more personal questions related to their particular relationships. Thus, after general introductory questions, I asked each woman to tell me in her own words when and where she met her partner and how long the relationship lasted. I would then move to questions that explored the relationship more closely, looking at the interviewee's motivations and expectations by asking why she got involved in the relationship and if it provided her with socio-economic and other kinds of support. I asked each woman about her understanding of her relationship, whether she ever felt pressured to stay in the relationship, and how the relationship came to an end. I also asked about power in the relationship, how they defined sexual exploitation and what they thought about prostitution in PKOs.[83]

The questions for Group B aimed to provide insight into the views of local women who were employed within UNMIBH about policy responses to sexual relationships and prostitution in PKOs. These questions were aimed at exploring their views about whether sexual relationships and/or prostitution constituted sexual exploitation, and how they saw the consequences of these activities for the mission as whole. After general background questions, I asked about their perceptions and knowledge of sexual relationships between BH women and peacekeepers during UNMIBH. I then asked if these relationships caused any institutional problems and what kind of problems such relationships might cause for PKOs. I also asked them whether they thought there was a distinction between prostitution and sexual exploitation in the context of PKOs. Finally, I asked them how they distinguished, for themselves, between sexual relationships, prostitution and sexual exploitation.[84]

The questions for Group C were designed with a looser structure than the questions for Groups A and B. Since I expected to interview people who undertook various duties within peacekeeping missions, I left room for asking additional questions, in order to explore any particular knowledge that the interviewees may have had. For example, I was not sure how many of my interviewees might have been directly engaged in drafting the SGB policy, how many of them would have experience in applying the policy in their everyday work, or how many of them would have served as peacekeepers in the field and thus be directly affected by the policy. Keeping this in mind, I designed a few additional questions for those who had been responsible for applying the policy. The interview format retained the

[83] For the interview schedule for Group A see Appendix A.7.

[84] For the interview schedule for Group B see Appendix B.5.

same structure as the other two groups, and was divided into the same two themes of sexual relationships and prostitution. As with Group B, the aim was not to explore the personal experiences of peacekeepers in sexual relationships and/or prostitution, but rather their understandings about whether they should be treated as forms of sexual exploitation.[85]

4.3.3 Ethical Considerations

The research was approved by the Human Research Ethics Committee at the University of Melbourne (HREC 0722985. 1 2008). The main ethical considerations consisted of ensuring that the interviews were conducted in a manner that respected the confidentiality of the interviewees, and ensuring that all documents related to the research were kept in a secure place to which only I have access. It also included producing the plain language statement (PLS) and consent letter for all interviewees explaining the objectives of the study, confidentiality, reference persons and the detailed procedure of conducting an interview. All face-to-face interviewees signed the consent forms, except for two from Group C. They both gave oral consent, one because she was uncomfortable about signing the consent form without giving me any explanation, and the other because he was openly afraid of repercussions from supervisors, although I reassured him about confidentiality. Due to geographical distance, I had to do the majority of interviews with Group C via phone, and in all those cases I was given oral consent by the interviewees. In any case, all my interviewees had been sent both the PLS and consent letter well in advance of the interviews, to inform them about the project and to let them decide if they wanted to participate. In addition, before each phone interview I asked interviewees if they had read the documents and if anything was unclear.

For Group A, confidentiality was very important, given the small size of BH and the cultural context, where patriarchal values and conservative sexual mores were particularly dominant in the post-conflict environment. Although I was not asking Group A about sexual abuse, they were considered by the Ethics Committee as a 'high risk' group due to the sensitive subjects I was exploring and the post-conflict context, which was considered risky for field research. Therefore, for Group A, in addition to ensuring absolute confidentiality and anonymity, I took a few extra measures to protect them from possible stress and psychological harm. I carefully examined all the risks that interviewees might be exposed to if they decided to talk to me, and determined how to avoid, or at least minimise them. I also identified free services that could provide psychological support to interviewees if needed.

[85] For the interview schedule for Group C see Appendix C.3.

In addition, I left it to each woman to decide on the time of the interview and to choose a place where they would feel the most comfortable.

Confidentiality was also important for Group B, but since they were not being asked about personal experiences of sexual relationships with peacekeepers, they were at less risk than Group A. Because I was asking them to reflect on my questions from the perspective of UN employees in UNMIBH, I did not have to take any extra precautionary measures.

Confidentiality was also important for Group C. I was aware that many potential interviewees in this group might jeopardise their employment if they agreed to talk to me. Due to their different geographical locations around the world, I made sure they had at least a week before the interview to read through all the documents related to the research and decide whether they wanted to take part. I was aware that the themes of my research were not popular within the UN since they highlighted difficult issues for the UN and that some UN staff had lost their jobs after publicly speaking about peacekeepers' involvement in cases of sexual exploitation and sexual abuse.[86] I was also aware that Group C might discuss highly confidential matters related to their work that they might not otherwise discuss outside the workplace. On the other hand, the fact that this group of interviewees was not asked about their personal experiences in sexual relationships or in prostitution with local women meant they were less personally vulnerable.

In sum, without ensuring confidentiality for all three groups of interviewees, this research would not have been possible. All participants were allocated identifying numbers and any other identifying features have been removed from my analysis of the data in Chaps. 5 and 6.

4.3.4 *Finding the Interviewees*

Groups A and C were the most difficult interviewees to find. Since there are no public data or statistics about Group A, the only way of reaching them was through women's NGOs and my personal contacts in BH. Knowing the cultural context of BH where most social interactions happen over coffee in casual places such as pubs and cafes, and not through the internet, I was positive that once I was in the country it would be easier to find Group A interviewees. Having family and friends in the two largest cities in BH, Sarajevo and Banjaluka, enabled me to connect with women who might know of potential interviewees. I relied largely on a 'snowballing' technique, building on personal and family contacts, as well as through the civil society organisations that mushroomed in post-conflict BH. As Liamputtong argues, snowballing as a recruiting strategy seems to be appropriate

[86] The most famous case was of Kathleen Bolkovac, a civilian police officer who lost her job in UNMIBH after publicly stating that peacekeepers were directly involved in trafficking of women in BH.

particularly when researchers work through community leaders.[87] The researchers may commence with a group of people they know and then recruit more potential participants through the contacts of the original group members.[88] In this way the potential pool of research participants can be enlarged.

Once in BH, I told some of my friends about my research project, and they offered to help me find participants. The gatekeepers are those who directly or indirectly provide access to the key resources needed to do research and who facilitate 'opportunities to interact with others in the chosen research site'.[89] Kitchin and Tate identify them as a 'practical consideration' when planning a research project.[90] In my case the gatekeepers were the people who helped me gain access to the women I wanted to interview. They would tell me they 'know someone' who had been in a relationship and that they thought they would be willing to talk to me. I then asked them if they would contact their friend or colleague, briefly explain my project and ask if they would be willing to participate. The 'snowballing' technique in my research proved to be an effective method of helping me 'to be known by others by the process of positive recommendation'.[91]Having intermediaries was essential because many of these relationships were hidden, and the only possible way to find women willing to participate in my research was by someone close to them suggesting they talk to me. However, the role of the intermediary ended once contact was made with a potential interviewee.

Also, before I went to BH, I had distributed an email template-letter through local women's organisations. In the template letter I briefly described the project and its aims, and invited women from Groups A and B to join the project.[92] I chose local women NGOs because they could reach potential women interviewees, although I was aware that this could result in a particular group of women recruits namely, urban, educated and middle class women who are members or supporters of NGOs. I asked the NGOs, as third parties, to distribute the letter to potential interviewees through their networks. The role of the NGO intermediary was completed once they had sent off the letter. If a woman identified herself as a potential participant and wished to join the project, she was asked to contact me directly. Thus, privacy and confidentiality were assured since the third parties (after passing on the template letter) did not have any further knowledge about

---

[87] Prenee Liamputtong (ed.) *Doing cross-cultural research: Methodological and Ethical Consideration* (Springer, 2008) 69.

[88] Phyllis Eide and Carol B Allen, 'Recruiting Transcultural Qualitative Research Participants: A Conceptual Model' (2005) 4(2) *International Journal of Qualitative Methods* 50.

[89] Robin Kearns, 'Being there: Research through observing and participating' in Iain Hay (ed.) *Qualitative research methods in human geography* (Oxford University Press, 2000)114.

[90] Rob Kitchin and Nicholas Tate, '*Conducting Research in Human Geography: Theory, Methodology and Practic*e (Harlow, 2000) 39.

[91] Eide and Allen, above n 88, 6.

[92] See attached 'Template Letter of Invitation to Participate in Research Project', Appendix A. 1 and A. 2.

participants' interest in the project. However, only three potential Group A interviewees replied to my email expressing some interest in participating, and ultimately none of the women in Group A came from the email strategy. This means that all of my interviewees were recruited through the snowballing technique and personal contacts.

The reason that so few women replied might simply have been a lack of internet access and a lack of familiarity with using it to communicate. Perhaps some women did not understand enough about the research or were not ready to talk and share their stories for fear of a breach of confidentiality, which could cause possible problems with present-day partners and the wider community. I was aware that sole reliance on email contacts was not enough, but being in Australia I did not have many alternatives. Finally, some women from Group A who participated in the interviews told other women about my project, and this helped me to reach other potential interviewees.

For Group B I interviewed two women who initially contacted me as a result of the email template letter I sent through local women's networks.[93] Also, I had a few personal contacts with women who had worked for UNMIBH. As I had expected, they were not worried about talking to me about their views and experiences of the mission. As with Group A, I found the majority of Group B participants through the snowballing technique. After I had interviewed a woman, she would often suggest contacting a friend or colleague who she had worked with during the mission. The Group B interviewees were very pro-active about this, making initial contact with these other women for me. Ultimately, 7 of the 13 interviewees in Group B were referred to me by other women I interviewed.

For Group C, I undertook a combination of snowballing techniques and email approaches. As I did for Groups A and B, I sent off a template letter that explained the aims of my research and invited all those willing to talk to me to contact me.[94] I emailed this letter to a few key UN institutions, such as the Conduct and Discipline Unit (part of DPKO) at UN Headquarters in New York City and to the Director of the Australian Defence Forces (ADF) Legal Services in Canberra. The letter introduced them to my research project and asked if they would help me recruit interviewees. While I had a few replies from different people in the ADF, I was unable to take it any further and arrange interviews. I also received two replies from the DPKO, but making concrete arrangements for interviews proved very difficult as, over a period of 12 months, I was switched from one person to another, and communication often seemed to stall. It took almost a year to set up an interview and the two people who initially were delegated to talk to me were unable to by then, so I spoke to someone else from the DPKO. Two DPKO staff declined to be interviewed. Both advised me to talk to women's groups, NGOs, whistleblowers, forced resignees and UN people who had retired. They suggested these people

[93] Ibid.

[94] See attached 'Template Letter of Invitation to Participate in Research Project', Appendix C. 1.

would make better interviewees for my research and had the 'most knowledge', while people who are still in the system 'just give official lines anyway'. They both implied that their views might conflict with the official position of the DPKO and that an interview would present difficulties for them in balancing their personal views with loyalty towards their organisation.[95]

Despite these obstacles, as with Groups A and B, the main method was snowballing. Some people who have served as peacekeepers put me in contact with their colleagues, and I also contacted some interviewees through academic circles. Without the support of other academics, I would not have been able to arrange most of these interviews. While I initially hoped to find at least 10 peacekeepers willing to talk to me, I ended up with 20, which was a good result. They represented all categories of peacekeeping personnel: the UN military component, UN civilian police officers and military observers, UN volunteers, individual contractors and consultants working on behalf of PKOs. At the beginning of this project I thought it would be good to interview those peacekeepers who had served in BH and who could talk about their experiences within the UNMIBH. However, I soon abandoned the idea because I realised how difficult it would be to reach peacekeepers willing to be interviewed in general, hence limiting my search to such a specific group ultimately would not be productive. Another reason was the fact that the UNMIBH ended almost a decade ago and I assumed that peacekeepers would in any case draw on their experiences from other missions. I think interviewing peacekeepers from various missions strengthened my research data because of the broader spectrum of experiences they were able to reflect upon.

4.3.5 Conducting the Research

Group A

I interviewed 11 women from Group A (BH women who had sexual relationships with peacekeepers). Seven interviews were conducted face-to-face in BH and four over the phone with two women residing in Cambodia, one in eastern BH and one in Serbia. Five of the seven face-to-face interviews were conducted in public spaces at the women's request and two in their homes. Six of them were residing in Sarajevo at the time of the interviews and one in Banjaluka. The interviews by phone took place while the interviewees were in their homes alone, in private. Although all the women were proficient in English, the interviews were conducted in

[95] See, Aviad Bar-Haim, 'Rethinking organizational commitment in relation to perceived organizational power and perceived employment alternatives' (2007) 7(2) *International Journal of Cross Cultural Management*; Monir Tayeb, 'Conducting research across cultures: overcoming drawbacks and obstacles' (2001)1(2) *International Journal of Cross Cultural Management*; Terrence Jackson and Artola Marian Calafell, 'Ethical Beliefs and Management Behaviour: A Cross-Cultural Comparison' (1997) 16(11) *Journal of Business Ethics*.

Bosnian/Croatian/Serbian (BCS), the mother tongue of both the interviewees and the interviewer. The length of each interview was approximately 60 min, but often the interviews were followed by informal discussions about their experiences. Since interviews with this group were particularly sensitive, it was important that the interview setting should be as pleasant and comfortable as possible, whether it was in a public or a private place, face-to-face, or over the phone.

Prior to the interview all the women were emailed copies of the PLS and consent form, and asked to read them and to inform me if they had any questions or comments. Before I started each interview, I asked the interviewees if they had read the PLS and consent form that I sent to them. Although they all had, I repeated to each of them that the interview was confidential and anonymous and that their personal details would not be revealed at any stage of the research. I recorded all the interviews. Prior to the interview I also asked each woman for permission to record the interview. All of them gave their consent.

When conducting interviews face-to-face in public spaces it usually took some time prior to the interview to order coffee, part of the traditional culture in BH. Talking over coffee is an expression of friendliness, of trust and of pleasure, and BH people treat the ritual of its drinking as very special. As Bringa argues, 'having coffee' is, on a 'day-to-day' basis, the most sustained informal interaction between households, friends and colleagues in Bosnia and Herzegovina'.[96] Therefore, drinking coffee during the interviews provided a close and intimate atmosphere.

I met four of the face-to-face interviewees after working hours in the early evening, two in a pub and two in their homes. I met with two women who were unemployed during the day in a coffee shop and I interviewed one woman in her office during working hours. Out of the 11, only 2 were married, both to the peacekeepers they had met during UNMIBH and with whom they now lived in third countries. The rest of the women were single at the time of the interviews.

Although I expected that some women might need counselling services, ultimately there was no need for referrals since none of the discussions were traumatic to the extent that they needed professional services. Since I expected that the women might be overwhelmed by the interviews which could resurrect many suppressed emotions, I ensured that we had some time to debrief after the formal end of the interviews. Eight of the women afterwards explored their feelings about the issues raised during the interview in informal discussions, while the rest did not want to discuss them. While none of them openly told me they felt stressed, all except one said that they had 'never thought' about some things connected to their relationship. Because of the de-briefing, the interviews with women from Group A tended to take more time than I initially had planned to spend. As a feminist researcher, I was reluctant to interrupt the women while they were talking. Some women went into considerable detail and two women wanted to talk about their present lives with the peacekeepers they had married.

---

[96] Bringa, above n 8, 91.

Group B

I interviewed 13 women from Group B (BH women who worked within UNMBIH). Nine were face-to-face interviews and four were by phone, since the interviewees were located out of Sarajevo and Banjaluka.

Six interviews took place in Banjaluka. Two were interviewed at their workplace after working hours, one in a café in the evening over coffee and cake, and three in their homes in the evening. In Sarajevo, I interviewed three women at their workplace during working hours. In general, the women with whom I conducted interviews at home were more willing to talk and were not as hurried as those who decided to meet me during working hours. I spoke to the rest of my interviewees (four) by phone.

As with Group A, I conducted interviews in BCS, but sometimes would use English if the translation of some questions sounded awkward or unclear. Because the interviewees had not had sexual relationships with peacekeepers, they were not so personal as with Group A, so the interviews with this group were shorter and it was not necessary to de-brief after the interviews.

Group C

For Group C, I interviewed 21 peacekeepers who were applying, administering or working under the umbrella of the SGB. Between them, the interviewees had served in Haiti, East Timor, Sudan/Darfur, Lebanon, Afghanistan, the DRC, Georgia, Afghanistan, Sierra Leone, Cote D'ivoire, Liberia, Kosovo and BH. At the time of the interviews, nine were still within field missions, including Afghanistan, Lebanon, Georgia, Liberia and Sierra Leone. Eight interviews were conducted face-to-face, and the remaining 13 were conducted via phone from Australia. Six face-to-face interviews were conducted in Melbourne, one in Brisbane and one in New York City. All the interviewees, except two, had long-term experience with PKOs, ranging from 2 to 15 years. Four of them were in military contingents, three civilian police officers and the remaining 14 were civilian personnel within PKOs. Four interviewees had served in PKOs in the former Yugoslavia.

The seven face-to-face interviews in Australia took place in public spaces like pubs and restaurants, chosen by the interviewees. The New York interview was conducted in the office of the interviewee. All these interviews lasted approximately 60 min. Two interviewees from this group refused to be recorded. While they did not give me explicit reasons for this, I had the feeling that they feared the recording might be used for other purposes. There were 13 male and 8 female participants.

Interviews with Group C were all conducted in English. The majority of my interviewees were interested in my cultural background and I did not mind sharing it as a way of building trust and confidence. Since we spoke in English, there were no language obstacles with this group of interviewees. Also, since the interviewees from Group C did not have to talk about their own experiences, but rather their views and perceptions, there was no de-briefing required with this group.

4.3.6 Research Challenges and Limitations

Although in-depth interviews provide rich information that can contribute to enhancing understanding of women's lives and the issues being investigated, they are time-consuming and require particular skills on the part of the interviewer, including flexibility, active listening skills and good communication skills. While I had been trained to do interviews in the field and by phone, once I started them for the purpose of my study, I found myself faced with several challenges.

The biggest challenge was language, interpreting and translation. The wording and translating of some questions that I had originally written in English for Group A proved to be especially problematic. Working in between the languages—English and BCS—was difficult because some original terms and expressions of the SGB could not be clearly translated. When I was faced with questions about such terminology I would ask the question in both languages because all the women spoke English. As much as possible I wanted to make sure that the interviewees understood the questions I was asking to avoid misunderstanding. One term that was difficult to translate was 'non fraternisation', which is not translatable into BCS. Even the term 'consensual sexual relationships' sounds awkward in BCS. However, it helped that all of my interviewees were proficient in English. For example, when I used the term 'strongly discouraged' in English, they immediately understood it. Although it was awkward to ask the questions in both languages and to spend time defining concepts, I made sure we understood each other and found creative ways to get ideas across.

A second challenge, which I did not expect, was related to my background and familiarity with the country and its people. Some potential interviewees from groups A and B were suspicious of me because of my ethnic background, as I have already mentioned. I had believed that because I am a woman who grew up in BH and spoke local languages, that I was well placed to undertake the research, especially with BH women. However, I had failed to take into account that the discussions in BH along geographic, ethnic and gender lines, would be affected by women's loyalties. I had initially assumed that I would not have many problems finding women willing to talk to me, but I was wrong. As Chaitin argues in the context of Israeli/Palestinian research,

> carrying out qualitative research in conflict-ridden contexts, in which people have experienced much social trauma in their lives, is a difficult task. The task becomes even more difficult when you are a member of such a society, when you are not a third party who can maintain neutrality.[97]

I did not predict that some women would not be willing to talk to me because of my ethnicity and because I spent the war time as a refugee in Serbia, a country perceived by the Muslim and Croat communities as responsible and accountable for

[97] Julia Chaitin, '"I Wish He Hadn't Told Me That": Methodological and Ethical Issues in Social Trauma and Conflict Research' (2003) 13 *Qualitative Health Research* 1146.

the atrocities Serbs committed in BH. As I said earlier, although no one asked me about my ethnic origins, my name is purely Serb. Two women asked me 'where were you during the war?', and when they heard my answer they said they could not help me.[98] Initially, they had both agreed to an interview. While they did not explicitly say that they changed their mind due to my ethnic background and the time I spent in Serbia, I assumed this may have been the reason. I was not prepared for such reactions from women, although I was aware, as some feminists have pointed out, that Serb women, as part of the Serb ethnic group, were perceived as 'guilty' because they were mothers, wives, sisters and daughters of Serb men who committed the crimes.[99] Zarkov, for example, emphasises this when citing a Croatian woman who said, 'I am not sorry for Serb women. Bosnian [meaning Muslim] and Croat mothers were crying when they had to send their sons into war, and Serb mothers were singing'.[100] However, I had thought that the experiences of all BH would unite us as women. Henry et al discuss the 'multiplied positionalities' of a researcher and how they are challenged, constrained and/or transformed by research.[101] They raise important questions about whether it matters if a researcher is white and female, or are race and gender irrelevant in the peacekeeping context?[102] From my own experience, ethnicity was seen as more important than the fact that I am, first and foremost, a Bosnian woman. Despite all this, half of the interviewees from Groups A and B were Bosnian Muslim women and the other half were Serb, Croatian and Jewish.

The third challenge that I faced was due to cultural reticence to discuss sexual relationships. As I mentioned earlier, BH is a patriarchal society where talk about sex is not welcome and where discussion about sexual relationships happens only within very close and private circles. Stigma and prejudices about women involved in relationships with foreigners, such as UN staff, are still present. One woman who married a peacekeeper who served in BH and who now lives abroad said to me that she 'doesn't want to talk' and explained that she was afraid how 'her partner might react'.[103] It may be, as Jackson argues, that love is seen as too individual, too personal to be subjected to investigation.[104] It can also be seen as making women vulnerable to being hurt by men.[105] In that sense the Bosnian woman married to a peacekeeper, perhaps was afraid of what the reaction of her current partner might be if he found out that she was involved in a romantic relationship with a peacekeeper.

---

[98] Both through e mail correspondence.

[99] As I argued elsewhere in this Chapter.

[100] Zarkov, above n 48, 184.

[101] Marsha Henry, Paul Higate and Gurchathen Sanghera, 'Positionality and Power: The Politics of Peacekeeping Research' (2009) 16(4) *International Peacekeeping* 468.

[102] Ibid 469.

[103] Private conversation in Banjaluka with a woman married to a peacekeeper.

[104] Stevi Jackson, 'Even Sociologists Fall in Love: An Exploration in the Sociology of Emotions' (1993) 27(2) *Sociology* 201.

[105] Ibid 205.

Love cannot be treated independently from the cultural and social context within which it is experienced.[106]

I was aware of the sensitivity of the topics and that any talk about sex and emotions might cause some stress for the women in Group A. Although the women with whom I spoke did not show signs of distress after the interview, two of them did express feelings of guilt for ending their relationships. Thus, as Lee and Renzetti argue, studies in personal sexual relationships can be in 'some way threatening to those being studied' by involving 'costs' such as feelings of shame, guilt or embarrassment.[107] This was indicated in my research as well. I was also aware that all the women who were willing to talk to me felt good about themselves and their relationships. As Henry et al argue, those 'subalterns' [original quotation marks] who can or are willing to speak, often tend to be individuals with formal and higher education, and they are a minority of the local population.[108] The research project was limited in that respect to self-selecting interviewees who had good experiences, while women who might have had bad sexual relationships with peacekeepers did not approach to me to be interviewed.

In addition, as Mills discusses, groups construct socially acceptable motives for and evaluations of social behaviour, and describe their behaviours in these terms. They verbalise certain motives rather than others and accept them as justifications for past, present and future acts.[109] Mills stresses that social action is defined and takes on meaning within specific contexts, groups and networks. He examined 'vocabularies of motive' and linked the study of linguistic behavior with social structure. 'Vocabularies of motive' related the attribution of motives to the interests, patterns of power and social positions that give rise to particular ways of talking about social relations and human actions. According to Mills 'different situations have different vocabularies of motive appropriate to their respective behaviors'.[110] Similarly, Mannheim argues that 'both motives and actions very often originate not from within but from the situation in which individuals find themselves'.[111] Thus, the motivational structures of individuals are relative to societal frameworks, so the views of the women interviewees have meaning within a Bosnian social and cultural context and can not necessarily be replicated in other contexts.

---

[106] Ibid 202.

[107] CM Renzetti and RM Lee, 'The problems of researching sensitive topics' (1990) 33(5) *American Behavioral Scientist*, 515.

[108] Henry et al, above n 101, 471.

[109] C. Wright Mills, 'Situated Actions and Vocabularies of Motive' (1940) 5(6) *American Sociological Review*, 907.

[110] Ibid, 906.

[111] Karl Mannheim, *Men and Society in an Age of reconstruction* (Routledge, 1940) 249.

The final challenge I experienced was resistance from interviewees in Group C related to their organisational loyalty. I found policy makers reluctant to be forthcoming about their current plans to revise codes of conduct in relation to the SGB, or about details of any of the case studies they had encountered in their professional careers. Also, when I conducted the interview with a DPKO policy maker in New York City, I was unable to get any documents from their office, not even leaflets relating to preventing and combating sexual exploitation and abuse which are produced for distribution in PKOs. I was told they did not have any in the office. In fact, as this interview did not provide any new or particularly relevant information for my project, I decided not to include it in the analysis.

It has been argued that a good employee contributes to success of the organisation.[112] Article 100 of the UN Charter emphasises that UN staff 'shall refrain from any action which might reflect on their position as international officials responsible only to the Organization'. Also, article 101 prescribes 'the highest standards of efficiency, competence, and integrity' as 'the paramount consideration in the employment of the staff'. In accordance with article 101, the SG promulgated Staff Regulations which outline provisions relating to service of staff.[113] Its section on 'General rights and obligations' states that 'staff members shall exercise the utmost discretion with regard to all matters of official business and shall not communicate to any Government, entity, person, or any other source any information known to them by reason of their official position that they know or ought to have known has not been made public, except as appropriate in the normal course of their duties or by authorization of the Secretary-General'.[114] This provision may explain why some Group C interviewees were guarded about what they said to me.

In sum, while I faced a number of limitations and challenges, I managed to overcome them by being flexible and adaptable to the situations I found myself in. While language represented a challenge, it ultimately did not affect my research data since women from both Groups A and B were proficient in English and were willing to spend some time exploring the concepts and their meaning in BCS. My personal background created some difficulties for my research since, contrary to my expectations, some women were also divided across ethnic lines. However these divisions did not prevent me from ultimately interviewing women from all three ethnic groups. Further, although BH is a patriarchal society and some women refused to talk about their sexual relationships due to the fear that anonymity and confidentiality might be breached, I managed to interview enough women from both Groups A and B to obtain in-depth data for the research. Finally, reluctance from policy makers from Group C to share data was something I expected prior to my field work and had taken into account in the planning stage of my research.

[112] L.R. Jauch et al, 'Organizational Loyalty, Professional Commitment and Academic Research Productivity' (1978) 21 (1) *Academic Management Journal* 84.

[113] *Staff Regulations*, ST/SGB/2001/8 (27 September 2001) .

[114] Ibid sec 1.2 (i).

While I anticipated that I would not be able to find a large number of peacekeepers willing to talk to me due to their professional codes of conduct, the final number was quite impressive and enabled good data collection.

4.4 Conclusions

This chapter explored the context of my case study and its research aims and methods. The first part of the chapter showed that while women in BH enjoyed many sexual rights and freedoms before the war, these rights were restricted by the conservative post-war climate. The number of inter-ethnic sexual relationships and marriages declined during the war. In addition, during the war, divisions across ethnic and gender lines emerged not only among various ethnic groups, but also among women belonging to various ethnic backgrounds. However, women's solidarity was not entirely destroyed as some women crossed ethnic lines to work together for peace. During the post-conflict period there was a revival of tradition, conservative gender politics and the gradual restriction of women's sexual freedoms by male-dominated national, militarised and religious politics. This period also saw the arrival of tens of thousands of male peacekeepers, many of whom were interested in sexual activities with women in BH. Finally, I argued that, as a Bosnian woman who speaks local languages and is familiar with the politics and culture of the country, I was well placed to research the experiences of the BH women who had sexual relationships with peacekeepers and those who worked within UNMIBH, about both sexual relationships and prostitution involving local women and peacekeepers during the mission.

The second part of the chapter set out the aims and methodology of the research. It described the process of designing the questions, finding the interviewees and conducting the research, and outlined ethical issues, and research challenges and limitations. The aims of my study were to explore the views and perceptions of three groups of interviewees (A, B and C) about the SGB provisions regarding sexual relationships and prostitution. While I faced a number of challenges in undertaking the research, I nevertheless succeeded in collecting useful data, which provide the basis for the qualitative analysis in the following two chapters.

Chapter 5
Sexual Relationships in UN Peacekeeping Operations

5.1 Introduction

This chapter analyses the results of interviews with the three groups of participants in the research: women who were involved in sexual relationships with peacekeepers during the UN Mission in Bosnia and Herzegovina (UNMIBH) (Group A); women from Bosnia and Herzegovina (BH) who were employed in UNMIBH but did not have sexual relationships with peacekeepers during this period (Group B); and peacekeepers in general who are bound by the SGB (Group C). Its purpose is to explore how the interviewees from the three groups view sexual relationships in the context of peacekeeping operations (PKOs), and their reactions to the approach taken by the Secretary-Generals' Bulletin (SGB). As I noted in Chap. 3, the views of local women in countries where missions are active and who are directly affected by the SGB were not taken into account in drafting the SGB, nor have their views been sought by previous researchers. This chapter brings their voices into the discussion and fills a void in understanding the impact of the SGB on its subjects. It also brings peacekeepers' perspectives on the SGB into the discussion, and their response to its 'strong discouragement' of sexual relationships between local people and peacekeepers.

As outlined earlier, the SGB takes the view that there is an 'inherent inequality' between 'beneficiaries' and peacekeepers, and therefore 'strongly discourages' sexual relationships between them.[1] Those who wish to engage in such relationships are required to first seek approval from the Head of Mission.[2]

In order to explore the attitudes of interviewees to sexual relationships between peacekeepers and BH women, I selected interview questions that related most closely to this issue and focused on the interviewees' answers to those questions.

---

[1] Secretary-General's Bulletin, *Special measures for protection from sexual exploitation and abuse*, ST/SGB/200313 (9 October 2002), para 3.2 (d).

[2] Ibid para 4 (4) and 4 (5).

O. Simic, *Regulation of Sexual Conduct in UN Peacekeeping Operations*,
DOI 10.1007/978-3-642-28484-7_5,

After closely reading the interview transcripts, I identified the main themes in the responses of my interviewees, which I have used to structure the presentation of their views in this chapter and the conclusions that I draw from them. I have made liberal use of direct quotations in an effort to ensure that the voices of the interviewees come to the fore and are the primary driver of the analysis that is developed. In conclusion, I reflect on their responses and compare them with the approach taken by the SGB.

5.2 Group A

When interviewing BH women who had sexual relationships with peacekeepers, the core questions that related to the theme of sexual relationships were: Why did you engage in a sexual relationship with a peacekeeper? What did you expect to gain from this relationship? Who had the power in the relationship? Do you think that UN staff have 'inherently unequal power' in relation to BH women? Do you think that such sexual relationships jeopardise trust in the UN, its credibility and integrity? What do you think about the SGB's provision that 'strongly discourages' such relationships? From their responses to these questions, five themes emerged which I have used to organise my discussion: reasons for entering into their relationship, expectations from their relationship, perceptions of power in their relationship, UN credibility and integrity, and their response to the 'strong discouragement' of sexual relationships.

As I have said, there were 11 interviewees in Group A. At the time they met their UN partners, they were all employed in what they considered to be good jobs, and they were all happy with their salaries. As one interviewee who was employed in the mission said:

> A8: The salary was terrific having in mind circumstances at that time in Sarajevo and BH.

The women were aged 25–29 when they met their partners. In nine cases their partners were a few years older and in one case he was 18 years older. Ten women met their partners through work, either within the UN mission or with local groups (often NGOs) working closely with the UN on the implementation of various projects in the country. While all the women were single at the time they met their partners, two of the UN partners were married at that time. Both of them later divorced their wives, one during the relationship with the interviewee, and the other after the relationship with the BH woman had ended. Five partners were deployed as military personnel and six as civilian personnel. Seven relationships were serious and long-term, with prospects of marriage. In two of these relationships the women became engaged to their partners, but the relationships ended before marriage, while two other relationships led to marriage, and both women were still married to the same partners at the time of their interview. The shortest relationship lasted for 8 months and, apart from the two relationships that ended in marriage, the longest lasted for 5 years. Of the nine relationships that ended, five were ended by the partner, two by the woman and two by mutual agreement.

5.2.1 *The Reasons for Entering into Their Relationships*

The reasons most of the interviewees (8 out of 11) gave for getting involved in relationships with peacekeepers were no different from the reasons that would be expected in normal peace-time circumstances. The main reasons were love, attraction and friendship. Nine of the women reported that they were in love and were physically attracted to their partners, while two said that the relationship was based on a combination of friendship and attraction. None of the women entered their relationships because they wanted to leave the country.

> A6: Simply, I had a feeling I had found a soul mate. I really fell in love with him from the very beginning and I think he was in love with me too.

> A9: We became very close friends who shared a lot…it could happen that he would stay over night in my place as a friend, I slept in his place as a friend, etc. It was a really great relationship. Then we took a step further and it became a sexual relationship and our emotional relationship became even stronger.

The interviewees, either 'fell in love' or their sexual relationships developed from friendships. Of the nine who reported they were in love, two said they were attracted by the 'exotic' origin of their partners, who they described as Chinese-Hawaiian and African-American respectively.

> A2: His origin was Chinese Hawaiian. He was very exotic, interesting and I liked very much that he picked up some of our language (laugh) like 'dobar dan' (good afternoon). He really showed an effort and was interested in everything. You can feel the difference if someone learns the language and culture because if he knows the language he will get P grade [promotion], or because he really wants to learn it. He knew our jokes and slang and I liked that.

> A7: It was a very interesting combination of his personality, his experiences, education and knowledge. All that in the same person and of course, the attraction between us which was evident from the very beginning. The combination was very strange, that an American soldier, an African-American, could speak our language. In a way that was fascinating. He spoke our language very well and we were immediately pushed towards each other through the job.

Both women described a fascination with the different racial and cultural background of their partners, in particular with their efforts to learn the BH language and culture. However, neither of them connected their feelings of attraction with the post-conflict BH environment in which they lived.

Other interviewees were able to distinguish between different types of sexual relationships and said they felt clear from the beginning about what type of relationship they were entering into and what kind of feelings they had.

> A7: I think it was more an adventure for me, definitely an adventure.

A2: He was my first boyfriend, my first love. There was lots of chemistry there as well. I don't know...I have to say that these beginnings were like 'puppy love', something so beautiful that I remember.

A3: It was not a physical attraction for sure [giggle]. If you could see him, you would know why, but he had some charm and some black humour that I liked.

Only three women, A3, A7 and A11, referred to the post-conflict context as playing an important role in their decision to start a relationship. A3, who worked for 10 years in a military base as an interpreter, spending 2 weeks in the base and then 2 weeks as a civilian at home, believed that the context did influence her decision to enter into a relationship.

A3: I think it is inevitable, if you live twenty-four hours a day in an environment which is closed, which is like a 'state within a state', and you are directed towards the people that you meet on a daily basis and when you are isolated for twenty-four hours a day with these people, that somehow all the attention and all that you need, acknowledgement of you as a woman, as a person, you get all these from people who are really not that important to you. You are a foreigner and you try to reject all these things, but by the time you finish your two weeks of service and go back to your real world, all of them do not exist. Then when you return [to the base] it all seems sweet...and attractive in some way...that intimacy and 'forbidden fruit'...

For A3 there was a clear contrast between 'real life' and life on a military base, which offered shelter from the harsh reality of everyday, post-conflict BH life. She also referred to the attractions of 'forbidden fruit', particularly within a military context where roles are clearly defined, indicating that local women serving in the base were at that time already absolutely forbidden to have sexual relationships with military personnel, and that the ban made such relationships even more desirable, at least for some women.

A7 highlighted the importance of her relationship as an outlet for feelings and desires that were suppressed during the war. She felt that she needed this outlet and the connection with 'someone who was not from here'.

A7: In the period after the war I thought it was a strong emotional and passionate journey for me. I felt that I wanted a change in my life and that four years [of war] suppressed a lot of energy in me that I needed to let go. I needed that communication with other people, with someone I could connect with and that he was not from here, from this context where I live, was very attractive in that period...

On the other hand A11, who also referred to the post-conflict context as an important factor in her decision-making about her sexual relationship, discussed the complexity this created for her. Although she eventually married her partner, she avoided going out with him for a quite some time and, if he had not been persistent, she would probably never have started the relationship.

A11: I had prejudices if I can call them prejudices, because he was a foreigner, because of the kind of job he did, because I knew he wouldn't be in the country long, so if I fell in love, I would be in trouble, because he would leave, so at the beginning I did not want to go out with him...

Therefore, the main reasons women entered into their relationships with peacekeepers were love, friendship and attraction. The post-conflict context mattered a lot to three of them, two of whom felt the context made their relationships more likely, while the third was reluctant to enter her relationship because of the uncertainty of the context. Although these interviewees thought that the context played a significant role, none of them considered the context in the way the SGB does. While the SGB, as the rationale for strong discouragement, indicates a need to protect the most 'vulnerable populations', none of these women saw themselves as vulnerable or in need of protection from such relationships.

5.2.2 Expectations from Their Relationships

When I asked about what they expected to gain from their relationships, none of the women referred to any financial benefits, to the possibility of getting out of BH to live a more comfortable life, or to any other 'economic' motivations. Rather than being motivations for commencing a relationship, some of these expectations did become realistic considerations once the relationship had developed.

> A4: When it started, it started like an affair, some adventure. . .you don't plan this sort of stuff at the beginning of any relationship, thinking 'oh, now I will get married' etc. Then it became a real relationship. However, we never thought at the beginning that we would go to a third country and live together.

Seven interviewees eventually expected to get married and leave the country as a result of their relationships developing, while four reported that they never had any serious long-term plans for their relationships. Two described their relationships as a short-term adventure which they had no wish to pursue further. Importantly, and perhaps not surprisingly, all those who had expectations of marriage were in long-term relationships and four of them had met their partner's family by visiting them in their home country. Their hopes and expectations developed as the relationship developed and both partners made a commitment. For example, A1, who was in a relationship for 2 years, said:

> A1: I had a plan to get married, to move to Norway or to stay here. I was thinking it would be better to live in Norway because salaries were higher there, but then our relationship ended and I dropped off my studies because I had to support my family.

A1 had been engaged to her partner and they had serious plans for marriage, so it seemed quite normal to plan a future together, and the better quality of life in Norway made it the obvious place to live, rather than BH.

For three of the seven women who hoped to leave BH with their partner, this hope was not shared by their partner. A2 was one of them.

> A2: There were expectations. I intended to live abroad with him, but that was not his desire. We spoke about it before he had to leave, but he was not ready for marriage regardless of the fact that I visited him and met his family. I was ready to leave, to find a job and everything, but he wanted to work on his career.

A7 and A8 were among those who had no such expectations.

A7: The fact is that I was not thinking about responsibilities, obligations, leaving my country or marriage. . .when we came to the point of talking about it, I ran away from the whole idea. . .

A8: I did not expect anything. I enjoyed this relationship in that period of my life because I did not expect anything from it, because at that time I had just left a difficult relationship with one of the local guys. So, I did not expect anything from this relationship. It was some sort of 'intermezzo' for me, which impressed me because I was with a man with whom I could talk about anything, with someone who was funny, someone who made my day, but we never had any plans for the future.

Clearly, future plans and expectations for most of them depended on the importance and seriousness of the relationship, as one would assume to be the case in a non post-conflict situation. One woman, who later married her partner, said that she had not expected anything and had initially rejected his marriage proposal:

A10: He proposed to me after eight months, but I rejected him because we had not been in a relationship long enough. I was afraid that he only wanted to do me a favour and take me out of this place and then later live his life. Also, I was wounded during the war and was afraid I would have some health problems and I did not want to be a burden to him.

While A10 probably had very good reasons for wanting to leave the country because of her medical condition, she did not want to take advantage of her partner feeling sorry for her. She asserted her pride and dignity and did not want to be patronised.

In sum, the expectations of interviewees about their relationships varied. While the majority (seven) spoke of their relationships becoming more serious over time, eventually leading to an expectation of marriage and leaving BH as a result, four had no long-term expectations and were in the relationships for adventure and enjoyment.

5.2.3 *'Inherently Unequal Power'*

I asked the interviewees whether they thought UN staff enjoyed 'inherently unequal power' in relation to the local population in general. I also asked them who had the power in their relationships and what makes women powerful in sexual relationships. While the majority of interviewees thought that UN staff had 'inherently unequal power', they thought this was primarily because of the legal immunities they enjoyed. Thus, when describing power between peacekeepers and BH people more generally, they described it in legal and 'imperial' terms, which might be considered 'inherent', but perhaps not in the way the SGB understands 'inherently unequal power'. Most interviewees described the power differences in their relationships in terms of intellect, age and education, rather than as something 'inherent'.

Two interviewees explicitly stated that they had the power in their relationship.

A3: I had the power. I was dominant in this relationship. He was a very weak man. First, he was not well educated, he was very young and he did not have opinions and positions about issues. He would always agree with what I said. However back then it did not bother me. I enjoyed that he was a nice, easy going person...

A8: He never had power in this relationship. Definitely, I had it because I had a lead on lots of things. I would always plan what to do, what to see. He was kind of clumsy.

For both women, power was about leadership and being in control of what happened in the relationship, rather than financial status or anything 'inherent' in the nature of relationships between UN staff and local women. Another three women also defined power in terms of who made the decisions within the relationship. However, they described their partner as having this power for various reasons, including age and maturity.

A2: I was twenty when I met him, so I was very submissive. I thought that he was always right and he knew best. I think I was not really grown up at the time, did not have much of a personality back then. That was at the beginning of our relationship. Three years later, he could not recognise me because I had changed, become self-confident and our relationship was not functional any more...

A4: I think he had it in the beginning because I allowed it. He was married at the beginning so, for example, I would let him decide when we could go on holidays, because first he had to go with his family, and then we could go, that sort of thing. But I am the sort of person who would let someone else decide things as long as it suited me, as long as he made decisions that I supported or liked that was not problem for me at all...

On the other hand, A11 described her lack of power in the relationship as stemming from her partner's lack of agency and his inability to make decisions, in particular about marrying her. She felt she lacked power because the future of their relationship was uncertain. However, after they married she felt the power shifted to her.

A11: I did not feel I had the power in our relationship. He was very insecure and he still is. Now it is different, in our marriage I decide about lots of things. I feel powerful now, but before I did not feel that way because he was insecure about marriage.

Although A5 spoke of her partner as having more power in their relationship, she thought of this as a reality that she accepted, rather than that it was humiliating or degrading for her. This is the only response that could be read as referring to peacekeepers enjoying 'inherently unequal power', although A5 did not see this as a problem.

A5: He was more dominant than me, in intellectual and economic ways as well.

All four of the other interviewees said that power in their relationships was equally shared.

A1: In our relationship no one had more power and because of that I liked our relationship which was based on mutual agreements and communication.

A7: We had agreement on everything we did at every moment. I absolutely was never forced to accept anything. There was incredible attraction and love between us.

A9: I think we had a very balanced relationship. We had similar opinions, political views, we understood each other very well and did not have that problem of inferiority and superiority.

A10: I think that we made decisions together. . .sometimes he would make decisions about some things, sometimes me. . .

None of the interviewees, except perhaps A5, thought there was inherently unequal power in their relationship, as assumed by the SGB. Thus, while the SGB 'strongly discourages' sexual relationships because of the 'inherently unequal power' of peacekeepers, my interviewees did not experience such inequality in their sexual relationships.

In answer to more general questions about what makes women powerful in sexual relationships, five interviewees stated that it is primarily self-confidence.

A1: The fact that she is self confident, that she knows what she wants.

A2: Self confidence, her own personality. . . it is not about 'you complete me', but you 'complement me'. . .

A4: If she herself knows what she wants and if she is quite confident about how to get that, how to access that, that's it then. No one can give you that. Someone can give you financial security, but if you don't know what you want to do with yourself and with any money you may have, you don't get anything from it.

A10: A woman can control a relationship, regardless of education and money. She can still be the one who makes decisions.

Two women thought that financial security played a crucial role in giving women power in a relationship.

A11: Financial security primarily. It gives a woman security and power.

A6: That she is loved, that gives her the biggest strength. . . and that she is financially equal. . .for example, if she doesn't work that she has a right to access his bank account so she doesn't have to ask him if she can buy bread for their children. . .

The other four interviewees thought that a woman's power comes from mutual understanding and partnership in a relationship. These views are important because they demonstrate that women's power in relationships is not only about their socio-economic position, but also about agency, education, self-confidence and partnership.

However, when I asked interviewees about power more generally, all but A5 agreed that UN staff had 'inherently unequal power' in relation to the local population. A5 thought the UN staff had no power in BH:

A5: If you mean the power to change things, no, especially not here. It would be good if they had. In that case they could have changed something in this country. . .

It is notable that A5 was the only one who could be understood to have described power in her relationship as 'inherently unequal'. While she claimed that her partner was 'dominant' in their personal relationship, she did not think that peacekeepers as a collective had power to 'change things' at the country level.

Although all the other interviewees thought that UN staff had 'inherently unequal power', they did not think this because of their experiences of power in their personal relationships, but rather because of the legal immunities UN staff members enjoy and the deference that the local population accords them. Three interviewees specifically referred to the legal immunities.

A3: Yes, in many ways... Some people had immunity...In general they were very well protected here.

A6: Definitely, because they had amnesty for crimes. If they killed someone they wouldn't be prosecuted. Of course, their countries should have prosecuted them but that never happened. No one has been prosecuted so far, but they were not as bad here as what I read they were doing in Afghanistan or Iraq.

A11: Definitely, they come into a country to control the situation after some problems occur. They can do whatever they want, speeding, everything. Our police can't even ask them anything, so that gives them power.

The power that came from the immunities enjoyed by UN staff, and the consequent freedom to do what they liked, was seen as problematic. These interviewees were all critical of the misuse of legal immunities, and the impunity that resulted.

Three women talked about what might be described as the 'imperial power' of foreigners in the UN mission.

A1: Our people, with their Balkan mentality, think that every foreigner who comes here automatically has more power because foreigners have always been bosses and conquerors. A foreigner was better and more powerful, so automatically he was something special in the eyes of the local people. They thought that a person is better just because they are foreign, not necessarily because they are better in some particular way, so we give them intellectual power, and financial power is assumed. This is a kind of general subservience in our people.

A8: They have economic power. The western world has power over weaker states and we are no exception from that...

A11: Definitely...they are coming into a country to control the situation after some problems occurred, they can do a lot of things. The money gives them power.

A1 had in mind the complex history of the last 500 years of the Balkan region, occupied by the Ottoman Empire and, later on, the Austro-Hungarian Empire. Similarly, A8 and A11 implied that, regardless of the fact that this was a PKO, many Balkan people saw them as an occupying force.

Only one interviewee understood 'inherently unequal power' in gendered terms, as in the SGB's usage.

A1: If a girl is poor, unemployed and uneducated, or doesn't speak languages, for example like the girls from Indonesia who marry old guys from the US, there is definitely control in such relationships because those women were not raised to take care of themselves and be independent...

Two things are notable about this observation. Firstly, while A1 suggests that there is a possibility that UN staff might have 'inherently unequal power' over local women, she refers to women in Indonesia, rather than in BH. She disconnects 'poor, unemployed and uneducated women' from her own context as if such women do not exist in BH. Secondly, she also suggests that these 'other' women were not raised to 'be independent'. A1 appears to believe that BH women are raised to be independent and educated, which may suggest that she has 'blind spots' about women in her own country, or that she believes the SGB should apply different rules in BH because women there have more power than women in developing countries.

In sum, the majority of my interviewees understood 'inherently unequal power' in legal and 'imperial' terms rather than gendered and financial terms as the SGB implies. Although they thought that peacekeepers enjoyed 'inherently unequal power' generally, they did not think that this played out in their sexual relationships.

5.2.4 UN Credibility and Integrity

When asked whether consensual sexual relationships could jeopardise UN credibility and integrity, nine women said that they thought not, while two interviewees thought that it depended on the cultural context within which PKOs operate. Three thought that such relationships could improve the credibility of the UN.

> A5: I don't see how that is possible.

> A6: I would not say so. People expect the UN to bring peace and I can't see how these relationships can jeopardise the credibility of the UN.

> A10: No.

> A11: No. I don't think so.

> A7: I think no. On the contrary, if you respect the basic human rights on choice, I can't see how that [consensual sex relationships] would jeopardise credibility and integrity.

Three women suggested that these relationships could in fact increase UN credibility.

> A1: On the contrary, I think that they can increase UN integrity because the UN staff have a chance to learn about local people. . .they also help in building trust between UN staff and local people. They increase the possibility for developing good relationships between people from different countries. . .

> A9: On the contrary, I think they have advantages. I think sexual life is an important part of human life and should be respected.

> A3: It is possible that because of the relationship you are in, you could develop some positive emotions about the country. . .

The two interviewees, who thought that sexual relationships could reflect badly on UN integrity, said it depended on the cultural context of the peacekeepers' work and the seniority of the UN staff member involved.

> A4: Maybe at the beginning of the mission, if there is still conflict in the country. . .it depends on the cultural context where peacekeepers work. . .

> A2: I think yes. . .you can't be objective and impartial when you are in these relationships. . .

In sum, only one interviewee (A2) clearly expressed a concern that these relationships could jeopardise UN credibility, while another interviewee thought they might, depending on the cultural context. The majority of my interviewees did not think that these relationships could jeopardise the UN in any way. Rather, three of them suggested that these relationships could increase organisational credibility and integrity.

5.2.5 *Response to 'Strong Discouragement' of Sexual Relationships*

With respect to the SGB's assumption that local women in the PKO context are very vulnerable, the majority of women from Group A agreed. While they acknowledged that the context of PKOs often increases women's vulnerability, they did not think that sexual relationships should be 'strongly discouraged' as a result. Only one interviewee said she did not have any opinion about this question, while two interviewees said that they didn't think women in post-conflict situations were particularly vulnerable. Eight women explicitly stated that local women were more vulnerable as a result of the war. For example:

> A4: They are a vulnerable group and have a higher risk of exploitation, although I haven't had that experience. We all experienced the war and traumas.

While A5 and A9 agreed that the post-conflict circumstances make women more vulnerable, and may lead to them making different decisions than they would in normal circumstances, they nevertheless thought those decisions were valid.

> A5: When you live under abnormal conditions, such as war, it is possible that you will look for some consolation, for some way to a normal life. It is difficult to make a clear distinction between what is normal and what is not. I think it is normal that I can consent, but in a war environment the circumstances where relationships develop are not normal.

> A9: Local women are vulnerable. However, I think that women can clearly decide what a normal relationship is. They are totally conscious of what is what, but they don't have any other way out in the circumstances. It is a very difficult and intimate decision, but what you do with your body is your own choice.

Two interviewees did not think that women were made more vulnerable than anyone else by the post-conflict conditions, although A7 did say she thought this perhaps made women more vulnerable to manipulation than men.

> A7: I would not accept that argument because I would not say that women are the only group which is particularly vulnerable. We were all in an abnormal situation, but maybe women were at higher risk of manipulation. What I experienced in the war was that norms become harsher, i.e. what is acceptable or unacceptable. Control within the family becomes stronger, not only because of security, but because if you are a woman, a daughter, that control is even higher. So when you run from such pressures you can become the victim of some sort of manipulation because you don't know the culture, the communications, social networks that exist in missions.

> A8: We are all vulnerable. I wouldn't accept that argument.

Although the majority of my interviewees thought that women in the post-conflict context were vulnerable, when asked whether sexual relationships between local women and peacekeepers should be 'strongly discouraged' as a result, all but one interviewee said 'no'. Ten interviewees thought that consensual sexual conduct should not be regulated at all. They were concerned that such regulations would be patronising, endanger the right to private life and free choice, and unrealistic.

A1: No. It should be regulated by usual moral norms, but not legal pressures because then you assume that local populations are victims. No one should regulate private things.

A7: I don't think so. I think the people themselves should decide about their relationships.

A6: I don't think they should prohibit sex. If they prohibit it, there will be even stronger desires for these relationships. They are lonely when they are in missions, they are far away from their homes and it is human that they want to have someone from here.

A3: Consensual sexual relationships should not be regulated.

One interviewee was not clear.

A11: I am not sure if it is OK to prohibit all sex between peacekeepers and local women. It is difficult to answer this question because some relationships are normal, some are not.

In sum, although the majority of interviewees agreed that women in war-time are more vulnerable, they did not think that this was a reason to establish special rules, such as 'strong discouragement', to regulate consensual sexual relationships between women and peacekeepers. Despite their vulnerabilities, the interviewees thought that women were capable of choosing whether to engage in a sexual relationship or not.

5.2.6 Conclusions

All of the Group A interviewees reflected on their relationships from a personal perspective and their expectations varied according to the nature of their relationships. The women who were in long-term relationships had expectations that extended to their future lives together, while those women in short-term relationships lived more day-to-day. While only a few of them referred specifically to the post-conflict context and how it affected their decision-making about their relationship, none of these context-specific considerations raise concerns that would justify the protective regulation of sexual relationships along the lines of the SGB.

As explained in Chap. 3, the SGB appears to rest on several assumptions. The empirical research findings challenge those assumptions. First, although the majority of the women saw themselves as more vulnerable as a result of the war, they did not think this was a justification for the SGB's 'strong discouragement' rule. They thought that consensual sexual relationships were a private matter and should not be regulated by legal or administrative policies.

Second, when asked about the distribution of 'power' in their relationships, all of the women responded in terms of who had the decision-making power. Only one described her relationship in terms that could be understood as 'inherently unequal power'. In their responses, the interviewees understood 'power' rather differently from the SGB's understanding. The majority agreed that 'imperial' power and legal immunities gave UN staff power when compared with local people. However, they thought that this general inequality in power did not affect power in their intimate relationships with peacekeepers. The interviewees also did not define power in economic or gendered terms, but as being based on education and agency.

As A3 said, 'I had the power. I was dominant in this relationship. . .he was not well educated. . .and he did not have opinions and positions about issues'. Their views contradict the assumption made by the SGB: that UN staff have inherently unequal power over beneficiaries in all of their interactions, including in sexual relationships.

Third, the SGB assumption that peacekeepers' involvement in sexual relationships with local women will likely be exploitative has also been challenged. Most interviewees thought that such relationships were not different from the relationships that would be expected in normal peace-time circumstances. As A9 said, '. . .we understood each other very well and did not have that problem of inferiority and superiority'.

Fourth, the SGB assumes that sexual relationships between UN staff and local women jeopardise UN credibility. However, the majority of Group A thought that it is the immunities UN staff enjoy, from the application of local criminal law and civic regulations, which negatively affects its integrity. A few of them also suggested that sexual relationships can help to build trust between local people and the UN, and thus improve the reputation of the UN.

While Group A was comprised of relatively self-confident, middle-class and educated women, at the very least their experiences show clearly that women 'beneficiaries' are not a homogenous group, as is assumed by the SGB, and that not all women are sexually 'vulnerable' and in need of the protection that the SGB seeks to provide. Furthermore, their experiences suggest it may also be unsafe to make these assumptions about other less privileged women who engage in sexual relationships with peacekeepers, as it can be expected that their relationships may also be motivated by such ordinary desires as sexual attraction, love, friendship and a sense of adventure.

From the perspective of my interviewees, the SGB approach is over-inclusive when it assumes that local women are in a position of 'inherent inequality' and therefore need protection when it comes to sexual relationships with peacekeepers. Effectively banning them may even increase the attractiveness of sexual relationships to those involved, as one of my interviewees acknowledged when she referred to 'forbidden fruit'.

5.3 Group B

When interviewing BH women who were working within UNMIBH about sexual relationships, the questions that I asked were: What did you think about UN staff who got involved in sexual relationships with local women? Why would local women be interested in UN staff? Did you think that UN staff had 'inherently unequal power' in relation to the local population/women? Did you think that sexual relationships between local women and UN staff could undermine UN credibility and integrity? What do you think about the SGB's provision that 'strongly discourages' such relationships? The responses to these five questions make up the five themes in this section.

As I outlined earlier, there were 13 interviewees in Group B. Four of the women still work for international organisations in BH. The interviewees were aged 25–38 when they started to work within the mission. Two women were working with the military contingent of the mission, while the rest were with civilian organisations.

5.3.1 Perceptions of Reasons for UN Staff Entering into Relationships

When responding to the question about why peacekeepers got involved in relationships with BH women, seven thought the reasons were no different than they would be under normal peace-time circumstances. Another four thought that BH women were attractive to foreign men because they were more traditional and submissive in sexual relationships. Two women disapproved of these relationships if they were only for the purposes of having sex.

Seven interviewees thought that peacekeepers got involved in sexual relationships with BH women for the usual reasons, ranging from love to sexual desire. For example:

> B4: There were cases where people met and fell in love, got married, which is completely normal. On the other hand, there were a lot of cases where these relationships were result of a pure human nature, sexual need and desire...

> B9: When I think about these relationships I think as I would about any other relationships between men and women. There is nothing particular about them. It just happens that he is a foreigner, she is a local, and that's it.

> B13: There were lots of various relationships. If people found each other I never judged them. It was a chance to meet a soul mate. I looked at these relationships as normal.

Four interviewees thought that UN staff were more interested in 'our women' because they are 'more traditional and raised in a patriarchal society' (A4), and therefore very attractive to them.

> B5: In principle women here are different than women there [in the West]. Women there are more oriented towards careers and women here more towards family. Some of them [UN staff] might like it, so maybe our women would be more interesting to them than theirs.

> Me: You think that 'our women' are more conservatively raised...to please men?

> B5: Yes...

> B7: I think that our women are still traditional and patriarchal and it is very easy to get used to that. If they come from a country where that does not exist, it is very reasonable that they will choose someone who will, I don't know, accept his family name and completely identify with him, as traditional Balkan women would...and we have certainly more of them here than they have in Norway.

> B10: I think they were interested in our women because they had very bad experiences with their own. I don't know why. I met lots of their women when I went to visit them [in their

home country]. They were very nice and kind, but they were very selfish as well. The majority of them don't work, while their partners, soldiers, work in the field and live their lives. . .you know, they have too much freedom. The soldiers like the mentality of our women more. They were fascinated by us, our dedication to family and that way of life.

B11: I think someone told me that one of the reasons why Norwegian people easily communicate with Bosnian women is because they feel better with our women than they could feel in Norway. It's because the mentality of the women here and there is different.

These interviewees did not have a problem with UN staff being attracted to the traditional submissiveness of BH women, while B10 was clearly proud of this tradition.

Two women condemned relationships based on anything other than love. One of them was concerned that the main reason that UN staff entered into relationships with local woman was to have sex, while the other supported these relationships only if they were based on love. According to her, relationships with 'legitimate reasons' were those that could lead to marriage or that were committed.

B1: Everyone thought that UN staff only want sex from locals. Everyone thought so, both men and women, and that there was no need to show love.

B2: I don't have anything against people who fall in love with each other, even in the work place. I don't have anything against it, if it is for legitimate reasons, regardless of whether the man is a foreigner or local. . .if people love each other, if they enjoy each other, why not have a relationship. . .I don't see a problem with people who came here [internationals] starting a relationship, getting married or having any relationship that leads to marriage. . .

The majority of the women thought that UN staff entered into sexual relationships with local women for 'normal' reasons ranging from love to casual sex. However, four thought that the traditional upbringing of local women was attractive to UN staff members. Even these did not suggest that the 'traditional submissiveness' of BH women is a reason to 'strongly discourage' these relationships.

5.3.2 *Perceptions of Reasons for Local Women Entering into Relationships*

When asked why local women would be interested in having a sexual relationship with UN staff, the interviewees defined a wide range of reasons including sex, money, love, 'getting out of poverty' and 'leaving the post-conflict situation'. Some interviewees did not have problems with any of these reasons, while some were concerned about some of them.

B7: I looked at those as something very positive. If people are happy it does not matter if the relationship is for sex, money or love. These relationships can be healthy and based on love for sure. . .

Four interviewees thought that the reasons local women entered into relationships with peacekeepers were connected to the post-conflict context and its difficulties, like wanting to leave the country and escape the looming poverty.

B11: I believe there were lots of reasons…from 'let me get out of this poverty', to unreal expectations of a better life abroad because no one could know what was waiting for them there when they got married to someone who is not from here…but also there were real, honest love relationships…

B8: I know women who were running after these guys just to get married and go to England. Some of them desperately wanted to do so, but I can't judge them. I don't know what kind of circumstances they were living in. Maybe they thought it was the only way out, or maybe they were alone during the war after losing their parents, so the only solution they could see was to get married.

B1: I believe that many women who entered into these relationships at that time wanted, after everything that had happened in our country, to leave, to migrate abroad. However, they would very soon realise that these guys were absolutely not interested in anything like that. I would not encourage these relationships.

B10: There were women who entered into these relationships just to get passports and get out of poverty. But many more really fell in love because they [international men] were different from our men. They were very independent, earned good money, were ready to iron their clothes, wash and cook, and they were so caring. They were as loyal as puppies. I was fascinated by that.

One interviewee talked about two-way 'exploitation' suggesting that both parties can profit from such relationships. She did not perceive 'exploitation' to be negative, but rather as the pursuit of personal interest that can be based on emotional or material needs.

B6: You could look at these women as if they wanted to achieve something. I don't know. Some of them left this region and went to the US, England, etc. But this exploitation is always the same. A local woman can see a local doctor and say 'I will marry a doctor' if that is her aim. It doesn't matter if he is local or a foreigner if she wants to do so. They could even exploit each other to achieve some of their goals. He might not want to be alone, to make his life easier until he gets back home and she might have the reasons I mentioned.

B3 summarised a problem that was raised in nearly all of my interviews: the stigma attached to women who entered into relationships with UN staff.

B3: You know we always had some sort of prejudice that Bosnian woman would enter into a relationship with a policeman from who knows where because of her self interest, and maybe this prejudice exists even more among those who came here [internationals] than those who were here in the community. This sort of prejudice and stereotype was unforgivable because it was discriminatory and humiliating for a local person who by accident met someone who was English, French or Chinese. This stereotype was especially common here during the war. That emotional dimension, your own independence, your dignity and right to decide if you want to be in a relationship with someone is nullified and becomes a part of that general stereotype which exists even now. It was a stereotype held by foreign men, but also foreign women. I was present twice when women [international staff] commented on relationships between a Bosnian woman and someone from the mission. They implied that by default the relationships were based on self-interest and not on emotions or anything else. That was totally incorrect. Of course, if you have thousands of relationships, some of them will be based on self-interest, or pressure, or love. It is not for me to encourage or discourage these relationships.

It seems that Group B interviewees accepted the significance of the post-conflict context as a reason for local women to enter into sexual relationships with UN peacekeepers. It was not clear whether interviewees based their opinion on facts or assumptions.

5.3.3 'Inherently Unequal Power'

Although the number of interviewees in this group who thought that there was 'inherently unequal power' between UN staff and local women were barely in the majority (7 out of 13, like the women in Group A, they did not think this inequality was a problem for sexual relationships between them. Most of them thought there was 'unequal power' between UN staff and local people because of their better economic position, privileged status and better education, and, like Group A, many also mentioned the legal immunities they enjoyed.

> B1: Yes, probably because of money and financial imbalance, his origin, the country where he came from, the position he had in the mission. . .we thought that all these people were very educated and well-off back in their countries because their government sent them as experts.

> B4: I think that their status gave them some power, but I did not think it should. I think that local people had perceptions that these people had power over them, unfortunately. . .they did have power, for example, that they could park a car in front of the cathedral in the centre of the city and no one could do anything about it. They would not get a ticket or be punished because of that. . .in such a way you encourage them to behave badly and differently, so they feel they can abuse that power. . .

> B7: It was a fact that some positions were reserved only for foreigners, such as a high level positions. . .this tells us that they came into the country with some sort of power and that they have some power over the local population and local employees. . .

> B8: Possibly, yes. They sometimes behaved as if no one could do anything to them and did as they liked, which of course resulted in resentment from the local people. . .

Four interviewees expressed more nuanced views on power. They were not convinced that UN staff enjoyed unequal power, at least not all of them.

> B10: I don't know. . .maybe at the beginning, but later this power became less, or less visible. . .I don't think they were seen as authorities. . .they had economic power. . .

> B11: Hmm, not sure. . .they were in a better position in some ways. . .maybe they did not have as much power as people liked to think they did. . .

> B12: I am not sure. It depended on individual people and how they were perceived. . .they had some power, they were always in a position of authority. . .we have never been in a position of authority over foreigners. . .we were in a position of subordination. . .

> B6: I don't think so. It depends on their regulations, what they were allowed to do and prohibited from doing. . .I never thought of them as having any power. . .

The other two interviewees, B2 and B5, like all the respondents from Group A, acknowledged that there was, in general, inequality in power but that this inequality did not affect or invalidate genuine and non-exploitative sexual relationships.

> B2: I agree that some sort of power imbalance did exist. However, if people honestly found their soul mate, loved each other, etc. . .I did not see why the relationships should be banned and how this was connected to the power they had. I didn't think that the foreigners who came here to work were, by default 'above us', so to speak.

B5: I could not see that. I did not see connections between their relative power and their relationships…that [power] had nothing to do with relationships. As a group they [UN staff] could represent their power, but as individuals I am not sure they represented it or had power as such…I did not see these relationships were more risky than other sexual relationships [between locals].

Although the interviewees from Group B were concerned about general inequalities in power, they differentiated between general power and individual power in sexual relationships. Like Group A, Group B understood power in terms of education, age and legal immunities. There was overall discomfort about immunities and the kind of disrespectful and illegal behaviour they encouraged. Like Group A, they also expressed concern about the UN's 'imperial' power and local people perceiving themselves as in a position of subordination. Similarly to Group A, they did not believe that general inequalities in power were necessarily reflected in individual sexual relationships.

5.3.4 UN Credibility and Integrity

When responding to the question about whether sexual relationships between local women and peacekeepers can jeopardise trust in the UN's credibility and integrity, five interviewees felt that they could have a very positive impact on the local credibility of the UN by building trust, connecting with the community and breaking down stereotypes. Two said that such relationships did not have any detrimental impact on the UN, while the other six said that it depended on the type of relationship.

Similarly to two of the interviewees in Group A, five thought that sexual relationships could have a positive impact.

B7: I don't see that they can endanger credibility of the organisation if it is a healthy relationship. They can only increase its credibility because these people are seen as tolerant, as people who accept differences as a part of their life, and emotionally and rationally engaged in a relationship.

B8: I think these relationships help build trust. Many of them who came here had prejudices about us, that we are some sort of backward people, but then they were surprised to learn that we are more sophisticated that they thought…once they met us and learned about us they were happy to spend time with us…they changed their opinions about us because they spent time with us and hung out with us…there was nothing to endanger their credibility and integrity…

B10: Absolutely not. They hated us [Serbs] and at the beginning of the mission they were full of all sorts of prejudices about us…later on they saw that nothing the media said about us is true, and that it was all propaganda against us…after hanging out with us they changed their opinion…I think dating and socialisation is great because they have an opportunity to accept us…if a peacekeeper can date one of our women, then he thinks positively about us as well, for sure…

B13: I think it can only advantage an organisation. I don't think there was any possibility that these relationships endangered the organisation in any way.

Both, B5 and B9 were emphatic that these relationships did not have a detrimental impact on UN integrity.

B5: No.

B9: Absolutely not. I don't think so.

The other six interviewees said that whether these relationships jeopardised the credibility of the UN depended on the people involved and the type of relationships they were engaged in. However, some of the interviewees did not have consensual sexual relationships in mind when making their response, but rather were referring to sexually exploitative behaviour.

Two interviewees referred to prostitution, sexual harassment and exploitation as 'relationships' that have a negative effect on UN credibility.

B1: Yes, they can... you would expect that these people are strictly professional and when they offer you something that can almost be identified as prostitution, then it is undermining not only trust, but the morals of the organisation that came to help.

B3: Eventually they could if a relationship has elements of harassment or exploitation, of course it can have implications for credibility...

Two were concerned about workplace relationships and 'unprofessional behaviour' in the work place due to sexual relationships.

B2: I think no, however, if people behave unprofessionally because of their relationships, or they can't separate their private life from their professional life, then it can become a problem.

B4: In principle, yes. I am thinking about concrete examples and when some people don't have any criteria for choosing their local partners I think that their credibility as UN staff, and also perceptions of the organisation, can be undermined...we had a case in our organisation, a relationship between international and national staff, which was very bad and people knew about it, not only from our organisation, but from outside too.

Another two interviewees thought that it depended on the type of relationship the people develop and how it is perceived by the public.

B6: ...a relationship should not be a problem, but it depends on how this relationship develops and looks in the public eye, I guess...

B11: With respect to consensual sexual relationships...I think these relationships can jeopardise credibility because you don't know what kind of relationships people engage in and what will result from them.

None of the women from Group B thought that consensual sexual relationships could be damaging to the UN, although six thought that 'relationships' that have sexually exploitative elements may negatively affect UN credibility. Five interviewees thought sexual relationships could be positive for the UN and its reputation.

5.3.5 Response to 'Strong Discouragement' of Relationships

None of the women from Group B supported the SGB's 'strong discouragement' of sexual relationships in PKOs. The reasons given included the idea that regulation of consensual sex would patronise people involved in them, disrespect their privacy, jeopardise individual human rights and freedoms, and encourage racism.

> B1: I think there should not be explicit bans on sexual conduct. I think it should be left to people to decide about their relationships. The UN does not encourage these relationships, but it shouldn't ban them either. If there are some feelings between people, there should be no barriers to those feelings.

> B2: If people are adults they should have the responsibility for their own conduct. I would never ban consensual sexual conduct. If people want to have sex and they are adult, then that is their thing and I absolutely support it.

> B6: Some code of behaviour should exist, but any sort of banning is ridiculous. It treats us like some backward country...I think it is not acceptable...there should be some regulations in countries that have strict codes of behaviour, like some Islamic countries where women can have problems...I don't think they should ban relationships if people want to have it or fall in love. Which rules can tell adult people that they can't have sex?!

> B8: I think it is ridiculous to ban adult people from having sexual relationships...it won't work...if people fall in love, they will be together...

It is notable that B6 suggests the potential need for 'some regulations' in contexts such as 'Islamic countries'. This view echoes the opinion of A1 who also suggested that women from some countries, such as Indonesia, may need some protection, but not BH women. Both of these women supported some regulation, depending on the context, but did not support regulation in BH. Nevertheless, B6 did not believe that rules can prevent adult people from falling in love or having sex.

Seven of the interviewees were concerned that 'strong discouragement' of sexual relationships would jeopardise the human rights of people who want to engage in sex, as well as encourage discrimination.

> B3: They can ban people having friendships and relationships, but I don't see reasons for it in some contexts. If they have a zero tolerance policy on such relationships, that opens a debate about human rights and individual rights...What if people fall in love? To whom do they have to prove that their relationship is based on love and honest emotions?

> B5: I can understand that the UN wants to regulate relationships, but I don't approve of any sort of ban. If people work together and have relationships, that should be somehow regulated, but not by banning. Maybe they should not work at the same place, but I don't see how consensual sexual relationships can endanger local populations or UN missions. It is not acceptable and infringes basic human rights. No one has a right to regulate personal relationships.

> B9: It is an impingement on the intimacy of two adult people who are in a sexual relationship. On the one hand you have a war which completely diminishes your human rights and on the other hand you have an organisation which also infringes your human rights by not allowing you to exercise them...I think this is completely wrong and unfair, at least where Bosnia is concerned ...it would be terrible if someone could be repatriated because of a sexual relationship. For example, if my partner was instructed to break up with me, even if it was only a purely sexual relationship. I think that is so wrong.

> B11: I don't think it is OK to strongly discourage sexual conduct. No, it is not OK because in this way they build walls and fences between people...we are all humans and you encourage racism if you ban people from falling in love, from mixing with one another, from dating.

> B4: To me it is an impingement on human rights and freedoms because I can't see very good reasons why one would discourage these relationships. It is a sort of discrimination against both the local woman and the peacekeeper, the UN staff member.

> B12: I think that strong discouragement won't work, because it does not make sense. I don't think it is OK. People should be free to make decisions about their lives.

> B13: I think that rules, bans and any sort of regulation are wrong. You can't regulate love or sexual life without impinging on human rights.

One interviewee expressed concern that the 'strong discouragement' rule was based on prejudices against local women.

> B7: I don't support the principle of strong discouragement because I don't see why there is such a strong perception that a local woman, by default, can be sexually exploited by a peacekeeper. All sexual relationships that I have witnessed so far were everything else, but not sexually exploitative. No, I don't support this principle.

Notwithstanding that some interviewees in Group B were concerned about the motivations of the peacekeepers and local women for engaging in sexual relationships and the general inequality of power between them, none of them supported the SGB's policy of 'strong discouragement'. On the contrary, they were emphatic in their insistence that such a policy is 'unfair' and endangers human rights and freedoms. They were also concerned that the policy is patronising and is based on prejudices and negative stereotypes of local woman.

5.3.6 Conclusions

The majority of the interviewees in Group B perceived the reasons for local women entering into sexual relationships with peacekeepers as more contextualised to the post-conflict environment and the Balkan region than those in Group A. They believed that due to the dire economic circumstances resulting from the conflict, local women saw these relationships as an 'escape' from hardship. However, one interviewee from Group B (B3) expressed concern that such views stigmatised local women, both locally and internationally, and that they were unfair and did not allow women to make their own choices. It is instructive that none of the women from Group A talked about escaping hardship as a reason for entering into their relationships. By treating sexual relationships as suspicious, and local women as 'inherently' vulnerable, the SGB risks encouraging stigmatisation and perpetuating the kind of prejudices expressed by Group B. Paradoxically, the view of local women manipulating peacekeepers in order to 'escape' is inconsistent with the SGB view that it is local women who are vulnerable and need protection from exploitation by peacekeepers.

The majority of respondents from Group B believed that the reasons for peacekeepers entering into sexual relationships with local women were no different than they would be under peace-time circumstances. However, four thought that the reasons foreign men were attracted to BH women were because they are submissive and traditional in sexual relationships. As B7 puts it '...our women are still traditional and patriarchal...' None of these interviewees thought that such 'submissiveness' should be the reason for 'strong discouragement' of such relationships. While the SGB indicates suspicion that peacekeepers would sexually exploit local women, none of the interviewees from Group B thought so.

While the majority of interviewees from Group B agreed that UN staff had 'unequal power' in a general sense, like the majority in Group A they did not necessarily think that these power discrepancies would be reflected in sexual relationships between peacekeepers and local women. These views clearly contradict the SGB assumption that the 'inherently unequal power' of UN staff trickles down to their sexual relationships. Also, like Group A, Group B did not define unequal power in gendered or economic terms, but rather in terms of the immunities that UN staff enjoy.

The majority of the interviewees in Group B, like the majority in Group A, thought that sexual relationships do not jeopardise the credibility and integrity of the UN, but rather that the organisation's credibility is jeopardised by immunities which lead to a lack of accountability for crimes and regulatory breaches committed by peacekeepers in host countries. Also, similarly to Group A, several interviewees suggested that such relationships can increase the UN's integrity by promoting tolerance and building trust between local people and the UN. Some of them also expressed concern that such an approach by the SGB can encourage racism and stigmatisation. As B11 said, '... you encourage racism if you ban people from falling in love, from mixing with one another...'.

Despite their different and sometimes contradictory views on the motivations of women and peacekeepers entering into relationships, and the degrees of inequality between them, only one of the women from Group B agreed with the SGB that these relationships should be strongly discouraged. All of the others thought that the virtual prohibition of sexual relationships is unfair and may impinge on individual human rights and freedoms.

5.4 Group C

In my interviews with peacekeepers, both civilian and military, the following questions were directly related to the question of sexual relationships: Would you agree that peacekeepers have 'inherently unequal power' in relation to people in the local population? What kind of institutional problems can sexual relationships between peacekeepers and local people raise for PKOs? What do you think about the approach to sexual relationships taken by the SGB? Three themes, around which the following discussion is organised, emerged from the answers given by my interviewees: 'inherently unequal power', UN credibility and integrity, and their response to the 'strong discouragement' of sexual relationships.

As outlined earlier, there were 20 interviewees in Group C, 13 males and 7 females. All of the interviewees knew at least one case of a colleague having a sexual relationship with a local woman or man while on mission, but had not experienced this personally. The nationalities of Group C included Australian, American, Brazilian, Canadian, English, Italian, Nepalese and South African. Between them, they had experience of service in Afghanistan, BH, Cote D'ivoire, East Timor, Georgia, Haiti, Kosovo, Lebanon, Liberia, the DRC, Sudan/Darfur and

Sierra Leone. Three had been deployed as civilian police officers, 4 as soldiers and 13 as civilians. They had from 8 months to 15 years experience with PKOs.

5.4.1 'Inherently Unequal Power'

All but two of the peacekeepers interviewed agreed with the SGB's statement that peacekeepers have 'inherently unequal power' in relation to local people. They defined 'power' in terms of their legal immunities, economic status, 'imperial' position and greater security. Also, all but one answered the question with reference to the local population generally, rather than women specifically. Like the majority of the women in Group A and Group B, interviewees in Group C thought that the diplomatic immunities and special legal status enjoyed by UN staff bestowed considerable power and a position of superiority when compared to the local community.

> C7: In principle, you do have power in conflict-affected countries where peacekeepers operate. There is extreme poverty and people are in need of basic things. As international staff you have a relatively OK salary and also have power over resources, etc. Those put you in a position of inherent power in comparison to the majority of the population and in some places to the whole population.

> C8: Wherever they are deployed [peacekeepers] it is because there is a problem. There may be civil war, a country may be in distress. . .they come there to help, to maintain peace or solve whatever problem is there, so people see them as saviours of some kind.

The following two interviewees gave a more nuanced account of 'inherently unequal power'. They were concerned about diplomatic immunities and impunity the UN staff enjoy. Although they referred to sexual relationships, it seems that they had exploitative sex in mind.

> C3: They [UN staff] have a range of diplomatic immunities which may or may not relate to specifically sexual relationships. . .It comes down to money, accountability and all of these. . .they have more money, they are not accountable to local structures and they can leave any time.

> C12: If it is a police officer who committed the crime, it directly compromises the victim because of their inability to make reports and seek redress—that kind of overt power. Then there is the more general power of a UN peacekeeping mission and its personnel, who are often above local law so they can act with impunity. This does not have to be about sexual relationships, but rather across the board. They speed, they drink and drive, they do all kinds of things and there is no kind of regular law accountability for that. . .because of their 'super god' status generally within that community.

Another two were the only interviewees who answered the question with sexual relationships with local women in mind.

> C20: In these relationships there was a fairly unequal power dynamic and the man had no long-term intentions. I heard about very short-term prostitution relationships, sort of disguised ones. For example, relationships where a woman or woman's family benefit from the relationship. It was more of a convenient arrangement. . .East Timor is a very

conservative Catholic society so these things are quite disguised. There were a few night clubs where you had the impression that this type of activity occurs, but it wasn't overt.

C2: We go to a third world country ravaged by war…the people are poor, they have lost their brothers, husbands…economically they are vulnerable. It is human nature if you are vulnerable and you see a way out through marrying somebody of higher economic standing, doing something that will benefit you economically. You are trying to find a way out from that environment. She knows you won't stay there, she will hate the situation she is in. Is she just using you to feel good about herself? Maybe she will see the peacekeeper and think it can be like in a Hollywood movie, but ultimately the peacekeeper will leave so she wants to benefit from our position of authority.

Neither interviewee allowed for any possibility that sexual relationships might be long-term, genuine or that the women involved might have emotional or other motivations for engaging in sexual relationships with peacekeepers. They both referred to the 'unequal power dynamic' in sexually exploitative relationships and prostitution.

When asked about 'inherently unequal power' almost all of Group C talked about local populations as if there was no diversity or difference between their gender, class, education, skills, age and so on. They described local people, in contrast to peacekeepers, as having little education and limited experience and knowledge.

C6: Local populations are largely illiterate, poor. They are affected by conflict, traumatised…

C9: We are physically there to protect the locals, as they are incapable of doing it for themselves…in my experience. They are susceptible to exploitation…

C17: A lot of these people [local] did not have the benefit of an education, have never travelled a lot. UN staff are very, very worldly people. They have lived and travelled all over the world. They are constantly travelling and they have exposure and I guess a degree of worldliness that the local people can't compete with. So when you combine the huge differential between earning and knowledge, then you end up with a very, very powerful incentive for women to get involved with peacekeepers.

While these views may be true, they strip away the ability of local people to do something for themselves as they are seen as lacking financial resources, education and security. C17 suggested that the education and knowledge that peacekeepers have is what gives them power over local people, but that this is also why local women may want to get involved with peacekeepers. However, these views are in stark contradiction to the views expressed by Group A who did not think of themselves as powerless, at least not when compared to their partners. Some of them also did not think of themselves as less educated or knowledgeable than peacekeepers. In fact some women felt powerful in their relationships and that they were superior in education and intellect.

When I asked C17 if there were any relationships between local women and peacekeepers that seemed different from her stereotypical description, ones in which local women were not necessarily illiterate and marginalised, an example easily came to mind, although she said that this was the exception rather than the norm.

> C17: For example, one of my staff members [based in Sierra Leone] is a Ghanaian and he chose a local woman as a partner. She had a local position with the UN as well. That relationship was widely known and worked because, despite the fact that there was a huge salary differential between the two of them, she had a lot of power. You know, she was a very powerful woman in her own right and had high standing, more or less, in the international community. That relationship worked and was readily accepted by everyone, but that is by far the exception rather than the norm.

C17 suggested that some relationships between local women and peacekeepers are exceptions although she had in mind UN employees rather than local women. C20 also thought that some relationships are genuine despite the imbalance of power that potentially exists between peacekeepers and local women.

> C20: . . .they have inherent power in a number of ways, for example they can just leave the country. . .in terms of power relations between them and local women, there is a potential for inherent unequal powers, but discouragement is ridiculous because some of these relationships are genuine.

Group C defined power in various ways including economic power, security, legal immunities and 'imperial' power, as well as worldliness and knowledge. Two interviewees from Group C did point to a possible distinction between general inequalities and inequality in individual relationships in the ways that interviewees' from Group A and some from Group B did. They did not think that the general inequalities necessarily have to trickle down into personal relationships between UN staff and local women. However, the views of Group C were generally more consistent with the SGB concept of 'inherently unequal power'.

5.4.2 UN Credibility and Integrity

When asked what kind of institutional problems sexual relationships between peacekeepers and local people could cause for PKOs, all of the respondents in Group C were concerned that sexual relationships can jeopardise UN credibility. The problems they thought may arise included conflicts of interest for the peacekeepers, the danger of threats to local women from jealous local males, the risk of stigma from 'peacekeeper babies', negative public perceptions and, more generally, the distraction of peacekeepers from performing their professional duties, thus undermining the credibility of UN work. However, three interviewees thought that such relationships could be an advantage for the UN.

The following five peacekeepers thought that sexual relationships would destabilise and degrade the security environment within which PKOs operate. According to them, such relationships could disrupt military discipline and create competing interests and divided loyalties which could put the whole mission in danger, as well as those involved in the relationship. Some of them were also concerned about the physical safety of the people involved in these relationships and stigma attached to women who may enter into these relationships.

C9: You are there to do your job and look after the people and that is what you are supposed to do...you have to have self discipline and you should be able to control yourself. I absolutely agree with the non-fraternisation policy. If you have to protect one village and your girlfriend and her family are in another village, you might say, 'Oh, no, I am going there, my girlfriend is there'. So, you see, it is actually very dangerous for you to have a conflict of interest.

C11: What happens if the security environment suddenly deteriorates and you need to evacuate? Where is your focus going to be? On your role, or the person you have a relationship with? The reasons our operations are unaccompanied is because our environment is not safe and you have to focus on the mission, not significant others...so having anyone may compromise the mission's integrity.

C10: One of the most dangerous things that can happen in the mission is that someone who has a relationship with a local puts the life of that local in danger... let's take Bosnia as an example. It was hard enough for a woman in that context to be an interpreter...If she was my interpreter, for example, I would make an assumption that local intelligence organisations would be in contact with her... and I would tell her that I have no problems with her being open about what was occurring. If, on the other hand, I was engaged in a sexual relationship with her, it would then put her under increasing pressure because now there would be emotional pressure about her answering questions etc. The second issue about her safety would be about her being allowed to go back to a traditional community and risk being ostracised in that community...the third is that I would always be concerned as to whether she was pressured to have a sexual relationship with me by the local intelligence community...moreover, if you are a 22-year-old woman and you are engaged in a sexual relationship, there are other local men of that age who would see you as a potential partner... you threaten all the males in that community and you limit their options as to who they can have as their life partners...

C6: Here [Afghanistan], it could be a great security risk. It [sexual relationships] would be so unacceptable for the community...also, if a local becomes pregnant, they can lodge a complaint and ask for maternity costs for the child that the UN has to pay...

Another five peacekeepers also expressed concerns about 'peacekeeper babies' who may be born from these relationships, and the negative consequences for the mothers, the children, and also the UN.

C1: If peacekeepers exploit local people, it is a matter of betraying a trust...they should not exploit the people because they are there to maintain the peace in the country and if they have sex with a girl and she gives birth, then that creates a social problem for the mother and child...

C5: I think people would be very concerned about a woman being abandoned, once they found out she was in a sexual relationship with a peacekeeper, because she would then be considered damaged goods or unmarriageable...also, people would be concerned about children not being supported if a local woman becomes pregnant in a relationship and then a person just goes back to where they were from...it affects the UN, but the UN doesn't involve itself in these problems [peacekeeper babies].

Eight interviewees were concerned about the negative public perceptions of the UN that any sexual relationships with local women may engender.

C4: The institutional problem is the reputation of the UN, which is in a position of power and authority ...it is about the reputation of an organisation that is there to bring peace, stability and development, and not having its individuals exploiting the difficult realities...

C8: When peacekeepers relate socially or sexually with a local population there will always be some power dynamics that may undermine the credibility and integrity of the work of the UN...you need some kind of measures so the institution does have control...

C20: It could cause a negative perception of the UN, that certain people behave inappropriately. There will be rumours, etc.. . .so, this can lead to damaging the UN's reputation. . .I guess there are problems with children who are born from these relationships and what the UN should do about them. . .

One interviewee was concerned that sexual relationships may distract UN staff from performing their duties.

C2: . . .for the institution, sexual relationships can mean that no work can be done, we can become obsessed with free sex as we often are, regardless if whether is in the UN or elsewhere. . .you can get offspring and diseases from these relationships. . .

Three interviewees thought that whether sexual relationships might cause problems for the mission depended on the peacekeeping context, which differs from country to country.

C7: It depends in which country you are, in which context you are working. . .in some countries it is unacceptable and in some countries it is fine, people don't really mind. . .I know colleagues of mine who married women or men who they met in the Balkans. . .and it seems to me that there was no strong cultural condemnation for that. . .if you have, for example, a peacekeeping operation in Columbia, I don't think consensual sexual relationships would be a big issue. . .

C13: It depends on the context. Countries where we work are often extremely conservative and a relationship can pose a threat and security stress for our personnel. . .so, sometimes it can pose a security threat and it can be very, very bad for our relationships with the local community and in an environment like that, where we have a serious threat against UN personnel, it is really important that we have the trust of the community. . .

C14: In my experience sexual relations between UN peacekeeping personnel and local populations are common. However, there is a difference between these relationships back in the former Yugoslavia and in Haiti. Whereas in Haiti, given the dire straits of the economy and the vulnerability of the local population, sexual relationships between peacekeepers and the local population I would characterise as more concerning to me to the extent that it was quite obvious that you would definitely be exploiting the imbalance of power in relationships which may be sexual, but also power of influence.

Like interviewees A1 and B6 these two peacekeepers thought that the specific cultural context of a PKO determined whether sexual relationships would endanger the credibility of the UN or not. While A1 and B6 referred to Indonesia and Islamic countries as places where there would be a need for a 'code of behaviour', like C7 they thought that the Balkans would be more accepting of such relationships. Similarly to some views in Groups A and B, two peacekeepers thought that sexual relationships could also bring some advantages, either to the people involved or to the UN.

C3: The only advantage is that true love can come out of it. . .

C12: . . .it can also be positive [to have a sexual relationship] because you can gain a greater insight into the local community, you can get the real story, you can predict certain difficulties. It depends on what your job is of course. . .

C20: . . .some Timorese like to see their women married to foreigners, since then they become part of their culture. In that sense, it is really seen as a positive thing that foreign people are embracing Timorese culture and becoming part of it. . .there is a potential for these genuine, cross-cultural relationships. I think they enhance the UN credibility because these peacekeepers can have access to information that other people can not have because they were immersed into the community. . .

While all of the interviewees were concerned that sexual relationships may negatively affect UN credibility and integrity, like the SGB, they mostly had exploitative sexual activity in mind. Thus, while the SGB concerns UN credibility and integrity because of sexual relationships between UN staff and local women, it seems that the concern my interviewees expressed was more related to sexually exploitative behaviour than sexual relationships. Also, while the cultural context of the PKO played an important role for all three Groups of interviewees, it is different from the context the SGB assumes. While the interviewees distinguished between post-conflict contexts (some of them more traditional and conservative and thus less accepting of sexual relationships than others), the SGB has one approach that applies to all PKOs. Finally, two peacekeepers, like some interviewees from Groups A and B, surmised that such relationships could in some cases have a positive effect on UN credibility and integrity.

5.4.3 *Response to 'Strong Discouragement' of Relationships*

Most interviewees in this group (13) supported the SGB's 'strong discouragement' of sexual relationships between peacekeepers and local women because of the complications that sexual relationships may introduce, including conflicts of interest. Six interviewees suggested a total ban on sexual relationships while three interviewees explained that 'strong discouragement' was interpreted in their mission as a total ban. Another four interviewees thought that the rule should be more flexible, depending on the context in which it is applied. Finally, none of the interviewees had heard about the exception from the SGB 'strong discouragement' provision, the exercise of discretion that the Head of Mission has when applying this policy.[3]

Support for the ban of sexual relationships was expressed in the following ways:

> C2: At the end of the day, [local] women want to somehow benefit from it [sexual relationship] either to be taken out of that area or to be benefit economically, so they target somebody. You can't be in a normal boyfriend-girlfriend relationship. So, it is better not to have any relationships.

> C6: I think that sexual relationships between local women and international staff are sexually exploitative. It is impossible to know if something is truly consensual, therefore it is better to avoid the whole thing by prohibiting any form of sexual relationships.

> C11: UN peacekeepers are deployed to a mission for a specific purpose and that purpose is not to enter into a relationship with local populations, but to focus on their primary role. If they want to enter into a personal relationship with somebody from the local population, then they should step out of the mission and find a way to pursue that relationship.

---

[3] The Head of Department, Office or Mission may use his or her discretion in applying the standard prescribed in section 3.2 (d), where beneficiaries of assistance are over the age of 18 and the circumstances of the case justify an exception. Sec 4.5 of the Secretary-General's Bulletin, above n 1.

C9: We have a non-fraternisation policy which is interpreted as 'don't touch locals'...it would be too complicated if you got involved with somebody because you can upset them...

C11: If UN personnel are engaging in sexual relationships with the local population that are consensual, I believe that it falls within the SGB's definition of sexual abuse.

C14: Zero tolerance. Sexual relationships are considered to be sexual exploitation. There is zero tolerance for both sexual relationships and sexual exploitation [in the Haitian mission].

The following three interviewees said that the application of 'strong discouragement' meant, in practice, that sexual relationships were effectively prohibited, suggesting that there was a big discrepancy in missions between the written rule and how it was implemented on the ground.

C2: Our rule [in Sierra Leone] was that you should not have any sexual relationships with locals. That was the rule for all UN staff. You can be a friend, but no sex under any circumstances.

C6: It was interpreted in my mission that there should be no relationships with beneficiaries, with Sudanese women. That is the point that he [the commander] made...

C19: No relationships are allowed with locals [in Liberia]. You know, even emotional relationships are not permitted.

The interpretation of 'strong discouragement' as a ban demonstrates that sexual relationships are 'considered to be sexual exploitation' in some field missions, in accordance with the intent of the SGB.

Another four interviewees observed that the interpretation of the 'strong discouragement' provision differed from mission to mission and was flexibly interpreted. The response of one interviewee, who worked in a mission-based Conduct and Discipline Unit (CDU), seemed to confirm their views:

C13: We don't know what it ['strong discouragement'] means. It doesn't really tell you. We don't have a definition, so it leaves a lot of discretion for officers who come from a range of countries...I mean, I can tell you how I interpret it, how we interpret it when we have cases, but my interpretation is not the same as the interpretation of a CDU officer in Liberia, Congo or...and this is why there are problems with the SGB because we don't know what it means.

The wording of the SGB on sexual relationships certainly leaves responsible officers in each UN peacekeeping mission to interpret 'strong discouragement' as they see fit. This allows for flexibility, for looking at cultural contexts and taking other circumstances into account when interpreting the 'strong discouragement' provision. In missions where 'strong discouragement' is interpreted strictly and sexual relationships are effectively banned, peacekeepers who have sexual relationships with local women may be repatriated, disciplined and even lose their jobs, while in others where there is a more flexible approach, they may be able to continue their service and their relationships. Thus, repatriation for having a sexual relationship seems unjust in itself.

Five interviewees who did not interpret the SGB's wording on sexual relationships as a total ban were concerned that such an approach was too absolute, that it could jeopardise sexual rights and freedoms, and that it was not fair.

C1: The SGB policy is very strict. If anyone is found having a sexual relationship or giving food for sex, they will be repatriated. The zero tolerance policy should restrict relationships, but not absolutely because people have human desires to have sex... but it shouldn't be exploitative sex.

C5: I can actually see relationships around me that are genuine and consensual, the relationships that I think are legitimate...it is a right of those people to be in their relationships and there should not be any sanctions for that...

C13: It's a difficult one...There is definitely some exploitation going on there as I see so many peacekeepers getting involved in relationships and making some kind of promises that there will be marriage in the end...but this can happen anywhere and I think that women in these countries are not naïve. So, yes, there is some exploitation there, but I do not think it is to the extent that the UN would need to take formal or disciplinary measures to respond to it.

C18: It [sexual relationships] is a bit of escapism...to have a better life and if you are in a relationship you may be able to escape this current life. I don't know, but I am sure that lots of them do have true feelings and then how do you police true feelings? How do you distinguish between genuine and other relationships? ...you definitely have to have guidelines, but if you make it black and white there are going to be occasions where people have true feelings for each other, it is just human nature...and I would hate to think that someone was penalised for having true feelings...

C20: I think that is ridiculous to ban sexual relationships...I think there are some genuine relationships that should not be prohibited... I don't think it is fair to include those...

To summarise, five interviewees expressed concern about the injustice and strictness of the 'strong discouragement' SGB rule if it was applied as a ban. They thought that sexual relationships in PKOs can be genuine, consensual and legitimate. This is clearly something that the SGB ignores when it insists on 'strong discouragement', regardless of the type of sexual relationships people are involved in. While there was general support of the 'strong discouragement' provision, the majority of peacekeepers were concerned about its application and interpretation in the field when it was applied as a ban. There was also a view that the policy needs to be applied flexibly so that different socio-economic and cultural contexts can be taken into account.

5.4.4 Conclusions

Compared to Groups A and B, Group C expressed more of an institutional perspective, from the point of view of the mission as a whole and its role. Interviewees in Group C talked about their responsibilities as peacekeepers, as participants in peacekeeping missions on behalf of the UN and their home countries, although individual perspectives also came through. Group C's responses largely reflected institutional interests, while members of Groups A and B offered perspectives based on their personal experiences and views. Group C interviewees were also generally concerned with protection of the whole population, rather than individual beneficiaries.

When responding to the question of 'inherently unequal power', the majority of interviewees held strong views about the lack of power of the local population they were commissioned to protect, based on the fact that local people are largely traumatised due to the conflict and dependent on the UN mission. In the view of most of the interviewees, these factors create 'inherently unequal power' between local people and peacekeepers, which is consistent with the SGB approach. However, two interviewees (C17 and C20) did not support the institutional approach and distinguished between these general inequalities and differences of power in sexual relationships, like all of the interviewees from Group A and most of the Group B. They thought that, despite the fact that peacekeepers have unequal power, genuine sexual relationships exist in the context of PKOs. One of them was more specific and referred to local women employed within UN missions. According to this interviewee, sexual relationships between those women and peacekeepers were an exception to relationships which involved 'inherently unequal power'. It is significant that these two interviewees, despite their institutional allegiances, thought that sexual relationships between local women and peacekeepers could be genuine, despite one confining his/her comments to local women employed within the mission.

Because most interviewees considered sexual relationships to be sexually exploitative due to unequal power dynamics, they expressed concerns about the impact that sexual relationships with locals may have on the credibility and integrity of the UN. However, three peacekeepers (C7, C13 and C14) departed from the institutional perspective, echoing the views of some of the women from Groups A and B, drawing attention to the context within which PKOs work, and suggesting that at least in some post-conflict contexts, such as the Balkans, the credibility of the UN would not necessarily be jeopardised by sexual relationships. According to these interviewees, in some regions the local people were less vulnerable and had more liberal views on such relationships. They thought that in 'extremely conservative' (C13) countries where 'the dire straits of the economy and the vulnerability of the local population' (C14) exist, it would be more problematic to have such relationships. Thus, while the SGB homogenises all post-conflict societies, these three interviewees differentiated between them, taking into account socio-economic and cultural circumstances.

Like some of the interviewees from Groups A and B, three peacekeepers (C3, C12 and C20) thought that these relationships could enhance UN integrity, rather than jeopardise it as the SGB assumes. Likewise, these three interviewees also expressed concern about the lack of local accountability of peacekeepers and the immunities they enjoy, which can have a negative affect on UN integrity.

Although the majority of interviewees in Group C supported the SGB approach, eight peacekeepers expressed concerns about the interpretation of 'strong discouragement' as a total ban. They thought that it was unfair to penalise genuine sexual relationships and respond to them with formal disciplinary measures. However, while Group C overwhelmingly supported the SGB's 'strong discouragement' approach, it is significant that some interviewees expressed concern about such an approach when it was enforced as a total ban. Despite their institutional loyalties, they saw such a ban as an unacceptable impingement on participants' sexual rights and freedoms.

5.5 Conclusions

This chapter has explored the views of the interviewees about the SGB's provision for 'strong discouragement' of sexual relationships between local women and peacekeepers. Local women's views have been given particular prominence, since they have not been considered in previous research.

During the interviews, two competing perspectives emerged concerning the SGB's provision for 'strong discouragement' of sexual relationships between local women and peacekeepers. One perspective, expressed by the overwhelming majority in Group C and one local interviewee (from Group B), was in favour of the SGB policy. These views conform with the SGB assumption that women are 'inherently' vulnerable and in particular need of protection in post-conflict societies. The views of Group C reflected an understanding of the role of peacekeepers as protectors and, in that context, emphasised the undesirability of sexual relationships. They argued that local people in post-conflict societies are vulnerable, powerless, traumatised, live in a context that is highly insecure, and need protection from any sexual encounters with peacekeepers because they are all likely to be sexually exploitative, including sexual relationships. This view is supported by the radical feminist argument that sees women as victims of dominant male sexuality and as subordinated sexual objects that men seek to possess.[4] It also stereotypes peacekeepers as men who can not treat women with respect. However, the support of most of Group C for the SGB's 'strong discouragement' approach was not because it protected women in particular. Rather, the 'strong discouragement' approach was seen as a measure justified by the general need of all beneficiaries for protection from those involved in the UN mission.

The second view, held by all but one of the local respondents in Groups A and B, disagreed with the SGB 'strong discouragement' provision. This is consistent with the 'sex positive' feminist view which argues that, even if they live in patriarchal societies, women can not simply be reduced to the status of 'passive victims'.[5] These interviewees strongly challenged the assumption that because of the post-conflict context, characterised by 'vulnerability' and 'inherent inequality', women need protection from every sexual encounter. As Kapur argues, such assumptions result in imperialist interventions in the women's lives in the developing world. They recreate the imperialist image of native women as backward, illiterate and

[4] Andrea Dworkin, *Pornography: Men Possessing Women* (Perigee Books, 1981); Catherine MacKinnon, *Towards a Feminist Theory of State* (Harvard University Press, 1989).

[5] Sylvia Walby, *Theorizing Patriarchy* (Wiley-Blackwell, 1990) 125.

victimized.[6] Zarkov believes that victimization and agency should be only two of the many possible narratives of the positioning women within a violent conflict.[7] As A9 said, 'Local women are vulnerable. However. . .women can clearly decide what a normal relationship is'. The interviewees voiced their concerns about sexual autonomy, agency, and the sexual rights and freedoms of the participants in such relationships. For example, A9 stated that 'sexual life is an important part of human life and should be respected'. Indeed, as Justice Blackmun in his dissenting opinion in the US Supreme Court case of *Bowers v. Hardwick*[8] suggested, 'sexual intimacy is a key relationship of human existence and central to the development of human personality'.

Concerns were also raised about the patronising language that the SGB employs, and the stigma that such language can place on local women. It is notable that, despite their institutional views and favourable consideration of the SGB in general, eight peacekeepers supported the local women's concerns, and thought it unfair to ban all sexual relationships between local women and peacekeepers because some of these may be legitimate and genuine.

While almost all of the interviewees agreed that peacekeepers had inherently unequal power, local women were critical of the SGB assumption that these general power differences necessarily affect the power dynamics in personal sexual relationships. More importantly, many interviewees conceptualised power in a way that diverged significantly from the SGB assumption that 'inherently unequal power' is based on gendered and financial power, since Group A defined power primarily as being based on education and agency. Thus, while the SGB defines power as domination and 'power-over', local women tend to conceptualise power as 'power-to' and the capability to assert oneself, as some 'sex positive' feminists do, such as Hartsock who understands power 'as energy and competence rather than dominance'.[9] They suggest that power understood exclusively as domination is particularly masculine and women tend to reject this definition, understanding it as 'a capacity to transform or empower oneself'.[10] As A3 argues, 'I had the power. . .in this relationship. He was a very weak man. . .not well educated. . . and he did not have opinions and positions about issues'. Thus, although peacekeepers were

[6] Ratna Kapur, 'The Tragedy of Victimization Rhetoric: Resurrecting the "Native" Subject in International/Post-Colonial Feminist Legal Politics' (2002) 15 *Harvard Human Rights Journal* 11.

[7] Dubravka Zarkov, 'Towards a new theorizing of women, gender and war' in Evans M, Davis K and Lorber, J (eds) *Handbook of Gender and Women's Studies* (SAGE, 2006) 231.

[8] *Bowers v. Hardwick*, 478 U.S. 186, 196 (1986).

[9] Nancy Hartsock, Money, *Sex and Power: Towards a Feminist Historical Materialism* (New York, Longman, 1983) 12, 224.

[10] Sarah Hoagland, *Lesbian Ethics: Toward a New Value* (Institute of Lesbian Studies, 1988); Starhawk, *Truth or Dare: Encounters with Power, Authority, and Mystery* (Harper, 1987); Thomas Wartenberg, *The Forms of Power: From Domination to Transformation* (Temple University Press, 1990).

stereotyped as holding 'inherently unequal power', the interviewees in Group A did not agree with that.

Group B, like Group A, identified a range of reasons that they thought might motivate BH women to enter into sexual relationships with peacekeepers, including sex, money and love. However, one of the interviewees expressed concerns about the stigma that is likely to be attached to women involved in such relationships due to the attitudes of peacekeepers, as well as local people. Local women are stereotyped as desperate to escape their situation, and therefore prepared to enter a sexual relationship deceptively in order to achieve this goal. When discussing the motivations of local women, a majority of the interviewees from Group B relied on this stereotype. Significantly, such stereotyping is out of step with the SGB's view of the 'vulnerability' of local women and the need to protect them from sexual relationships because they are likely to be exploited by peacekeepers.

The experiences of Group A, none of whom had entered their relationships in order to leave the country, point to the inaccuracy of the stereotype of local women as generally exploitative and scheming. One respondent from Group B (B3) highlighted this dimension of the complexity of sexual relationships between peacekeepers and local women, which the approach of the SGB threatens to entrench by treating these relationships as always suspect, albeit for different reasons. As she argued, 'This sort of prejudice and stereotype was unforgivable because it was discriminatory and humiliating for a local person...' Overall, Group B was in agreement with Group A in that they did not believe that BH women enter sexual relationships with peacekeepers primarily for reasons based on their vulnerability and 'inherent inequality'.

While the majority of peacekeepers argued that sexual relationships could undermine the credibility and integrity of the UN, only a few local interviewees expressed similar sentiments. Instead, local interviewees felt that the SGB assumption that sexual relationships between local people and peacekeepers would jeopardise UN credibility could encourage racism towards, and prejudices against, local people. Contrary to the SGB, these interviewees and three interviewees from Group C, argued that sexual relationships had the potential to increase the UN's credibility because staff engaging in such relationships might be seen as tolerant and embracing the values of multiculturalism. As noted in Chap. 2, former Secretary-General Hammarskjod argued that building positive relationships with local people is a key to the success of any PKO.[11] This means that relationships between locals and peacekeepers could be viewed as mechanisms for building trust between UN staff and the local population, and for breaking down the prejudices and stereotypes that some UN staff may have had before meeting locals. As A7 stated, '...they [sexual relationships] can increase UN integrity because the UN staff have a chance to learn about local people...'

[11] Secretary-General's Final Report on UNEF I, UN Doc. A/6627, 12 July 1967 in Katarina Mansson, 'The Forgotten Agenda: Human Rights Protection and Promotion in Cold War Peacekeeping' (2005) 10 (3) *Journal of Conflict and Security Law* 379, 382.

When asked about negative effects on UN credibility and integrity, the majority of local interviewees and several peacekeepers were more concerned about the negative effects of the immunities that UN staff enjoy, than about sexual relationships. According to these interviewees, the lack of accountability of UN staff for crimes committed while on mission is a much more serious threat to perceptions of the integrity and credibility of the UN.

This chapter has focused on the views of local women and peacekeepers on sexual relationships between local women and peacekeepers, elucidating points of difference and agreement. The SGB approach to sexual relationships stereotypes local populations as vulnerable and in need of protection, and effectively prohibits such relationships even though they may be consensual, genuine and legitimate. The fieldwork findings highlight the complexities and realities that make it difficult to create a policy for managing sexual relationships, as the SGB proposes. It is a serious concern that the SGB and its 'strong discouragement' provision, when interpreted in the field, often leads to a total ban on sexual relationships. The peacekeepers Jennings interviewed thought that it is difficult to deal with the 'strong discouragement' provision, so sexual relationships should be either banned or allowed.[12]

As the majority of local interviewees and some peacekeepers expressed, an absolute ban on sexual relationships may do injustice to genuine relationships and impinge on the human rights of the people involved, such as the right to privacy, sexuality rights and the right to equality. As I discussed in Chap. 3, the International Covenant on Civil and Political Rights (ICCPR) states that 'no one shall be subjected to arbitrary or unlawful interference with his privacy...'[13] and that 'everyone has the right to the protection of the law against such interference...'[14] Also, the right to equality before the law is denied, since local women and peacekeepers do not enjoy equal rights before the law in the way that other people who decide to engage in sexual relationships do. Article 26 of the ICCPR states, 'all persons are equal before the law...and the law shall prohibit any discrimination...on any grounds such as race, colour, sex...national or social origin...or other status'. However, local women and peacekeepers are 'strongly discouraged' from sexual relationships since peacekeepers derive their status from their professional roles with the UN.

By taking this approach, the SGB ignores the voices of those who it 'protects' and who are directly affected by its provisions, namely, local women engaged in sexual relationships. It relies on radical feminist perspectives which denies local women the right to be seen not only as possible victims of sexual exploitation, but also as agents who have power to consent to sex and freely chose their sexual

[12] Kathleen M Jennings, 'Protecting Whom?: Approaches to Sexual Exploitation and Abuse in UN Peacekeeping Operations' (Fafo, 2008) 23.

[13] *International Covenant on Civil and Political Rights*, opened for signature 16 December 1966, 993 UNTS 171 (entered into force 23 March 1976) article 17 (1).

[14] Ibid article 17 (2).

partner. The SGB perpetuates a conservative gender perspective that is out of step with broader human rights and is not flexible enough to respect the opinions of local women and allow for contextual legal, cultural and socio-economic considerations. This chapter shows that the SGB provision on strong discouragement of sexual relationships is over-protective, restrictive and patronising. In the next chapter I reflect upon the ways in which the interviewees understand sexual exploitation in the context of PKOs and, in particular, their responses to the SGB's ban on prostitution.

Chapter 6
Sexual Exploitation and Prostitution in UN Peacekeeping Operations

6.1 Introduction

Chapter 5 analysed responses from Groups A, B and C to the 'strong discouragement' of sexual relationships in the context of peacekeeping operations (PKOs) contained in the Secretary-Generals' Bulletin (SGB). This chapter explores their understanding of sexual exploitation and prostitution in PKOs, and their responses to the approach taken by the SGB. As I discussed in Chap. 3, the SGB includes prostitution as a form of sexual exploitation, stating that any 'exchange of money, employment, goods or services for sex, including sexual favours or other forms of humiliating, degrading or exploitative behaviour, is prohibited. This includes any exchange of assistance that is due to beneficiaries of assistance'.[1]

Although the SGB does not specifically use the term prostitution, as I previously discussed in Chap. 3, in its explanation of the foregoing provision the Department for Peacekeeping Operations (DPKO) leaves no doubt that prostitution is included.[2] Whether prostitution is a form of sexual exploitation has always been debated and even feminists are deeply divided on this question. Despite this, the SGB takes the firm view that prostitution is sexual exploitation and therefore it is prohibited in PKOs. By including prostitution in its definition of sexual exploitation, the SGB takes an objective point of view. There is no consideration of consent or other subjective components of the sexual conduct by either of the participants.

This chapter brings the voices of the people directly affected by the SGB into the discussion about whether prostitution should be understood as sexual exploitation, or as a form of employment (sex work). Although I asked the interviewees separate questions about sexual exploitation and prostitution, both became intertwined in

[1] Secretary-Generals' Bulletin, *Special Measures for Protection From Sexual Exploitation and Abuse*, ST/SGB/2003/13 (9 October 2003).

[2] DPKO, 'Standard Operating Procedure: Public Information Activities on Sexual Exploitation and Abuse' (3 April 2006).

O. Simic, *Regulation of Sexual Conduct in UN Peacekeeping Operations*,
DOI 10.1007/978-3-642-28484-7_6, © Springer-Verlag Berlin Heidelberg 2012

their answers. As a result, I have drawn all the comments related to prostitution together and analysed them as a theme that emerged in the context of discussing sexual exploitation. The personal struggles of interviewees to separate sexual exploitation and prostitution reflect the struggles of feminists to draw a clear line between exploitative and non-exploitative sexual conduct, although, as I argue, the interviewees did in fact identify some clear lines of distinction.

From the responses to the questions related to sexual exploitation and prostitution, three themes emerged in all the Groups, which I have used to organise my discussion: defining sexual exploitation, views about whether prostitution is sexual exploitation, and perspectives on the SGB's definition of sexual exploitation, which includes any exchange of money for sex, regardless of consent and the adequacy of the remuneration.

6.2 Group A

When interviewing women from Bosnia and Herzegovina (BH) who had sexual relationships with peacekeepers, the core questions related to sexual exploitation were: How do you understand sexual exploitation and the difference between 'exploitative' and 'non-exploitative' conduct in the context of PKOs? What sort of sexual conduct should be prohibited by the SGB?

The women in Group A needed more time to think over the questions about sexual exploitation before responding to them, compared to when I asked about their sexual relationships. I noticed that many had difficulties answering or understanding what I was asking them. They often asked me to make the question clearer or explain it in other ways, so I then asked additional questions, such as whether they thought prostitution was sexual exploitation. Even then, the interviewees had less to say about these questions than when they were asked to talk about themselves and their relationships. It seemed to me that the interviewees were all struggling to understand and explain what they thought amounted to sexual exploitation and why. The majority gave short answers and often did not answer questions directly, but used examples as a way of expressing their views. It may be that interviewees were less comfortable talking about experiences that were not their own.

6.2.1 Defining Sexual Exploitation

When responding to the question about how they understood sexual exploitation in the context of PKOs and how they would distinguish between sexually exploitative and non-exploitative conduct, the women from Group A made reference to a broad range of sexual activities. Leaving the question of prostitution aside for the moment, they referred to trafficking in women, sex with young girls, sex for survival, sexual activity without a woman's consent, and verbal and psychological sexual harassment as forms of sexual exploitation. As sexual harassment in the UN is dealt with under another policy[3] and another related administrative instruction,[4] I will leave it aside for present purposes.

> A2: BH became a destination for trafficking in women in that period. I remember there were raids on brothels around the country and the police were trying to differentiate between victims of human trafficking and prostitutes. I later found out that one of the IFOR police officers who was interrupting me while I was interpreting women's statements was directly involved in trafficking women.

> A4: Trafficking in humans is sexual exploitation. I also heard about young girls, 12–13 years old, having sex with UNPROFOR [United Nations Protection Force in the Former Yugoslavia] members.

> A8: Sexual exploitation can happen anywhere, in the workplace...It can be verbal, it doesn't only have to be rape. There are different types, physical and also mental exploitation.

Four interviewees talked about the distinction between exploitative and non-exploitative relationships in terms of consent and abuse of power.

> A6: If you make love with someone and don't expect anything that is not SE.

> A7: Exploitation of a woman's body without her consent [is sexual exploitation].

> A9: There are people who use their power for various things and sexual exploitation is one way of abusing a power you have... if you pay for sex with a kilo of flour or sugar, it is sexual exploitation. So, I don't blame a woman or man who decides to do it, but I blame those ones who don't properly pay them for the service.

> A11: Consent. If both parties are willing, there is no sexual exploitation, but if there is some sort of threat to a woman that she has to earn money for something and the other party pays for that, then that is sexual exploitation.

The majority of my interviewees made reference to a broad range of sexual activities when asked to define sexual exploitation. They spoke of trafficking, of verbal and psychological harassment, of sex for survival, of abuse of power and of sex without consent. Therefore, the Group was in general agreement with the SGB's broad definition of sexual exploitation, although they were also concerned with subjective factors, like the presence or absence of consent.

6.2.2 *Whether Prostitution Is Sexual Exploitation*

Of the 11 interviewees in Group A, four thought that prostitution was a form of sexual exploitation. Two thought that prostitution is sexually exploitative, but also that if it is fairly paid and already exists in a society, then it should be legalised. Four women were of the view that prostitution was not sexual exploitation,

---

[3] Secretary-General's Bulletin, *Promotion of Equal Treatment of Men and Women in the Secretariat and Prevention of Sexual Harassment*, ST/SGB/253 (29 October 1992).

[4] UN Secretariat, *Administrative Instruction on Procedures for Dealing with Sexual Harassment*, ST/AI/379 (29 October 1992).

although three of those thought that in some circumstances it may be. One interviewee did not have any position on prostitution.

Four interviewees thought that prostitution was sexual exploitation and explained this as prostitutes not having a 'real choice' about engaging in sex.

> A1: Prostitution is sexual exploitation. In prostitution, sex is a currency. Sexual exploitation is a product of many things. . .it is rarely the decision of the woman, as in, 'I will be a prostitute because I don't want to work'. The choice is conditional, imposed on them by the environment in which they live, so they don't have a choice.

> A6: I think that prostitution is sexual exploitation. I think that regardless of whether prostitutes want to do that job and do it for money, I think they are victims because these are women who are forced to do that.

> A7: Prostitution is absolutely sexual exploitation. They are forced to do that.

> A11: I don't think that voluntary prostitution exists. There is always some problem behind the decision a woman takes to become a prostitute. She always needs money and she definitely doesn't do it because she likes it. There are no women who like to work in the sex industry, it is definitely not their choice.

Two interviewees were unable to decide.

> A8: I would not distinguish between sexual exploitation and prostitution. For me prostitution is sexual exploitation, but I know that some women think it is not. I think it should not be legalised, but there are contrary arguments and I agree with them to some extent. If you already have prostitution and allow it to develop, then you should regulate it and ensure women's protection and health education.

> A5: Prostitution is sexual exploitation, but on the other hand the woman gets paid, so I don't know. I never thought about it.

Another four of my interviewees thought that whether prostitution was sexually exploitative or not depended on certain conditions being fulfilled, including consent, real choice and adequate pay.

> A4: Prostitution is not sexual exploitation. It is when one person consciously agrees to provide sexual services for money. There were a lot of stories about UN staff visiting brothels.

> A3: I don't have a clear opinion about prostitution. It depends on whether it is a real choice, or if a person is forced into prostitution by a third person. So it can be sexual exploitation, but it doesn't have to be. Prostitution has always been a part of human life. You can look at prostitution in various ways, depending on the context and circumstances.

> A2: During the post-war period in our context and our region, but also in neighbouring countries which were going through a period of transition, women did not have real opportunities to find jobs, to feed their families. I understand that they could think of prostitution as a way to earn an income. In other countries prostitution can be regulated and legalised. It can be thought of as a free choice by women because they are protected by the state and it is their right to choose it as a job. One example is Amsterdam. I don't think these women are forced to do prostitution. They are not in countries where their choices are few, so it is not the only thing they can do, as is the case here and in other countries which are in transition.

> A9: Unfortunately, many women work in prostitution in the peacekeeping context because they have no other ways of feeding their families. I don't consider this as a choice. Those who use their services, unless they pay properly, they exploit them. If they pay fairly, I don't have anything against it.

The various views expressed by the women from Group A reflect the complexity of this topic. Only four interviewees thought prostitution is sexual exploitation because they thought only women who had no other choices would engage in it. Others thought if a woman is adequately paid and she is making a choice to work in the sex industry, then prostitution is not sexual exploitation. They also recognised the complexity of the notion of 'free choice' by clearly taking a nuanced approach to the idea of consent. While the SGB firmly places prostitution as sexually exploitative activity, my interviewees were not so firm in their approach to prostitution.

6.2.3 Perspectives on the SGB's Approach to Sexual Exploitation and Prostitution

When responding to my question about what sort of sexual conduct should be prohibited, all the interviewees generally agreed that sexual exploitation should be prohibited. They were in agreement that sexual exploitation is trafficking in women, sex for survival, sex with young girls and sex without consent. Two interviewees also expressed concern about implementation of the policy.

> A3: After all these years working with NATO [North Atlantic Treaty Organization], the first time I saw a sexual harassment policy was only one year ago. That was the first time that we, as civilians, could say if we felt harassed by filling out a form which was available through our staff intranet. . .after all those years, and they said that our anonymity was guaranteed, etc. I think that no one reported anyone because they were afraid to lose their jobs. I think there should be some documents which you can use if something happens to you. I think something must exist.

> A4: I think some sex should be regulated. I knew an Australian who was working here in Bosnia, he was found with some teenage girls in brothels in Liberia, I think. The UN has good rules, but doesn't have any mechanism to process those who breach the rules. There are so many cultures in the UN and what is good for one may not be good for another.

These two interviewees suggested that regardless of what rules are adopted, it would be difficult to implement them. Also, A4 pointed out that it is hard to have a rule that applies to everyone because of the diversity of cultural perspectives in the UN.

6.2.4 Conclusions

When identifying forms of sexual exploitation, the women from Group A made reference to a broad range of sexual activities, such as sex with minors, trafficking in women, sex for food and sex without consent. Although they broadly defined sexual exploitation, in contrast to the SGB some women felt that subjective consideration of consent is a method of distinguishing non-exploitative sex from sexual exploitation.

When asked whether prostitution was sexual exploitation, the women from Group A expressed two different views. Four thought it was a form of sexual exploitation, taking the radical feminist view, while the other seven thought that prostitution was not sexual exploitation, provided that women were able to make real choices and received adequate pay. Therefore, they distinguished between sexual exploitation and prostitution in terms of choice, consent and remuneration. While the SGB deems prostitution to be sexually exploitative, the interviewees from Group A demonstrated that there is no general agreement on this point. Although some of them thought along the same lines as the SGB, the majority thought that prostitution is not sexually exploitative if it is freely chosen as a means of livelihood and adequately paid.

When discussing the SGB's approach to sexual exploitation and prostitution, all the interviewees agreed that sexual exploitation should be prohibited, while two were concerned about the difficulties of actually implementing these prohibitions. They thought that the culture of impunity and the lack of peacekeepers' accountability for crimes they commit may be a serious impediment to prosecuting and penalising such crimes.

6.3 Group B

When interviewing local women who were working with the United Nations Mission in Bosnia and Herzegovina (UNMIBH), I asked them: What forms can sexual exploitation take? Since many interviewees struggled to reply to this question, like Group A, I asked them additional questions, such as: What do you think about prostitution? What sort of sexual conduct should be prohibited by the SGB? Like the interviewees in Group A, the responses to these questions were shorter than the answers to questions about sexual relationships, and more time was taken to think before replying to them.

6.3.1 Defining Sexual Exploitation

The interviewees made references to three forms of sexual conduct as sexually exploitative. These were: trafficking for forced prostitution, sexual harassment, and sex with young girls. All interviewees expressed opinions about prostitution as well and I analyse their views as a separate theme.

> B2: Some women are forced into prostitution, like trafficking victims. . .it [sexual exploitation] is about financial exchanges or any other exchanges for sex. . .it can also be in the work place if your boss blackmails you, such as, 'you have to have sex with me otherwise you will lose your job'. . .

> B11: Trafficking in women. . .I suppose there are women who don't do that for survival, but for a better life. . .There were also some young girls, even children, who prostituted themselves for food and for money with UN staff and that is certainly sexual exploitation. . .

B12: I heard that SFOR [Stabilisation Force in Bosnia and Herzegovina] used sexual services from high school girls around bases...very cheap services...also, if someone blackmails you to have a relationship to keep your job, if there is force, then that is sexual exploitation...

Therefore, as with Group A, a wide range of sexual conduct was viewed as sexual exploitation. Also, like some interviewees in Group A, B11 had a subjective perspective, suggesting that it may be important to take into account women's choices, especially when it comes to sexual conduct that objectively looks like sexual exploitation.

6.3.2 Whether Prostitution Is Sexual Exploitation

Five out of the thirteen women thought that prostitution was sexual exploitation, regardless of choice or circumstances, while the rest (eight) of the interviewees said that under certain circumstances prostitution is not sexual exploitation.

The five interviewees who thought prostitution was sexually exploitative believed that a woman could not make a real 'choice' about it or that prostitution was by definition, humiliating.

B1: Yes, it is.

B2: Prostitution is definitely exploitation. The majority of women who work in prostitution and the sex industry don't do it because they want to, but because they can't work anywhere else.

B6: Yes, it is. Every form of sexual conduct that involves some force is exploitation.

B9: It is sexual exploitation, something horrific. For me there should never be a reason for a woman or man to find themselves in a situation where they need to earn money in that way. I don't understand how someone can allow herself/himself that sort of humiliation.

B12: I think it is...I can't see prostitution as a conscious decision of women to work in the sex industry...the majority of prostitutes did not decide to work as prostitutes, but were forced by difficult life circumstances...I think it is serious exploitation...

The rest of the interviewees thought that whether prostitution was sexual exploitation depended on whether the woman involved was in a position to make a real choice about such work. One thought that prostitution was not sexual exploitation because she viewed it as freely chosen work:

B10: I think it is not. It is the decision of a woman who does this job.

B3: I can't agree with prostitution as a way of life. I can understand that someone might work in prostitution in some contexts, such as in Holland where prostitution can be a profession. However, usually women choose this profession because they don't have any other choices and any other 'goods' to sell except their bodies, and that would be exploitation...

B4: Yes, in some circumstances...there are lots of women who do not want to do it... I think there must be something really bad in someone's life to make them work as a prostitute...

> B5: It depends. . .if prostitution is a choice then it is not. . .hmmm, still there is the question, if she could choose. . .

> B8: If a woman is doing that for money, I don't see why that would be exploitative. If she chooses to do that as her job and to take money for it, I don't see exploitation in that case. . .If she earns money, it means it is good for her and it's her decision.

> B11: It is a very complex question. . .it depends why a woman decides to work in prostitution. If she has chosen to, then it is not. . .but, there are women who don't have to be physically forced into it, but can be by life circumstances and in that case it is sexual exploitation. . .

> B13: There were women who voluntarily worked in prostitution in Bosnia . . .we all knew that in the period when the military came into the country [SFOR] young local women sexually serviced them. . .prostitution is sexual exploitation, I think. . .a woman must have a good reason to do it. . .very few women do that because they really want to, I mean voluntarily. . .

While five of the women thought that prostitution was itself sexual exploitation, the majority of the interviewees (eight) took a subjective standpoint that prostitution is not necessarily sexual exploitation if women are able to choose to enter the sex industry.

6.3.3 Perspectives on the SGB's Approach to Sexual Exploitation and Prostitution

When asked whether sexual exploitation in PKOs should be prohibited, all of my interviewees thought that it should be. Five supported the SGB's inclusion of prostitution in its definition of SE, while seven thought prostitution should not be banned if it is legal in the country of mission. One interviewee did not think prostitution should be banned in PKOs.

> B4: Some things should be regulated in some difficult contexts, such as exploitation of children and non-consensual relationships, etc. I think this general instruction [SGB] to UN staff does not make sense. I don't think that UN staff should be prohibited from using the services of prostitutes either. I don't see what would be the basis for not using these services. . .I think it is an infringement of human rights as well. . .

> B5: If prostitution is legal in the country of mission then peacekeepers should be able to use the services of prostitutes. If it is not, then they are banned, the same as the rest of the population.

> B8: They should respect the laws of the country they are in. If prostitution is legal in the country then I don't see why they should be banned from using it. I don't see anything wrong with using sex services if they use protection and all of that. . .

> B12: If prostitution is legal in the country where the peacekeepers are, I don't see the basis for banning peacekeepers from using these services. If a country legalises prostitution, then it should be legal for its citizens, foreigners, tourists etc., to use those services.

> B13: I think that prostitution should be banned if it is illegal. If it is legal in the country of mission, I think that peacekeepers should be able to use the services of prostitutes just like citizens of that country.

There was a strong view that the UN should respect local laws and if prostitution is legal in a country of mission, then the UN should respect it, rather than create its own rules that go against or supersede local laws.

6.3.4 Conclusions

As with Group A, the interviewees from Group B considered a range of sexual activities sexually exploitative, such as trafficking in women for forced prostitution, sex with young girls, abuse of power and sex for food. Their understanding of sexual exploitation is hardly surprising, because there is no general disagreement about these activities being sexually exploitative.

However, when it comes to prostitution, the interviewees were also split. Five women thought that prostitution was sexual exploitation, because they believed that women in the sex industry were economically forced into it. However, one woman did not think that prostitution was sexual exploitation at all, while, as with Group A, the majority (seven) thought that whether prostitution is sexual exploitation depends on consent and the ability to make free 'choices'. Thus, while the SGB defines all prostitution as sexually exploitative, the interviewees in Group B, as in Group A, viewed consent and choice as a way to distinguish sexual exploitation from prostitution. Seven interviewees from Group B thought that if prostitution is legal in the country of mission, then there is no legitimate reason why peacekeepers should be banned from using the services of prostitutes. I think that this legalistic approach towards prostitution comes from re-emphasising the local interviewees' sentiment that the UN should respect local laws, rather than create their own rules. At a minimum they point to the need for the UN to differentiate among various local contexts and respect local laws and cultures.

6.4 Group C

When interviewing peacekeepers, the main questions were: How do you understand sexual exploitation in the context of PKOs? How would you describe prostitution in the context of PKOs? What sort of sexual conduct should be prohibited by the SGB? In contrast to the interviewees in Groups A and B, the respondents from Group C had quite a lot to say. However, although they did not struggle with understanding the questions that I asked them, their answers intertwined sexual exploitation and prostitution, and were sometimes contradictory. As with Groups A and B, I separately analysed their replies that related to prostitution, since they discussed prostitution in response to all three questions that I asked them.

6.4.1 Defining Sexual Exploitation

Like Groups A and B, interviewees from Group C made reference to a broad range of forms that sexual exploitation can take, such as abuse of power, sex for survival and trafficking in women. Two raised 'peacekeeper babies' in this context, but this is not covered by the SGB and is beyond the scope of my book.[5]

Eight interviewees thought that peacekeepers were in a position of power over local people, which meant that sexual exploitation of local women was likely to occur.

> C5: I understand it [sexual exploitation] as where the UN is unquestionably in the position of economic and social power over people who are supposed to be recipients of the mission's benefits.

> C10: Sexual exploitation depends upon an imbalance in power. It would be the same for me as between an academic and a student, or between a superior military officer and a subordinate officer or soldier. There is an inequality because of the position held, in this context most often by men, so they hold a superior position in the sense that they are the boss of a woman and, in some peace operations, sexual exploitation may occur between an interpreter, for example, and the person for whom she/he is interpreting.

> C11: When a member of a UN mission uses their position of advantage, it is sexual exploitation. As a representative of the UN you are there to assist the country, not to cause more harm and so when they [peacekeepers] engage in sexual activities with the local population they are causing more harm than good. If you expect a sexual relationship with an individual because they work for you, or you are providing them with opportunities they would not have otherwise, then it is abusing your position and, therefore, exploitation.

> C18: My understanding would be taking advantage of locals. CivPol [civilian police] and the UN are seen as a greater force and we seem to have great wealth and they don't. When I was in the Solomon Islands, a lot of them [women] were interpreters and they did not understand why we just could not give them money and go. I saw there things I did not feel comfortable with. One of the sergeants used to organise trips for the local girls and take them for a swim. The girls all swam in their clothes, but it should have been a mixed group and it should have been something that we females did. He should not have been part of it. It did not sit comfortably with me: the old man getting his jollies from seeing young women swimming.

> C19: Sexual exploitation would be taking advantage of women who don't necessarily want to be involved, but because they are vulnerable, economically or socially, they are sort of exploited and used in that environment...

These interviewees suggested that it is easy for peacekeepers to abuse the power they have compared to local populations. The interviewees had a clearly objective approach to sexual exploitation when they suggested that because of this imbalance of power, all sex is potentially sexually exploitative. Others referred to survival sex, trafficking in women and sexual abuse.

[5] UN General Assembly, *United Nations Comprehensive Strategy on Assistance and Support to Victims of Sexual Exploitation and Abuse by United Nations Staff and Related Personnel*, A/RES/62/214 (7 March 2008).

> C16: There is sexual exploitation of the local community, kids, women and men. They don't have any other economic means to survive, so sex is the only service they can offer for survival. So, the UN workers can get cheap sex with locals...

> C12: Trafficking in women.

> C8: Forms of sexual offences committed by personnel. Sexual exploitation is sexual harassment, sexual abuse, sexual exploitation, all of it.

When answering my question about how they distinguished between 'exploitative' and 'non-exploitative' sexual conduct, the majority (14) of the interviewees said that it was 'very difficult' to draw this distinction. However, when pushed, they associated sexual exploitation with economic inequality and abuse of power, and non-exploitative sex with consent. Three interviewees thought it was not difficult to differentiate between them, while three did not know the answer to this question.

> C2: Sexual exploitation is economic exploitation, exploitation from the peacekeeper and the woman.

> C19: I always saw sexual exploitation as when someone profits from it financially. In a relationship if you have someone who has power and takes advantage of a person, I suppose that would come under the definition of sexual exploitation as well.

> C6: I guess it is a question of consent by the woman and whether or not there are any financial aspects to the relationship, and the level of education and status of the woman, and her vulnerability. If she is a very vulnerable woman who is not being paid, is uneducated and she is not truly consenting to what is happening, then I would say that is SE. There are different views of what is appropriate and what is not, and it is difficult to convince people from different backgrounds whether or not consent is really relevant because you can not really ever prove consent.

Three interviewees thought it was not difficult to differentiate between exploitative and non-exploitative sexual conduct.

> C1: A consensual sexual relationship is a love affair and loving, mutual sex. Prostitution is when you give money to have sex, and sexual exploitation is taking advantage of local people's weaknesses.

> C7: I don't think it is difficult to differentiate between them. If I have to judge the case maybe, but as a peacekeeper, I don't think so. It is quite obvious what relationship you are engaging in and what your intentions are.

> C16: A consensual sexual relationship is when you have two adults who consent to have sex. Sexual exploitation is when peacekeepers utilise sexual services in developing nations, paying for these services and taking advantage of the situation they are in. Prostitution can be consensual and in Australia it is consensual. It can be consensual in war time as well [prostitution] since you always have options, even though these options may be far more limited in a war zone.

All three interviewees pointed to subjective factors when determining the differences between exploitative and non-exploitative conduct. They saw consent as a key factor when making this distinction. C1 and C16 also thought that sexual exploitation is an abuse of power, while prostitution is an exchange of money for sex that can be consensual.

Another peacekeeper talked about a 'spectrum' of sexual conduct and where he would draw the line.

> C5: I think it is very difficult to differentiate. It is a spectrum where, on one hand, you have prostitution, for example in Timor, and you can say that women were forced into that economically. The next situation is when you don't have an exchange of goods, but you have one partner who is in a more powerful position. Finally, you have the situation where someone who works with the UN is involved in a consensual sexual relationship, even though you recognise there might be power imbalances. So, I think it is difficult to distinguish. For example, if I had a staff member involved in the first situation, I would report that [prostitution]; the second situation I probably would not report and I don't think that consensual relationships are reportable.

Group C, similarly to Groups A and B, named a range of sexual activities as sexually exploitative. However, it seems that power imbalance was the main way of describing sexual exploitation, which is in accordance with the SGB. Although the majority of interviewees initially thought it is difficult to distinguish between sexually exploitative and non-exploitative conduct, they associated sexual exploitation with factors such as economic inequality and abuse of power. Similarly to Groups A and B, the presence of consent was associated with non-sexual exploitation.

6.4.2 *Whether Prostitution Is Sexual Exploitation*

All of the interviewees in Group C were aware that prostitution occurred in their missions and in PKOs in general, and accepted it as a fact of life. While 14 interviewees did not consider prostitution to be sexual exploitation, nine of them believed that some forms of prostitution were sexually exploitative. They distinguished between child and adult prostitution, forced and voluntary prostitution, including survival sex and prostitution 'disguised' as a sexual relationship. The other six interviewees considered prostitution to be sexual exploitation in the context of peacekeeping.

Five interviewees thought of prostitution as a normal and inevitable social phenomenon that should be accepted rather than prohibited.

> C1: The policy on prostitution was very strict. Four peacekeepers at that time were repatriated for having sex with prostitutes. They did not go to brothels in the mission country, but went abroad [to the neighbouring country Uganda] and paid a middle man to bring them prostitutes. I did not see them as victims of sexual exploitation.

> C8: Military life can be very stressful. Soldiers are not deployed with their families, wives or partners. They are deployed for a year or more, and to say that they should not engage in sex with prostitutes or any local women is unrealistic. If someone chooses to engage in prostitution as a matter of choice, I don't see how that is sexual exploitation.

> C14: Prostitution in any of these places can be endemic and pervasive. One particular evening there was a music festival, very popular in Haiti, and before this evening was over there was sex trade with Haitian prostitutes servicing Pakistani police officers. It is not something that you would not find in any major northern American or European city. It is sexual trade, sex for money and it is economy-driven. The only difference is that if society functions well, you won't have it to the extent you have it in those places...

> C16: There were several brothels and prostitution in East Timor. In bars girls would talk to guys and go home with them. The guys may have given them some money for the evening they spent together. That was not organised prostitution. I would call it consensual sex. These girls actively sought partners and tried to make money. They would not have sex with just any guy, but with those they could get good money from…

> C4: The problems that I see are not in adult prostitution, but in child prostitution. I think it is possible to legalise the sex trade in these countries. Is prostitution greater exploitation than labour for slave wages? Is it in any way a more heinous social injustice than labour exploitation of any kind? It is no more exploitative than cheap labour.

It is notable that these interviewees did not see local women as victims or in need of protection, but as active agents who make a choice to work in the sex industry.

The rest of the interviewees distinguished between acceptable and unacceptable forms of prostitution, such as child and adult, and forced and voluntary prostitution, seeing the latter as prevalent in PKOs.

> C4: It is very, very prevalent [prostitution], particularly in the missions where I have had an opportunity to serve [Haiti, Liberia]. In local populations, involvement of boys and girls is particularly problematic. Under-age prostitution or child prostitution is problematic and seemingly much more prevalent than adult prostitution where they are voluntarily participating in the act.

> C2: There are voluntary and involuntary prostitution with local women and women abroad. I don't say that women are prostitutes because they want to be. They can be co-opted, coerced into sexual slavery. However, peacekeepers, clients, do not know the difference between them. It is well known that everywhere peacekeepers go, prostitution follows. In East Timor there were brothels with mainly non-Timorese women. Some of them could have been trafficked for sex.

> C11: I can say from my personal experience that prostitution is very prevalent. You drive to a restaurant in the evening and there are women and men who approach you to offer sexual favours. There are times when you find yourself in an uncomfortable position because people attempt to enter into an arrangement with you and this is an unfortunate reality. It was mainly street prostitution and both women and men were involved. My opinion is they were there because that was the only opportunity they had to make money. Whether they were forced into that through physical abuse, or threatened or forced because of their economic situation I haven't investigated, but based on what we have seen it was not what most people involved necessarily wanted to do…they were there because they felt they had no choice.

> C20: I heard about very short-term prostitution relationships, sort of disguised ones. For example, relationships where a woman or woman's family benefit from the relationship. In these relationships there was a fairly unequal power dynamic and the man had no long-term intentions. It was more of a convenient arrangement…East Timor is a very conservative Catholic society so these things are quite disguised. There were a few night clubs where you had the impression that this type of activity occurs, but it wasn't overt.

While these interviewees did not seem to have a problem with voluntary adult prostitution, they were concerned that most prostitution in PKOs was not voluntary and was likely to involve children.

Another six interviewees also thought that prostitution was not necessarily sexual exploitation, but that in the peacekeeping context it was likely to be exploitative because of power imbalances between peacekeepers and local people.

> C5: In the context of PKOs, prostitution is sexual exploitation. However, I don't think prostitution should be forbidden. I recognise it as a necessary economic evil.

C7: The countries where I served were extremely conservative countries [Sudan and Afghanistan], so the prostitution was not as open as it probably is in other countries, in other peacekeeping missions. Prostitution is sex in exchange for any material reward, it is a transaction and, in general, it was definitely sexual exploitation in countries where I worked.

C10: I would describe prostitution in the criminal context as an exchange of services between two partners, where the male offers some sort of benefit to the woman, and that can range from food to some financial benefit.

C14: Prostitution is sexual exploitation. It is clearly inappropriate that a UN peacekeeper would take a woman into his home under the guise of a domestic helper and then have 'consensual sex' with that woman for an extended period of time, effectively trading sexual favours for food and shelter.

C17: There is no difference between prostitution and sexual exploitation in the context of PKOs. If it is between two adults and there is no relative difference in authority and level of power, there is no big problem, but a lot of these [local] people have just come out of fifteen years of war and a lot of them are not educated. The women often can be very much taken advantage of, especially the younger women. There is a huge power imbalance most of the time and obviously there is a huge wealth imbalance as well.

C12: In the context of peacekeeping, I think it is primarily exploitative. I don't think that prostitution in every country, context or situation is. There certainly are women, probably a minority, who fully consent and choose prostitution, and even find it empowering.

One interviewee struggled with the contradictions between her personal belief of what constitutes prostitution and the position of the SGB. She also raised the complexities of various understandings of sexual exploitation by local women in Haiti.

C13: In my role, I am required to take action to inform UN personnel about means of prevention of breaching UN standards. In a professional capacity I regard any exchange of money, or services or goods, as prostitution and it is prohibited. However, from a personal perspective I would say that every relationship involves an exchange of sex and money, goods and services. There is an exchange for sure, but whether that is prostitution, I don't know. I worked in a mission in Haiti and I spoke with a number of women there and asked them 'what does exploitation mean to you? What does it mean to be sexually exploited?'. It is a very cultural thing there for women to be involved in something they call 'hassle' which means that they actively pursue sexual relationships with wealthy men, what we call 'sugar daddies', and there is no social stigma attached to that at all. It is well known and they are getting social and financial compensation for that. I would personally describe prostitution as when someone sells their body in exchange for money or goods, or any benefit without any intention of pursuing a relationship. So, it is an exchange that occurs without any relationship and commitment attached to that.

While the SGB would define 'hassle' as sexual exploitation, Haitian women engaged in the practice would not describe themselves as being sexually exploited. This example shows that the SGB's broad definition of sexual exploitation is out of step with local understandings of sexual exploitation, at least in Haiti. Further, contrary to the SGB, it shows that local women are not all vulnerable and at great risk of sexual exploitation.

The peacekeepers gave nuanced answers to the question of whether prostitution is sexual exploitation. They largely accepted prostitution in the context of PKOs as a fact of life in all missions. The majority thought that voluntary adult prostitution was not sexual exploitation, which clearly contradicts the SGB's approach. While six interviewees thought of prostitution as sexual exploitation, the rest distinguished between acceptable and unacceptable forms of prostitution. Thus, although the SGB treats all forms of prostitution as 'degrading or exploitative behaviour' that should be prohibited, the interviewees distinguished between child and adult, forced and voluntary, sex for survival, and prostitution 'disguised' as a sexual relationship.

6.4.3 Perspectives on the SGB's Approach to Sexual Exploitation and Prostitution

All the interviewees thought that sexual exploitation should be prohibited, and they supported the SGB in that sense. However, when they discussed prostitution, a majority of the interviewees (15) supported the SGB's approach to it, while five gave more nuanced answers with respect to the SGB definition and discretion in interpreting the SGB.

> C15: If one engages in sex with the local population, it is exploitation because you are in a better financial position than the local population. You are exploiting that opportunity and trust. It is a clear violation of the general UN rules.

> C12: I totally support it [the SGB]. I think that is the way of avoiding difficult situations that involve exploitation of local populations. They are not there to have a good time. They are there to perform a specific function, which is to fulfil a mandate.

Five interviewees had concerns about some aspects of the SGB, in particular prostitution, the scope of sexual exploitation definition and discretion in applying the SGB.

> C5: I know that the UN has a zero tolerance policy and I think that is appropriate. With respect to prostitution, I think is much better if you have laws about accessing prostitution, or living on earnings from prostitution. I don't think prostitution will go away and I recognise that for lots of women it is an economic option.

Two interviewees expressed concerns about the definition of sexual exploitation and its scope.

> C11: It comes down to the role of the UN and the personnel there, what perceptions are, and what the potential implications of UN personnel entering into relationships with the local population are. Is it something that contributing countries should repatriate their personnel for, or something that should be strongly discouraged? What does 'discourage' mean?

> C12: There is usually, not always, a major power imbalance between peacekeepers and a local person. I saw eight or nine cases where women ended up being abandoned by peacekeepers and...they suffer a stigma and have no prospects to remarry, so life can be very difficult for them in the future. But I also know people who married local people and live as normal families...These are consensual relationships...However, consent is always a complex concept, even within one culture, and we are dealing with transcultural issues and major power differentials between the parties involved...you can't make any generalisations and you have to look at each individual case...

Another two interviewees raised the issue of discretion in interpreting the SGB.

> C13: It comes down to using discretion in interpreting the SGB. I know, for example, that there are people selling sex on the street close to the mission offices...If a complaint comes to us, we will follow it up...However, this is not something that we would usually investigate because I know these women. They are making a choice to engage in sex. They are relatively affluent, confident, outgoing women.

> C15: It is rather difficult to police this because it comes down to education and clear understanding of the difference between genuine sexual relationships and sexual exploitation...It is one of those things that can be judged both fairly and unfairly.

In sum, while the majority of interviewees supported the SGB approach to prostitution, some recognised prostitution as an inevitable part of missions that gives women the opportunity to earn income. This is not recognised by the SGB.

6.4.4 Conclusions

With respect to forms of sexual exploitation that should be prohibited, the interviewees from Group C, like the interviewees from Groups A and B, referred to a range of sexual activities such as sex for food, trafficking in women and sex with minors. Also, similarly to the interviewees from Groups A and B, the majority in Group C thought that voluntary adult prostitution is not sexual exploitation. Five interviewees also viewed prostitution as inevitable in peacekeeping contexts, as a fact of life which is clearly not recognised by the SGB.

The majority of interviewees in Group C initially thought it was difficult to distinguish between exploitative and non-exploitative sexual conduct. When pushed to do so they identified consent, economic equality and free choice as important indicators of non-exploitative sexual conduct, which was similar to Groups A and B.

6.5 Conclusions

This chapter discussed and analysed the views of the interviewees regarding sexual exploitation and prostitution. There was considerably more agreement between the three Groups concerning these subjects than there was in relation to sexual relationships, as presented in Chap. 5.

Interviewees from all three groups argued that sexual exploitation should be banned, specifically sex for food, sex with young girls, trafficking in women and forced prostitution. A majority of the interviewees identified certain positive indicators that facilitate differentiation between exploitative and non-exploitative sexual conduct, such as subjective consideration of consent and ‘choice’, and also negative indicators, such as abuse of power or economic inequality. This latter view echoes the SGB approach, as two indicators of sexual exploitation are 'abuse of power' and 'abuse of a position of vulnerability'. The majority of Group C interviewees even used the same language as the SGB when defining sexual exploitation, probably because they are more familiar with the SGB than Groups A and B. It was notable that the majority of the interviewees (14) from Group C initially expressed concern about the difficulty of drawing a line between exploitative and non-exploitative sexual conduct, although when pressed they did not have a problem in making this distinction. The presumed 'difficulty' in drawing a line may be a key reason why the SGB treats all sexual conduct, including prostitution, as sexually exploitative and ignores subjective considerations of consent and 'choice' as a means of differentiation.

Overall, there were two competing views expressed about whether prostitution should be considered sexual exploitation. While the SGB's approach is to impose a blanket ban, the interviewees demonstrated that this is a controversial approach. One view was supportive of the SGB approach, which conceives of prostitution as a sexually exploitative practice that should be banned. This view reflects the radical feminist position which frames prostitution as an entirely negative activity that is always a source of harm and exploitation.[6] Several rationales supporting this position were voiced, such as a lack of other options to earn income and the existence of unequal power dynamics between peacekeepers and local women. Some interviewees thought that prostitution in some contexts (where poverty is extreme) should be prohibited because the need for protection from exploitation is higher. As C5 stated, '...you have prostitution, for example, in Timor...[where] women were forced into that economically'. It is notable that although peacekeepers recognised a lack of economic options as one of the reasons why women opt to work in prostitution, they were, paradoxically, in favour of the SGB which would effectively leave these women without means of survival.

The fact that women may choose prostitution as a strategy for economic survival is not recognised by the SGB. By simply imposing a ban, the SGB ignores the deeper socio-economic problems that often result in significant growth in the sex industry of a post-conflict society. As I illustrated in Chap. 4, BH became a centre of the sex industry after the arrival of peacekeepers. Since prostitution was illegal, women were forced to work underground and many of them were trafficked for the purpose of forced prostitution. As expressed by one interviewee from Group C, prohibition tends to move prostitution underground or encourage cross-border trafficking of women for the purpose of prostitution. As C1 stated, 'They [peacekeepers] did not go to brothels in the mission country, but abroad and paid a middle man to bring them prostitutes'. In denial of these facts, the SGB reflects

---

[6] Catharine A MacKinnon, 'Prostitution and Civil Rights' (1993) 1 *Michigan Journal of Gender and Law* 13; Laurie Shrage, 'Should Feminists Oppose Prostitution?' (1989) 99 (2) *Ethics* 347; Sheila Jeffreys, 'The Legalization of Prostitution: A Failed Social Experiment', a speech delivered at the Swedish mission side event at the Commission on the Status of Women (United Nations, New York, 5 March 2003).

the radical feminist approach to prostitution, which asserts that there is no difference between voluntary and forced prostitution and thus deems irrelevant any discussion of the conditions under which prostitution might be performed, including the fact that it can be consensual.

The second view, voiced by the majority of interviewees from all three groups, is that sex with minors, survival sex and trafficking in women for forced prostitution should be considered sexual exploitation, while voluntary adult prostitution with fair remuneration should not. This reflects a 'sex positive' position on prostitution which assumes that although a woman's economic class and socio-economic position may limit her options, she can still exercise the choice to enter the sex industry. This 'sex positive' position also advocates that legitimacy as workers should be accorded to prostitutes. As Nussbaum argues, while prostitution is usually a low-paid job, prostitutes have a degree of choice about which clients they accept and what activities they perform, so they 'should be allowed to pursue their trade'.[7] Kempadoo and Doezema also believes that sex workers should be treated in the same way as 'any other…migrant workers who need improved conditions, safety…and freedom from harassment and abuse'.[8] Doezema suggests that such the notion of 'suffering third world prostitute' has often been invoked to justify Western interventionist program.[9] Likewise, many interviewees argued that prostitution should be regulated and fairly remunerated. Although consent and age do not play a role in the SGB definition of sexual exploitation, to these interviewees, consent and age should be considered crucial factors in distinguishing sexual exploitation from prostitution. As A7 stated, 'Exploitation of a woman's body without her consent [is sexual exploitation]'.

By not acknowledging consent as a major point of reference for differentiating between sexually exploitative and non-exploitative conduct, the SGB embraces the radical feminist view that ignores a woman's sexual agency and responsibility because women's structural inequality is understood to preclude it. Opposing the SGB approach, many of the interviewees found an absolute ban on prostitution problematic in that it denies women's sexual agency and autonomy. A few interviewees in Group C thought that as prostitution is a fact of life in PKOs, it cannot be ignored or treated so simplistically. Thus, the majority of interviewees in each Group were not in favour of a blanket ban on prostitution.

International instruments have been careful to distinguish between forced and consensual prostitution, and between trafficking and prostitution. These distinctions make some forms of prostitution legitimate and acceptable. For example, the Beijing Platform for Action condemns 'forced prostitution', distinguishing between

[7] Martha C. Nussbaum, *Sex and Social Justice* (Oxford University Press, 1999) 281.

[8] Jo Doezema, 'Choice in Prostitution' in Conference Book: Changing Faces of Prostitution, Helsinki 3-5 May, 1995 (Helsinki: Unioni, The League of Finnish Feminists); Alison Murray, 'Debt Bondage and Trafficking: Don't Believe the Hype' in K. Kampadoo and J. Doezema, *Global Sex Worker's Rights: Rights, Resistance and, Redefinition (*Routledge, 1998) 128.

[9] K. Kampadoo and J. Doezema, Ibid 1,11.

free and forced prostitution.[10] Likewise, the Convention on the Elimination of All Forms of Discrimination Against Women (CEDAW) forbids only 'exploitation of prostitution and trafficking in women'.[11] In its concluding observations from 1999, the CEDAW Committee recommended that where prostitution and trafficking are rampant, 'the decriminalisation of prostitution' was a better way to regulate the sex industry, arguing that the illegality of the industry contributed to the problem.[12] Contrary to the aforementioned international instruments, the SGB does not recognise consent as a factor in distinguishing between sexually exploitative and non-exploitative prostitution. It simply bans all forms of prostitution, whether voluntary or forced, between adult local women and peacekeepers.

While the SGB responds to prostitution by imposing a blanket ban, the majority of interviewees in each of the three Groups make a case for introducing a distinction between prostitution and sexual exploitation, arguing that adult voluntary and adequately remunerated prostitution should not be treated as sexual exploitation. Prostitution in PKOs is a pragmatic strategy for some women, a reality that cannot be ignored or dealt with by a blanket ban. A ban on prostitution has ramifications for local women economically, as well as denying their sexual autonomy. Such a ban also risks pushing prostitution underground and encouraging trafficking in women. Neither the reality of these women's lives, nor the socio-economic issues in post-conflict societies that may place constraints on women's choices have been addressed by the SGB.

---

[10] The United Nations Fourth World Conference on Women, Platform for Action (Beijing, China, September 1995), para 39.

[11] *Convention on the Elimination of All Forms of Discrimination against Women* (CEDAW), opened for signature 18 December 1979, UNTS 13 (entered into force 3 September 1981) art 6.

[12] CEDAW Committee, 'Concluding Observations of the Committee on the Elimination of Discrimination Against Women: China', 20th sess (19 January-5 February 1999), para 288-289.

Chapter 7
Rethinking 'Sexual Exploitation' in UN Peacekeeping Operations

7.1 Introduction

In October 2003, the UN Secretary-General promulgated a Bulletin on Special Measures for Protection from Sexual Exploitation and Sexual Abuse (SGB) as a response to allegations about sexual exploitation by peacekeepers. The SGB, also known as the 'zero tolerance policy' (ZTP), bans almost all sexual activity between peacekeepers and local women in order to prevent sexual exploitation and abuse. As a result, the SGB not only prohibits sexual exploitation, but also any 'exchange of money for sex' (prostitution). It 'strongly discourages' sexual relationships between UN staff and 'beneficiaries of assistance', justifying this stance by asserting that such relationships 'are based on inherently unequal power dynamics…[and] undermine the credibility and integrity of the work of the UN'.[1] However, despite the adoption of the SGB, sexual exploitation allegations continue to present problems that need to be dealt with by the UN, particularly the Department for Peacekeeping Operations (DPKO).[2]

This chapter reflects on the main findings of this book, arguing that they demonstrate the need for a revision of the SGB in consultation with the people directly affected by its provisions, namely local women and peacekeepers. This research project has analysed the views of local women and peacekeepers regarding the inclusion of sexual relationships and (adult) prostitution in the definition of sexual exploitation adopted by the SGB. It found that this broad definition of sexual exploitation is not supportable. On the basis of this finding, backed up by 'sex positive' feminist theories, the inclusion of sexual relationships and prostitution in

---

[1] Secretary-General's Bulletin, *Special Measures for Protection from Sexual Exploitation and Abuse*, ST/SGB/2003/13 (9 October 2003)sec 3.2 (c) and (d).

[2] Office of Internal Oversight Services (OIOS), 'Statistics: Allegations for All Categories of Personnel Per Year (Sexual Exploitation and Abuse)', 13 April 2012 <http://cdu.unlb.org/Statistics/AllegationsbyCategoryofPersonnelSexualExploitationandAbuse/AllegationsforAllCategoriesofPersonnelPerYearSexualExploitationandAbuse.aspx>.

O. Simic, *Regulation of Sexual Conduct in UN Peacekeeping Operations*, DOI 10.1007/978-3-642-28484-7_7, © Springer-Verlag Berlin Heidelberg 2012

the definition of sexual exploitation contained within the SGB is problematic because it blurs the distinction between exploitative and non-exploitative sex, which is inconsistent with international human rights norms and participants' every day experiences. In this conclusion, I argue that future UN policies about sexual conduct in peacekeeping operations (PKOs) should be informed by local women's knowledge and peacekeeper's views, and also be grounded in the framework of international human rights law. Finally, I identify six considerations which will, I hope, provide guidance for UN policy makers in the future.

7.2 Distinguishing Between Exploitative and Non-Exploitative Sex in UN Peacekeeping Operations

As I argued at the beginning of the book, when the number of PKOs increased in the 1990s, there was a concomitant increase in everyday contact between local women and peacekeepers, which led to an increase in sexual activity between them. As a result, the number of reports of allegations of sexual exploitation by peacekeepers escalated. However, while many reports alleged that peacekeepers were involved in sexual exploitation, I argued that there was a failure to distinguish between exploitative and non-exploitative sex, which meant that many of the sexual exploitation allegations should have been more closely examined, and possibly dismissed. The later interviews I have done with local women and peacekeepers confirm the contested nature of many of these allegations.

As has been shown, the UN and DPKO responses to sexual exploitation allegations developed in three phases. They ranged from initial, ad hoc responses to increasingly coordinated responses that culminated in the promulgation of the SGB in 2003. The initial responses were developed by individual missions and were largely dismissive of the allegations of sexual exploitation, indicating a lack of political will to investigate them. However, in phase 2, the DPKO started to address the allegations by developing guidelines and training manuals on the topic which recognised and respected the sexual agency of local women and peacekeepers. Rather than stereotyping local women as inherently vulnerable and peacekeepers as predators, in phase two the DPKO assumed that both local women and peacekeepers could distinguish between sexually exploitative and non-exploitative behaviour in PKOs. The adoption of the SGB (phase 3) followed increased pressure from the international community and non-governmental organisations (NGOs) for more decisive action. This pressure became impossible to ignore with the publishing of a report by the United Nations High Commissioner for Refugees (UNHCR) and Save the Children in 2002, which reported that peacekeepers were exchanging aid for sex with children. As a result, the SGB was promulgated in 2003, adopting a zero tolerance approach to almost all sex.

By analysing the wording of the SGB provisions on sexual relationships and prostitution, and by using feminist theory and international human rights law,

I argued that the SGB is driven by radical feminist perspectives which consider all prostitution to be sexually exploitative and (hetero)sexual relationships conducted under the conditions of patriarchy to be suspect. The SGB provisions on sexual relationships and prostitution do not distinguish between sexually exploitative and non-exploitative sex, and as such are inconsistent with international human rights law since they deem both consent and age irrelevant to whether sexual conduct is exploitative.

By reviewing the four main empirical studies into adult sexual exploitation in PKOs conducted between 2002 and 2008, I found that only one raised concerns about the broad scope of the SGB definition of sexual exploitation.[3] While the majority of researchers did not question the broad scope of the SGB, the study by Kathleen Jennings started to question the lack of distinction between exploitative and non-exploitative sex by interviewing peacekeepers about their understanding of the SGB's 'strong discouragement' of sexual relationships.

To further clarify the distinction between exploitative and non-exploitative sex in PKOs, this book analysed the views of Bosnian women and peacekeepers from a range of missions on the SGB's 'strong discouragement' of sexual relationships between local women and peacekeepers. Two different views emerged. One view, held by the majority of peacekeepers, was in favour of the SGB's 'strong discouragement' because they felt that local people needed protection from sexual relationships with peacekeepers since their post-conflict circumstances made them highly vulnerable to sexual exploitation. The other view, held by a majority of the Bosnian women and two of the peacekeepers, was against the 'strong discouragement' of sexual relationships because it violated the sexual rights and agency of the participants in such relationships and made assumptions that were imperialistic and patronising. According to these interviewees, the SGB unjustly treats all women as victims and all peacekeepers as sexual predators.

I also examined whether and how the interviewees understood prostitution in PKOs. As with sexual relationships, two distinct views emerged. One was held by a minority of interviewees who considered that all prostitution, regardless of consent and age, is sexually exploitative activity that should be prohibited. The second view, held by the majority of Bosnian women and peacekeeper interviewees, maintained that prostitution is not necessarily sexually exploitative. These interviewees felt that adult, voluntary and adequately remunerated prostitution was not sexually exploitative and therefore should not be banned. Their views confirmed that consent and age should play an important role in distinguishing between sexual exploitation and (non-exploitative) prostitution. Drawing on the interviewees' perceptions, this book argues that by dismissing the relevance of consent, remuneration and age, the SGB blurs the division between voluntary prostitution and sexual exploitation, and consequently is inconsistent with international human rights law.

[3] Kathleen M. Jennings, 'Protecting Whom?: Approaches to Sexual Exploitation and Abuse in UN peacekeeping Operations' (Fafo, 2008).

7.3 Looking Ahead: Implications for UN Policymakers

My research shows how important it is for policy-makers to fully consider the views of the very people they want to protect from sexual exploitation in future decision-making that directly affects their lives. If they do not, there is a danger of producing ineffective policies and regulations, such as the SGB, which contain punitive and invasive measures that conflict with women's interests and needs. Such regulations may also draw attention to those issues that should be left to local women and peacekeepers to negotiate between themselves (sexual relationships) and distract from the more difficult problems of inequality and poverty, and the deeper socio-economic problems that remain unresolved in post-conflict societies in which PKOs are established. The SGB ignores the lived experiences of women that are targeted by the policy and for the policy to be efficacious, the proposed measures need to take these into account. The values, priorities and interests of local women, not of the UN, should shape policies that target their lives. Six major considerations for UN policy makers flow from this research. They outline a new framework for future UN policy making in relation to sexual exploitation. I have given particular weight to the perspectives expressed by local women, as these have not been considered in previous research.

First, this research shows that there is general support for a policy that bans sexual exploitation in PKOs. All of the interviewees thought that protection from sexual exploitation is necessary in PKOs, mentioning sex with minors, 'survival sex', forced prostitution and trafficking in women for the purposes of forced prostitution as examples. Accordingly, there is broad agreement that it is important to attend to the continuing problem of sexual exploitation, and that the UN must develop both proactive and responsive strategies. The strategies should address gender inequality, poverty and peacekeepers' immunity. The interviewees suggested that the UN should rethink the immunity peacekeepers enjoy, which they perceive to be one of the key obstacles to achieving justice for victims of sexual exploitation and abuse. The local interviewees felt that peacekeepers will not be held accountable for crimes they commit while on missions, including sexual offences. The UN should also address the overall lack of accountability for crimes committed in PKOs once peacekeepers return home.

Second, all the local interviewees, except one, and two peacekeepers thought that the policy as expressed in the SGB was over-inclusive and overprotective in relation to sexual relationships. They thought there was no need to protect women from consensual sexual relationships with peacekeepers, but instead to leave the decision to the people involved in such relationships. The regulation of sexual relationships was driven by the UN outrage at the apparent rapid growth in sexual exploitation and abuse cases. The SGB makes a number of assumptions about sexual relationships and the rhetoric in which these relationships are represented is contested. There is an assumption of 'vulnerability' and inherent victimhood of local women and of an 'imbalance of power' between them and peacekeepers. However, there is no empirical evidence indicating that consensual sexual relationships in PKOs are detrimental; rather it seems that the most pressing problem for women is a high rate of unemployment and a lack of income-generating opportunities. Yet, the economic oppression which women and the rest of the population face during and after war does not mean that the possibility of choice or agency should be negated. It also does not mean that their fundamental sexual rights, including the right to privacy, the right to choose partners, integrity, dignity and individual liberties, should be restricted. As the interviewees from Group A argued, although women live in war and post-war contexts, it does not mean that they cannot see the difference between good and bad sexual relationships.

Although Bosnian women are a specific cultural group, and caution should be adopted when generalising from their experiences, at the very least their perspectives show that women 'beneficiaries' are not a homogenous group, as the SGB assumes, and not all women are sexually 'vulnerable' and in need of the protection that the SGB seeks to provide. Their experiences also suggest that it may be unwise to make similar assumptions about other women in other contexts who engage in sexual relationships with peacekeepers, as it can be expected that their relationships may also, like the interviewees in Group A, be motivated by such ordinary desires as sexual attraction, love, friendship and a sense of adventure. The SGB policy on sexual relationships also perpetuates a negative stereotype of (male) peacekeepers as people who cannot treat women with respect and who are not capable of engaging in consensual and mutually rewarding sexual relationships. Overall, it ignores the complexities of women's interactions with peacekeepers and the nuances of their individual engagement with these practices. In sum, it should be left to local women and peacekeepers to negotiate sexual relationships between themselves.

Third, UN policy makers should recognise that prostitution, as the empirical research suggests, is a fact of life in peacekeeping contexts and acknowledge that it is the conditions under which prostitution takes place that determine whether it is sexually exploitative. The majority of interviewees from all three groups thought that voluntary and adequately remunerated adult prostitution was not sexually exploitative, but rather should be considered as a viable and legitimate economic option for women in post-conflict societies. With this in mind, the UN response to prostitution should be realistic, forward-looking and context-based. It should foster alternative economic options for local women, while recognising prostitution as a potentially important way for women to support themselves and their families. At the least, as long as there is no 'exit strategy' for women who work as prostitutes, prohibiting prostitution should not be an option. Further, prohibiting peacekeepers from paying money for sex denies prostitutes their right to work and to earn a living. Imposing a blanket ban on prostitution may not necessarily contribute to its prevention or decline because, as some interviewees suggested, prohibition may push prostitution underground, hiding it from view and limiting the scope of policy responses. Rather than investing resources and time in producing rules that ban prostitution, the UN should focus on supporting income-generating projects and lifting impoverished local economies in countries where PKOs are established.

By banning prostitution, the UN pushes it underground and places women in danger. Hidden from the public eye, women who work in the sex industry run the risk of being trafficked, abused, and their health and reproductive rights being jeopardised. The interviewees did not suggest that the UN should encourage prostitution, but rather accept it as a fact of life in peacekeeping contexts which will not go away simply by banning it.

No universally recognised legal norms either ban or permit prostitution. As discussed in Chap. 3, it is left to each nation state to regulate prostitution through its own laws. However, since a rapid growth in the sex industry often follows PKOs, the UN should help develop laws that reflect local conditions and accordingly protect women who work in the sex industry. Rather than pretending prostitution is not occurring, the UN should work with local governments and establish regulations to ensure that the activity is consensual, safety precautions are followed and that sex worker's rights are protected. Sex workers have human rights and freedoms, such as the right to work and generate income, the right to health care and reproductive rights. These are universal human rights and standards that should be exercised by sex workers and the UN should help make sure that this is the case.

The UN should work closely with local women who work in the sex industry in order to identify the ways in which it can address their needs and concerns. The UN should assist in implementing measures to help women address the abject poverty they often face after war by supporting them in their efforts to make a living without being exposed to abuse. Local women who do enter the sex industry should have the right to work, right to adequate remuneration and to protection from stigmatisation, harassment and discrimination. This can be achieved in each country where PKOs are established by assessing the conditions in which women live, the reasons they opt for sex work and what concerns they may have. Also, in collaboration with local women, the UN may analyse ways to improve their living circumstances. Providing women with income-generating schemes may help women in need to generate sources of income other than sex work. However, in cases where women do choose to provide sex services, the UN should not stigmatise them, but work with them to improve their working conditions and fully ensure their safety and human rights. A major problem associated with not recognising those in the sex industry as legitimate workers is the social stigma and discrimination that affect their ability to claim their own human rights. Peacekeepers should also be able to use sexual services as long as they use protection and adequately renumerate women.

The UN should invest in information and education of both local women and peacekeepers to help them make more informed decisions and take responsibility for their actions. It could provide more information to peacekeepers about the context they will work and live in during their posting and the socio-economic conditions local women face. It could also provide women information about peacekeepers, their origins, role and mandate. Such information would remake the environment in ways that supply more choices and information to both women and peacekeepers, encouraging individual responsibility for the actions they undertake and for sexual choices they make. Prostitution must be structurally addressed by looking at the broader socio-economic environment in which PKOs operate, and the ways in which this environment can become a safe place where local sex workers and peacekeepers can exercise their rights.

Fourth, the SGB justifies its call for 'strong discouragement' of sexual relationships and its ban on prostitution by claiming that they 'violate universally recognised international legal norms and standards'.[4] Yet the SGB breaches norms on sexual rights and freedoms, undermines women's agency and sexual autonomy, and blurs the division between consensual sex and sexual offences. It may be argued that the SGB violates universally accepted standards whereby consent helps differentiate sexual abuse from consensual sexual relationships. Negating local women's consent paradoxically breaches the norms the UN stands for and also removes the distinction between the capability of minors and adults to consent to sex.

Fifth, the interviewees did not agree with the SGB assumption that sexual relationships can undermine the 'credibility and integrity' of the UN. Instead, according to some interviewees, the prohibition of sexual relationships may have very serious consequences for the UN, because it may encourage racism, discrimination and stigmatisation. Such an approach may have a number of unintended consequences which create antagonistic relationships between local populations and peacekeepers. Some interviewees thought that rather than undermining UN credibility, sexual relationships between local women and peacekeepers can help to build trust and support multiculturalism: values that the UN stands for. They may help to deconstruct the prejudices and assumptions some peacekeepers have when they arrive in the in-mission country, as the analysis of the attitudes of Dutch peacekeepers towards Bosnian people in Chap. 2 demonstrated. Such relationships, according to the interviewees, help peacekeepers realise that people in mission countries are not barbaric and uncivilised. The empirical findings also suggest that the UN, rather than focusing on sexual relationships and prostitution, should reconsider the breadth of immunities that peacekeepers enjoy while on mission. All three groups of interviewees highlighted legal immunities, and the lack of accountability for crimes committed while on mission, as having serious consequences for UN credibility and integrity in the eyes of 'beneficiaries'. According to local interviewees the unequal power imagined in the SGB is a reality because of the broad immunities enjoyed by peacekeeping personnel, rather than because of unequal economic or gender power as the SGB seems to assume. Also, all three groups of interviewees suggested that the general inequality in power between peacekeepers and local women does not necessarily affect their sexual relationships. What concerns local women is immunity as a source of power rather than the material status of peacekeepers. The research findings indicate that local women interviewees were most worried about peacekeepers not being punished for crimes they commit and a lack of mechanisms for the enforcement of standards of conduct on those who perpetrate acts of sexual exploitation and abuse. The UN should invest its resources into developing policy and other responses which will

---

[4] Secretary-General's Bulletin, above n 1, section 3.1.

address the causes and consequences of sexual exploitation and abuse which undermine the 'credibility and integrity' of the UN, rather than consensual sexual relationships and adult, voluntary prostitution.

Sixth, the UN should shift its rhetoric from patronising and imperial language to the language of sexual agency and gender equality. By treating all women as a homogenous group the UN risks perpetuating conservative and imperial stereotypes about vulnerable women who need to be saved. Such an approach has consequences for their future leadership roles in post-conflict societies. If they are treated as child-like and patronised, it will be hard for them to obtain respect and to take leadership roles in their families and local communities. Women are victims, but they are also survivors and this acknowledgment needs to be embedded in all of the UN language. Women have to be treated with respect and their voice taken into account in any discussion that has a direct impact on their lives. This includes discussions and policy making in relation to adult sexual relationships between them and peacekeepers. The SGB relies upon and perpetuates negative gender and imperial stereotypes, and consequently encourages stigma and discrimination. Local interviewees considered such language and stereotypes counterproductive. The SGB also reinforces and acts upon negative stereotypes that exist about local women who are in sexual relationships, as expressed by some of the interviewees in groups B and C. It is of concern that these stereotypes, which seem to be prevalent among local and international populations, are legitimised and entrenched as rules in the SGB. Such a portrayal perpetuates the assumptions held by some women interviewees that peacekeepers are colonisers who look upon local women as backward and unworthy of being in sexual relationships with. Rather than reinforcing gender stereotypes, the SGB should promote gender equality and address the problem of sexual exploitation with a more targeted policy.

In conclusion, it is important to emphasise that this research was limited to adults, defined as persons 18 years and over. The main argument of this book is that women should not be treated as inherently vulnerable in post-conflict societies. While choice, agency and consent are socially constructed and constrained, they are pertinent when discussing consensual sexual relationships and prostitution, and that needs to be acknowledged by the SGB. Women should be consulted in the process of revising the SGB, even if the consultation is nuanced. In the course of researching my book I was not able to establish whether women's NGOs were involved in the process of drafting the SGB. However, even if they were, it has been 10 years since its promulgation and this book and a few other studies suggest that the policy has not delivered the expected results, namely a decrease in sexual exploitation. Moreover, the women who should be consulted should not be local women in positions of power, but women who work in the sex industry and women who have romantic relationships with peacekeepers. Often the women who are most affected by the policy are not heard, so it is important to listen to their voices and opinions on the concerns that directly affect their lives.

The book argues that it is necessary to have a policy that will ban sexual exploitation, but not prostitution and sexual relationships. While sexual relationships should be left to be negotiated by peacekeepers and local women, whose right to privacy should be respected, adult and voluntary prostitution could be at most 'strongly discouraged' and then, depending on local contexts, regulated if necessary. The Head of Mission could use discretion in the case of prostitution and apply it in a specific context, upon consultation with local women. It is important to highlight that discretion needs to be exercised consistently with human rights, namely rights to privacy, adequate remuneration and favorable working conditions. Any limitation must be necessary, proportional and not arbitrary. While discretion may not be the best option, it may be the best that can be achieved in a peacekeeping context. Otherwise, the UN's well-meant efforts to protect women's lives from sexual exploitation may, as the findings suggest, end up as moralising, intrusive, and punitive.

There is a real danger inherent in UN regulations that target local women's sexual lives and frame the need for protection on the basis of an assumption of vulnerability, poverty, and a lack of personal capacity and responsibility. Such imperial interventions into women's lives assume that they are 'good' for the targeted women. The SGB policy, which is based on assumptions of 'vulnerability' and 'imbalance of power', results in being punitive, ineffective and patronising, and may bring burdensome unintended consequences that hurt the group of women the UN claims it most wants to help. In order to avoid that, this book argues that the SGB needs to be revised in consultation with local women and peacekeepers, and with international human rights law in mind. For example, if the policy is to remain, at a minimum the UN should organise and invite local women in the country of mission, including women in relationships with peacekeepers and sex workers, to consult regarding application of the policy. The UN policymakers should develop specific institutional interventions that would recognise local women and peacekeepers as bearers of human rights. Future policies must take into account subjective considerations of age and consent, in order to establish the difference between exploitative and non-exploitative sex. Finally, UN policy makers should view local women as capable participants in their own lives and not ignore the perspectives of those on whose behalf it is claimed the peacekeepers are working.

Bibliography

1. Articles/Books/Reports

Abi-Saab, Georges, 'United Nations Peacekeeping Old and New: An Overview of the Issues' in Daniel Warner (ed), *New Dimensions of Peacekeeping* (Martinus Nijhoff Publishers, 1995)

Alvesson, Mats, *Postmodernism and Social Research* (Open University Press, 2002)

Andreas, Peter, *Blue Helmets and Black Markets: The Business of Survival in the Siege of Sarajevo* (Cornell University Press, 2008)

Anonymous, *A Woman in Berlin* (Secker and Warburg, 1955)

Archard, David, *Sexual Consent* (Westview Press, 1998)

Agustin, Laura, 'At Home in the Street: Questioning the Desire of Help and Save' in Elizabeth Bernstein and Laurie Schaffner (eds), *Regulating Sex: The Politics of Intimacy and Identity* (Routledge, 2004) 67

Augustin, Laura, 'Migrants on the Mistress's House: Other Voices in the "Trafficking" Debate' (2005) 12(1) *Social Politics: International Studies in Gender, State and Society* 96

Babbie, Earl, *The Practice of Social Research* (Thomson Wadsworth, 2004)

Beilstein, Janet, 'The Expanding Role of Women in United Nations Peacekeeping' in Lois Ann Lorentzen and Jennifer Turpin (eds), *The Women and War Reader* (New York University Press, 1998) 140

Barry, Kathleen, *The Prostitution of Sexuality* (New York University Press, 1995)

Batinic, Jelena, 'Feminism, Nationalism, and War: The 'Yugoslav Case' in Feminist Texts' (2001) 3(1) *Journal of International Women's Studies* 1

Banda, Fareda and Christine Chinkin, 'Gender, Minorities and Indigenous Peoples' (Minority Rights Group International, 2004)

Bakic-Hayden, Milica and Robert M. Hayden, 'Orientalist Variations on the Theme "Balkans": Symbolic geography in recent Yugoslav Cultural Politics' (1992) 51(1) *Slavic Review* 1

Bar-Haim, Aviad, 'Rethinking organizational commitment in relation to perceived organizational power and perceived employment alternatives' (2007) 7(2) *International Journal of Cross Cultural Management* 203

Beasley, Chris, *What is feminism?* (Sage, 1999)

Beals, Janette et al, 'The Prevalence of Posttraumatic Stress Disorder among American Indian Vietnam veterans: Disparities and Context' (2002) 15(2) *Journal of Traumatic Stress* 89

Beara, Vladan and Predrag Miljanovic, *Gde si to bio sine moj?* [Where have you been, my son?] (Drustvo za zastitu mentalnog zdravlja ratnih veterana i zrtava ratova 1991-1999, 2006)

Bell, Shannon, Reading, *Writing and Rewriting the Prostitute Body* (Indiana University Press, 1994)

Bellamy, Alex J. et al, *Understanding Peacekeeping* (Polity, 2004)

DOI 10.1007/978-3-642-28484-7,

Bellis, M A. et al, 'Adults at 12? Trends in Puberty and their Public Health Consequences' (2006) 60 (11) *Journal of Epidemiology and Community Health* 910

Benderly, Jill, 'Rape, Feminism, and Nationalism in the War in Yugoslav Successor States' in Lois West (ed), *Feminist Nationalism* (Routledge, 1997) 59

Bennett, Christopher, *Yugoslavia's Bloody Collapse: Causes, Course and Consequences* (New York University Press, 1997)

Berg, B. L., *Qualitative Research Methods for the Social Sciences* (Allyn and Bacon, 4th ed, 2001)

Bernstein, Elizabeth and Laurie Schaffner (eds), *Regulating Sex: The Politics of Intimacy and Identity* (Routledge, 2004)

Bindman, Jo Redefining Prostitution as Sex Work on the International Agenda (Antislavery International, unpublished report, 1997) http://www.walnet.org/csis/papers/redefining.html

Bieneck, Steffen et al, 'Adolescents' Sexual Scripts: Schematic Representations of Consensual and Nonconsensual Heterosexual Interactions' (2007) 44(4) *The Journal of Sex Research* 316

Bloom, JCH et al, 'Srebrenica a 'Safe' Area: Reconstruction, Background, Consequences and Analyses of the Fall of a Safe Area' (Netherlands Institute of War Documentation, 2002)

Blagescu, Monica and Albrecht Schnabel (eds), 'Reforming UN Peace Operations, New Challenges for Peacekeeping Training. Proceedings of the 2001 Annual Meeting of the International Association of Peacekeeping Training Centres' (United Nations University, 2002)

Bankus, Brent C. and William R. Flavin, 'Training US Army Peacekeepers' (2004) 15 (1) *Small Wars and Insurgencies* 129

Brahimi, Lakhdar et al, *Report of the Panel on the United Nations Peace Operations*, UN Doc A/55/305-S/2000/809 (21 August 2000)

Bringa, Tone, *Being Muslim the Bosnian Way* (Princeton University Press, 1995)

Brockman, Joan, 'The impact of Institutional Structures and Power on Law and Society: Is it Time for Reawakening?' (2003) 37(2) *Law and Society Review* 283

Brown, Wendy, *States of Injury: Power and Freedom in Late Modernity* (Princeton University Press, 1995)

Brownmiller, Susan, *Against Our Will: Men, Women and Rape* (Bantam Books, 1976)

Burns, Peter M. et al (ed), *Tourism Research Methods: Integrating Theory with Practice* (Centre for Agriculture and Bioscience International, 2005)

Burg, Steven, *The War in Bosnia and Herzegovina: Ethnic Conflict and International Intervention* (M.E. Sharpe, 2000)

Burgess, Robert, *Field research: a Sourcebook and Field Manual* (Routledge, 1986)

Campbell, Enid, Poh York Lee and Joycey G. Tooher, *Legal Research Materials and Methods* (LBC Information Services, 1996)

Carmichael, Jennine, *First, Do No Harm: Addressing the Problem of Sexual Exploitation and Abuse by International Aid Workers and Peacekeepers* (MA Thesis, the University of Melbourne, 2006)

Carmody, Moira, 'Sexual Ethics and the Erotics of Consent' in Mark Cowling and Paul Reynolds (eds), *Making Sense of Sexual Consent* (Ashgate Publishing Limited, 2004) 45

Chamallas, Martha, 'Consent, Equality, and the Legal Control of Sexual Conduct' (1998) 61 *Southern California Law Review* 777

Chaitin, Julia, '"I Wish He Hadn't Told Me That": Methodological and Ethical Issues in Social Trauma and Conflict Research' (2003) 13 *Qualitative Health Research* 1145

Chapkis, Wendy, *Live Sex Acts: Women Performing Erotic Labour* (Routledge, 1997)

Chinkin, Christine and Hilary Charlesworth, 'Building Women into Peace: the International Legal Framework' (2006) 27(5) *Third World Quarterly* 937

Cheng, Sealing, 'Romancing the Club: Love Dynamics between Filipina Entertainers and GIs in Military Camp Towns in South Korea' in Mark Padilla et al, *Love and Globalization: Transformations of Intimacy in the Contemporary World* (Vanderbilt University Press, 2007) 226

Clements, Kevin P. and Christine Wilson, *UN Peacekeeping at the Crossroads* (Peace Research Centre, Australian National University, 1994)

Cockburn, Cynthia, *The Space Between Us: Negotiating Gender and National Identities in Conflict* (Zed Books, 1999)

Cockburn, Cynthia and Dubravka Zarkov (eds), *The Postwar Moment: Militaries, Masculinities and International Peacekeeping* (Lawrence and Wishart, 2002)

Conaway, Camille Pampell, 'United Nations Reform: Improving Peace Operations by Advancing the Role of Women'. Report from expert group meetings in New York and Washington DC, November 14–16, 2006

Copelon, Rhonda, 'Surfacing Gender: Reconceptualizing Crimes against Women in Time of War' in Lois Ann Lorentzen and Jennifer Turpin (eds), *The Women and War Reader* (New York University Press, 1999) 63

Cousens, Elizabeth M., 'Building Peace in Bosnia' in Elizabeth M. Cousens and Chetan Kumar (eds), Peacebuilding as Politics: Cultivating Peace in Fragile Societies (Lynne Rienner, 2000) 113

Cossman, Brenda et al, 'Gender, Sexuality, and Power: Is Feminist Theory Enough?' (2003) 12 *Columbia Journal of Gender and Law* 601

Cowling, Mark, *Date Rape and Consent* (Ashgate, 1998)

Cowling, Mark and Paul Reynolds, *Making Sense of Sexual Consent* (Ashgate, 2004)

Crnobrnja, Mihailo, *The Yugoslav Drama* (McGill-Queen's University Press, 1996)

Defeis, Elisabeth, 'U.N. Peacekeeping and Sexual Abuse and Exploitation: An End to Impunity' (2008) 7(2) *Washington University Global Studies Law Review* 185

Denich, Bette, 'Women, Work, and Power in Modern Yugoslavia' in Alice Schlegel (ed), *Sexual Stratification* (Columbia University Press, 1977)

Denitch, Bogdan, *Ethnic Nationalism: The Tragic Death of Yugoslavia* (University of Minnesota Press, 1996)

Diamond, Irene and Lee Quinby, *Feminism & Foucault: Reflections on Resistance* (Northeastern University Press, 1988)

Diehl, Paul F., *International Peacekeeping* (Johns Hopkins University Press, 1993)

Doezema, Jo, 'Loose Women or Lost Women? The Re-emergence of the Myth of 'White-Slavery' in Contemporary Discourses of 'Trafficking in Women" (2000) 18(1) *Gender Issues* 23

Doezema, Jo, 'Choice in Prostitution' in Conference Book: Changing Faces of Prostitution, Helsinki 3-5 May, 1995 (Helsinki: Unioni, The League of Finnish Feminists)

Doezema, Jo, 'Ouch! Western Feminists' 'Wounded Attachment' to the 'Third World Prostitute' 67 (2001) *Feminist Review* 16

Donia, Robert, *Bosnia and Herzegovina: A Tradition Betrayed* (Columbia University Press, 1995)

Donini, Antonio, 'Local Perceptions of Assistance to Afghanistan' (2007) 14 (1) *International Peacekeeping* 158

Dripps, Donald, 'Beyond Rape: an Essay on the Difference between the Presence of Force and the Absence of Consent' (1992) 92 (7) *Columbia Law Review* 30

Duggan, Lisa and Nan D. Hunter, *Sex Wars: Sexual Dissent and Political Culture* (Routledge, 1995)

Duncan, Meredith, 'Sex Crimes and Sexual Miscues: The Need for a Clearer Line between Forcible Rape and Nonconsensual Sex' (2007) 42(4) *Wake Forest Law Review* 1087

Durch, William J. and James A. Schear, 'Faultlines: UN Operations in the Former Yugoslavia', in William J. Durch and James A. Schear (eds), *UN Peacekeeping, American Politics, and the Uncivil Wars of the 1990s*, (New York, St. Martin's, 1996) 193

Dudgeon v The United Kingdom, (Application no. 7525/76) European Court of Human Rights Judgment 22 October 1981

Dworkin, Andrea, *Intercourse* (Free Press, 1987)

Dworkin, Andrea, *Pornography: Men Possessing Women* (Perigee Books, 1981)

Ehrlich, Susan, 'The Discursive Reconstruction of Sexual Consent' (1998) 9(2) *Discourse and Society* 149

Eide, Phyllis and Carol B Allen, 'Recruiting Transcultural Qualitative Research Participants: A Conceptual Model' (2005) 4(2) *International Journal of Qualitative Methods* 1

Einagel, Victoria Ingrid, 'Lasting Peace in Bosnia? Politics of Territory and Identity' in Ola Tunander, Pavel Baev and Victoria Ingrid Einagel (eds), *Geopolitics in Post-Wall Europe: Security, Territory and Identity* (International Peace Research Institute, 1997) 235

Eisenstain, Zillah, 'Feminism and Feminisms: Socialist Feminism' in Wilma Mankiller et al, *The Reader's Companion to U.S. Women's History* (Houghton Mifflin Harcourt, 1998) 218

Enloe, Cynthia, Bananas, *Beaches and Bases: Making Feminist Sense of International Politics* (University of California Press, 1990)

Enloe, Cynthia, *Maneuvers: The International Politics of Militarizing Women's Lives* (University of California Press, 2000)

Fehlberg, Belinda, *Sexually Transmitted Debt: Surety Experience and English Law* (Oxford University, 1997)

Ferguson, Ann, 'Sex War: The Debate between Radical and Libertarian Feminists' (1984) 10(1) *Signs: Journal of Women and Culture in Society* 106

Fetcher, Holly B., 'Three Stories of Prostitution in the West: Prostitutes 'Groups, Law and Feminist "Truth"'(1994) 4 *Columbia Journal of Gender and Law* 26

Fetherston, A. B., *Towards a Theory of United Nations Peacekeeping* (St. Martin's Press, Macmillan, 1994)

Fischer, Martina, *Peacebuilding and Civil Society in Bosnia-Herzegovina. Ten Years after Dayton* (Münster Lit Verlag, 2006)

Fisk, Larry and John Schellenberg (eds), *Patterns of Conflict, Paths to Peace* (University of Toronto Press, 2000)

Fleitz, Frederick, *Peacekeeping Fiascos of the 1990s: Causes, Solutions and US Interests* (Praeger, 2002)

Franke, Katherine M., 'Theorizing Yes: An Essay on Feminism, Law, and Desire' (2001) 101(1) *Columbia Law Review* 181

Freeman, Jody, 'The Feminist Debate over Prostitution Reform: Prostitutes' Rights Groups, Radical Feminists, and the (Im)possibility of Consent' (1990) 5 *Berkeley Women's Law Journal* 75

Gallagher, Anne, 'Human Rights and the New UN Protocols on Trafficking and Migrant Smuggling: A Preliminary Analysis' (2001) 23(4) *Human Rights Quarterly* 975

Gavey, Nicola, *Just sex?: The Cultural Scaffolding of Rape* (Psychology Press, 2005)

Gelsthorpe, Lorain and Allison Morris, *Feminist Perspectives in Criminology* (Open University Press, 1990)

Gioseffi, Daniela, *Women on War: An International Anthology of Writings from Antiquity to Present* (The Feminist Press, 2003)

Glesne, C., *Becoming Qualitative Researchers: an Introduction* (Longman, 2nd ed, 1999)

Goldstein, Joshua S., *War and Gender: How Gender Shapes the War System and Vice Versa* (Cambridge University Press, 2001)

Goulding, Marrack, 'The Evolution of United Nations Peacekeeping' (1993) 3 *International Affairs* 451

Grady, Kate, 'Sexual Exploitation and Abuse by UN Peacekeepers: A Threat to Impartiality' (2010) 17(2) *International Peacekeeping* 215

Gustafsson, Daniel, *Peacekeeping and Prostitution: A Case Study of the Swedish Experience from Kosovo and Bosnia* (MA Thesis, University of Lund, 2005)

Halley, Janet, 'The Politics of Injury: A Review of Robin West's Caring for Justice' (2005) 65 *Unbound: Harvard Journal of the Legal Left* 1

Halley, Janet et al, 'From the International to the Local in Feminist Legal Responses to Rape, Prostitution/sex Work, and Sex Trafficking: Four Studies in Contemporary Governance Feminism' (2006) 29 *Harvard Journal of Law and Gender* 335

Hamilton, V. Lee and Joseph Sanders, *Handbook of Justice Research in Law* (Springer, 2000)

Hastie, Rachel, Disabled Children in a Society at War: A Casebook from Bosnia (Oxfam, 1997)

Hart, Deborah, *The Realism of Peace: George Gittoes* (Darwin, Museum & Art Gallery of the Northern Territory 1995)
Hartsock, Nancy, *Money, Sex and Power: Towards a Feminist Historical Materialism* (Longman, 1983)
Harvey, S. Marie et al, 'Relationship Power, Decision Making, and Sexual Relations: an Exploratory Study with Couples of Mexican Origin' (2002) 39(4) *The Journal of Sex Research* 8
Higate, Paul and Marsha Henry, 'Engendering (In)security in Peace Support Operations' (2004) 35(4) *Security Dialogue* 482
Higate, Paul, 'Gender and Peacekeeping Case Studies: The Democratic Republic of the Congo and Sierra Leone' (Pretoria: Gender and Peacekeeping, Institute for Security Studies, 2004) 91 Monograph Series
Higate, Paul, 'Peacekeepers, Masculinities, and Sexual Exploitation' (2007) 10(1) *Men and Masculinities* 99
Heiberg, Marianne, 'Observations of UN Peacekeeping in Lebanon' (Oslo, Norsk Utenrikspolitisk Institutt, 1994)
Henry, Marsha, Paul Higate and Gurchathen Sanghera, 'Positionality and Power: The Politics of Peacekeeping Research' (2009) 16(4) *International Peacekeeping* 467
Hoagland, Sarah Lucia, *Lesbian Ethics: Toward a New Value* (Institute of Lesbian Studies, 1988)
Horwood, Christopher, 'Sexual Abuse and Exploitation by Peacekeepers and Aid Workers' in Ward, Jeanne et al, The Shame of War: Sexual Violence against Women and Girls in Conflict (The Integrated Regional Information Networks, 2007) 80
Humphreys, Terry, 'Perceptions of Sexual Consent: the Impact of Relationship History and Gender' (2007) 44(4) *The Journal of Sex Research* 307
Hughes, Donna, Lepa Mladjenovic and Zorica Mrsevic, 'Feminist Resistance in Serbia' (1994) 2(4) *The European Journal of Women's Studies* 509
Husanovic, Jasmina, 'The politics of gender, witnessing, postcoloniality and trauma: Bosnian feminist trajectories', (2009) 10 (1) *Feminist Theory*
Integrated Regional Information Networks, 'The Shame of War: Sexual Violence against Women and Girls in Conflict' (IRIN, 2007)
Inter-Agency Standing Committee Task Force on Protection from Sexual Exploitation and Abuse in Humanitarian Crises, 'Final Report to the Inter-Agency Standing Committee Working Group on the Activities of the IASC Task Force on Protection from Sexual Exploitation and Abuse in Humanitarian Crises' (June 2004)
Inter Agency-Standing Committee, 'Report of the Task Force on Protection from Sexual Exploitation and Abuse in Humanitarian Crises' (13 June 2002)
International Peace Academy, *Peacekeeper's Handbook* (Pergamon, 1984)
Jackson, Stevi, *Heterosexuality in Question* (Sage, 1999)
Jackson, Stevi and Jackie Jones, *Contemporary Feminist Theories* (Edinburgh University Press, 1998)
Jackson, Stevi, 'Even Sociologists Fall in Love: An Exploration in the Sociology of Emotions' (1993) 27(2) *Sociology* 201
Jackson, Terrence and Artola Marian Calafell, 'Ethical Beliefs and Management Behaviour: A Cross-Cultural Comparison' (1997) 16(11) *Journal of Business Ethics* 1163
Jaggar, Alison, 'Globalizing Feminist Ethics' (1998) 13(2) *Hypatia* 23
Jaggar, Alison, 'Is Globalization Good for Women?' (2001) 53(4) *Comparative Literature* 298
Jaggar, Alison, *Feminist Politics and Human Nature* (Rowman and Littlefield Publishers, 1988)
James, Alan, *The Politics of Peacekeeping* (London, Chatto and Windus, 1969)
Jauch, L.R., W.F. Glueck and R.N. Osborn, 'Organizational Loyalty, Professional Commitment and Academic Research Productivity' (1978) 21 *Academic Management Journal* 8
Jeffreys, Sheila, *The Idea of Prostitution* (Spinifex, 1997)
Jeffreys, Sheila, The Industrial Vagina: The Political Economy of the Global Sex Trade (Routledge, 2009)
Jennings, Gayle, 'Interviewing: a Focus on Qualitative Techniques' in Peter M. Burns et al (ed), *Tourism Research Methods: Integrating Theory with Practice* (CABI, 2005) 99

Jennings, Kathleen M., 'Protecting Whom?: Approaches to Sexual Exploitation and Abuse in UN Peacekeeping Operations' (Fafo, 2008)

Kanetake, Machiko, 'Whose Zero Tolerance Counts? Reassessing a Zero Tolerance Policy against Sexual Exploitation and Abuse by UN Peacekeepers' (2010) 17(2) *International Peacekeeping* 200

Kapur, Ratna, 'The Tragedy of Victimization Rhetoric: Resurrecting the "Native" Subject in International/Post-Colonial Feminist Legal Politics' (2002) 15 *Harvard Human Rights Journal* 1

Kapur, Ratna, 'Post-Colonial Economies of Desire: Legal Representations of the Sexual Subaltern' (2001) 78 *Denver University Law Review* 855

Kazeem, Fayemi Ademola, 'The Challenges of Prositution and Female Trafficking in Africa: An African Ethico-Feminist Perspective' (2009) 3(1) *The Journal of Pan African Studies* 200

Kartusch, Angelika, and Mara Radovanovic, 'Report on the Combat in Trafficking in Women for the Purpose of Forced Prostitution in Bosnia and Herzegovina' (Ludwig Boltzman Institute of Human Rights, 2001)

Katayanagi, Mari, *Human Rights Functions of United Nations Peacekeeping Operations* (Martinus Nijhoff Publishers, 2002)

Kaufman, Joyce P. and Kristen P. Williams, *Women and War Gender Identity and Activism in Times of Conflict* (Kumarian Press, 2010)

Kearns, Robin, 'Being there: Research through observing and participating' in Iain Hay (ed.) *Qualitative research methods in human geography* (Oxford University Press, 2000)103

Kitchin, Rob, and Nicholas Tate, '*Conducting Research in Human Geography: Theory, Methodology and Practic*e (Harlow, 2000)

Kirshenbaum, Gayle, 'Who's Watching the Peacekeepers?' 12 Ms. Magazine (May/June 1994) in Ann Orford 'Politics of Collective Security' (1995–1996) 17 *Michigan Journal of International Law* 373

Kelly, Liz (ed), Surviving Sexual Violence (Polity Press, 1988)

Kempadoo, Kamala, 'Women of Color and the Global Sex Trade: Transnational Feminist Perspectives' (2001) 1(3) *Meridians: Feminism, Race, Transnationalism* 28

Kempadoo, Kamala and Jo Doezema, *Global Sex Workers: Rights, Resistance, and Redefinition* (Routledge, 1998)

Kent, Vanessa L, 'Peacekeepers as Perpetrators of Abuse: Examining the UN's Plans to Eliminate and Address Cases of Sexual Exploitation and Abuse in Peacekeeping Operations' (2005) 14(2) *African Security Review* 85

Kesic, Obrad, 'Women and Gender Imagery in Bosnia: Amazons, Sluts, Victims, Witches, and Wombs' in Sabrina Ramet (ed), *Gender Politics in the Western Balkans: Women, Society, and Politics in Yugoslavia and the Yugoslav Successor States* (Pennsylvania State University Press, 1999) 187

Kotiswaran, Prabha 'Preparing for Civil Disobedience: Indian Sex Workers and the Law' (2001) 21(2) *Third World Law Journal* 161

Korac, Maja, 'Women Organizing against Ethnic Nationalism and War in the Post-Yugoslav States' in Wenona Giles et al, *Feminists Under Fire: Exchanges Across War Zones* (Between the Lines, 2003) 25

Kumar, Krishna, 'Civil Wars, Women, and Gender Relations: An Overview' in Krishna Kumar (ed), *Women and Civil War: Impact, Organizations, and Action* (Lynne Rienner, 2001) 5

Kvinna Till Kvinna, *Engendering the Peace Process, A Gender Approach to Dayton-and Beyond* (Kvinna Till Kvinna Foundation, 2000)

Kwok, Wei Leng, 'Sex and Sexualities: Contemporary Feminist Debates' in Kate Pritchard Hughes (ed), *Contemporary Australian Feminism* (1997) 76

Lacombe, Dany, *Blue Politics: Pornography and the Law in the Age of Feminism* (University of Toronto Press, 1994)

Lane, Jan-Erik, *Globalization and Politics: Promises and Dangers* (Ashgate Publishing, 2006)

Liamputtong, Prenee (ed) *Doing cross-cultural research: Methodological and Ethical Consideration* (Springer, 2008)

Limanowska, Barbara, 'Trafficking in Human Beings in South Eastern Europe' (UNICEF, UNOHCHR, OSCE/ODIHR 2003)

LeMoncheck, Linda, *Loose Women, Lecherous Men: a Feminist Philosophy of Sex* (Oxford University Press, 1997)

Levin, Scott A., 'Sexual Exploitation of Refugee Children by U.N. Peacekeepers' (2003) XIX *New York Law School Journal of Human Rights* 833

Lobodzinska, Barbara (ed), *Family, Women, and Employment in Central-Eastern Europe* (Praeger, 1995) 237

Lupi, Natalia, 'Report by the Enquiry Commission on the Behaviour of Italian Peacekeeping Troops in Somalia' (1998) 1 *Yearbook of International Humanitarian Law* 375

MacCannell, Dean, 'Introduction to Special Issues on Semiotics of Tourism' (1989) 16 (1) *Annals of Tourism Research* 1

MacKinnon, Catherine, *Towards a Feminist Theory of State* (Harvard University Press, 1989)

MacKinnon, Catharine, 'Women's September 11th: Rethinking the International Law of Conflict' (2006) 47(1) *Harvard International Law Journal* 1

MacKinnon, Catharine A, *Are Women Human? And other International Dialogues* (Harvard University Press, 2006)

MacKinnon, Catharine A., *Feminism Unmodified: Discourses on Life and Law* (Harvard University Press, 1987)

MacKinnon, Catharine A, 'Prostitution and Civil Rights' (1993) 1 *Michigan Journal of Gender and Law* 13

Mannheim, Karl, *Men and Society in an Age of reconstruction* (Routledge, 1940)

Mansson, Katarina, 'The Forgotten Agenda: Human Rights Protection and Promotion in Cold War Peacekeeping' (2005) 10(3) *Journal of Conflict and Security Law* 379

Mardossian, Carine, 'Toward a New Feminist Theory of Rape' (2002) 27(3) *Journal of Women in Culture and Society* 743

Martin, Sarah, 'Must Boys be Boys? Ending Sexual Exploitation and Abuse in UN Peacekeeping Missions' (Refugees International, 2005)

Mazurana, Dyan E, Angela Raven-Roberts and Jane L. Parpart (eds), *Gender, Conflict and Peacekeeping* (Rowman and Littlefield Publishers, 2005)

McCormick, Naomi B., Sexual Salvation: Affirming Women's Sexual Rights and Pleasures (Praeger, 1994)

Mendelson, Sarah Elizabeth, *Barracks and Brothels: Peacekeepers and Human Trafficking in the Balkans* (Center for Strategic and International Studies, 2005)

Merriam, Sharan, *Case Study Research in Education: A Qualitative Approach* (Jossey-Bass Publishers, 1998)

Mgbako, Chi and Laura Smith, 'Sex Work and Human Rights in Africa' (2011) 33(4) *Fordham International Law Journal* 1178

Miler, Alice M., 'Sexuality, Violence against Women, and Human Rights' (2004) 7(16) *Health and Human Rights* 5

Milic, Andjelka, 'Women and Work in Former Yugoslavia and Their Present Situation' in Barbara Lobodzinska (ed), *Family, Women, and Employment in Central-Eastern Europe* (Greenwood Press, 1995) 237

Machel, Graca, *The Impact of War on Children: A Review of Progress Since the 1996 United Nations Report on the Impact of Armed Conflict on Children* (Hurst and Palgrave, 2001)

Mills, C. Wright, 'Situated Actions and Vocabularies of Motive' (1940) 5(6) *American Sociological Review* 904

Mladjenovic, Lepa and Donna M. Hughes, 'Feminist Resistance to War and Violence in Serbia' in Marquerite Waller and Jennifer Rycenga (eds), *Frontline Feminisms, Women, War and Resistance* (Routledge, 2001) 247

Mockaitis, Thomas R., *Peace Operations and Intrastate Conflict: the Sword or the Olive Branch?* (Praeger, 1999)

Modinos v Cyprus (Application no. 15070/89) European Court of Human Rights, Judgment 22 April 1993

Murray, A, 'Debt bondage and Trafficking: Don't believe the Hype' in Kamala Kempadoo and Jo Doezema (ed), *Global Sex Workers: Rights, Resistance and Redefinition* (Routledge, 1998) 51
Nagle, Jill, *Whores and other Feminists* (Routledge, 1997)
Ndulo, Muna, 'The United Nations Responses To The Sexual Abuse And Exploitation Of Women And Girls By Peacekeeping Missions' (2008) 27(1) *Berkley Journal of International Law* 127
Nikolic-Ristanovic, Vesna, *Social Change, Gender and Violence: Post-Communist and War Affected Societies* (Springer, 2002)
Nikolic-Ristanovic, Vesna (ed), *Women, Violence and War: Wartime Victimization of Refugees in the Balkans* (Central European University Press, 1999)
Notar, Susan A., 'Peacekeepers as perpetrators: Sexual Exploitation and Abuse of Women and Children in the Democratic Republic of the Congo' (2006) 14 (413) *American University Journal of Gender, Social Policy and Law* 413
Norris v Ireland (Application no. 10581/83) European Court of Human Rights, Judgment 26 October 1988
Norton, August and Thomas G. Weiss, 'Rethinking Peacekeeping' in Indar Jit Rikhye and Kjell Skjelsbaek (eds), *The United Nations and Peacekeeping: Results, Limitations and Prospects: The Lessons of 40 Years Experience* (Macmillan and International Peace Academy, 1990) 22
Nussbaum, Martha C., *Sex and Social Justice* (Oxford University Press, 1999)
Office of Internal Oversight Services, 'Report of the Office of Internal Oversight Services on the Investigation into Sexual Exploitation of Refugees by Aid Workers in West Africa' (A/57/465, 11 October 2002)
Olsson, Louise, 'Mainstreaming Gender in Multidimensional Peacekeeping: A Field Perspective' (2000) 7(3) *International Peacekeeping* 1
Olsson, Louise et al, 'Gender Aspects of Conflict Interventions: Intended and Unintended Consequences: Case studies on the United Nations Mission in Eritrea/Ethiopia (UNMEE), the NATO Stabilization Force in Bosnia and Herzegovina (SFOR) and the Temporary International Presence in Hebron (TIPH)' Final report to the Norwegian Ministry of Foreign Affairs (International Peace Research Institute, Oslo, 2004)
O'Neill, Maggie, *Prostitution and Feminism: Towards a Policy of Feeling* (Wiley-Blackwell, 2001)
O'Neill, John Terence and Nicholas Rees, *United Nations Peacekeeping in the Post-Cold War Era* (Routledge, 2005)
Organization for Security and Co-operation in Europe Vukovar, 'Report on Community Trauma in Eastern Croatia' (OSCE, 2002)
Otto, Dianne, 'Making Sense of Zero Tolerance Policies in Peacekeeping Sexual Economies' in Vanessa Munro and Carl F. Stychin (ed), *Sexuality and the Law: Feminist Engagements* (Routledge-Cavendish, 2007) 259
Otto, Dianne, 'The Sexual Tensions of UN Peace Support Operations: A Plea for 'Sexual Positivity' (2007) XVIII *Finnish Yearbook of International Law* 33
Otto, Dianne, 'Whose Security? Reimagining Post-Cold War Peacekeeping from a Feminist Perspective' in Robert G. Patman (ed), *Security in a Post-Cold War World* (Macmillan Press and St. Martin's Press, 1999) 65
Otto, Dianne and Sue Jackson, 'From Delicacy to Dilemma – A Feminist Perspective on Prostitution' in Kaye Daniels (ed), *So Much Hard Work –Women and Prostitution in Australian History* (1984) 366
Outshoorn, Joyce, 'The Political Debates on Prostitution and Trafficking of Women' (2005) 12(1) Social Politics: International Studies in Gender, State and Society 141
Overall, Christine, 'What's Wrong with Prostitution? Evaluating Sex Work' (1992) 17(4) *Signs: Journal of Women in Culture and Society* 705
Paris Roland, 'International peacebuilding and 'the mission civilisatrice' (2002) 28 (4) *Review of International Studies* 637
Pateman, Carole, *The Sexual Contract* (Cambridge, Polity Press, 1988)
Pheterson, Gail, *A Vindication of the Rights of Whores* (Amsterdam University Press, 1996)

Phal, Kien Serey, 'The Lessons of the UNTAC Experience and the Ongoing Responsibilities of the International Community in Cambodia' (1995) 7(2) *Pacifica Review* 129
Phillips, Anne, 'Feminism and Liberalism Revisited: Has Martha Nussbaum Got It Right?' (2001) 8(2) *Constellations* 250
Perschler-Desai, Viktoria, 'Childhood on the Market: Teenage Prostitution in Southern Africa' (2001) 10 (4) *African Security Review* 111
Pouligny, Beatrice, *Peace Operations Seen From Below: UN missions and Local People* (Kumarian Press, 2006)
Radulovic, Dragan, *Prostitucija u Jugoslaviji* [Prositution in Yugoslavia] (Filip Višnjić, 1986)
Ramet, Sabrina, *Gender Politics in the Western Balkans: Women, Society, and Politics in Yugoslavia and the Yugoslav Successor States* (Pennsylvania State University Press, 1999)
Ramet, Sabrina, *Social Currents in Eastern Europe: The Sources and Consequences of the Great Transformation* (Duke University Press Books, 1994)
Ratner, Steven R., *The new UN Peacekeeping: Building Peace in Lands of Conflict After the Cold War* (St. Martin's Press: Council on Foreign Relations, 1995)
Razack, Sherene, *Dark Threats and White Knights: The Somalia Affair, Peacekeeping, and the New Imperialism* (University of Toronto Press, 2004)
Rees, Madeleine, 'International Intervention in Bosnia-Herzegovina: The Cost of Ignoring Gender' in Cynthia Cockburn and Dubravka Zarkov (ed), *The Postwar Moment: Militaries, Masculinities and International Peacekeeping* (Zed Books, 2002) 51
Rehn, Elisabeth and Ellen Johnson Sirleaf, *Women, War and Peace: The Independent Experts Assessment on the Impact of Armed Conflict on Women and Women's Role in Peacebuilding* (UNIFEM, 2002)
Renzetti, CM and RM Lee, 'The problems of researching sensitive topics' (1990) 33(5) *American Behavioral Scientist* 510
Rikhye, Indar Jit and Kjell Skjelsbaek, *The United Nations and Peacekeeping: Results, Limitations and Prospects: the Lessons of 40 years of Experience, Issues in Peacekeeping and Peacemaking* (Macmillan and the International Peace Academy, 1990)
Roiphe, Katie, *The Morning After: Sex, Fear, and Feminism on Campus* (Little Brown and Company, 1993)
Rubin, Gayle, 'Thinking Sex: Notes for a Radical Theory of the Politics of Sexuality' in Carole S. Vance (ed), *Pleasure and Danger: Exploring Female Sexuality* (Routledge and K. Paul, 1984) 267
Rubinstein, Robert, 'Intervention and Culture: An Anthropological Approach to Peace Operations' (2005) 36(4) *Security Dialogue* 527
Rubin, Herbert and Irene Rubin, *Qualitative Interviewing: the Art of Hearing Data* (Sage Publications, 2005)
Scully. Pamela 'Vulnerable women: A critical reflection on human rights discourse and sexual violence' (2009) 23 *Emory International Law Review* 113
Scheurich, James, 'Social Relativism: A Postmodernist Epistemology for Educational Administration' in Spencer Maxcy (ed), *Postmodern School Leadership: Meeting the Crisis in Educational Administration* (Praeger, 1994) 17
Schellhaas, Constanze and Annette Seegers, 'Peacebuilding: imperialism's new disguise?' (2009 18 (2) *African Security Review* 1
Schultz, Vicki, 'Sex and Work' (2006) 18 *The Yale Journal of Law and Feminism* 223
Seaton, A. V. and M. M. Bennett, *The Marketing Of Tourism Products: Concepts, Issues And Cases* (International Thomson Business Press, 1996)
Secretary-General's Bulletin, *Special Measures for Protection From Sexual Exploitation and Abuse ST/SGB/2003* (9 October 2003)
Secretary-General, *Report of the Secretary-General on the Activities of the Office of Internal Oversight* Services, delivered to the General Assembly, UN Doc A/57/451 (4 October 2002)

Secretary-General, *Seventeenth Report of the Secretary-General on the United Nations Organization Mission in the Democratic Republic of Congo*, UN Doc S/2005/167 (15 March 2005)
Secretary-General, *Final Report on UNEF I*, UN Doc. A/6627 (12 July1967)
Secretary-Generals' Bulletin, *Promotion of Equal Treatment of Men and Women in the Secretariat and Prevention of Sexual Harassment*, ST/SGB/253, 29 October 1992
Shotton, Anna, 'A Strategy to Address Sexual Exploitation by U.N. Peacekeeping Personnel' (2006) 39 *Cornell Law Review* 97
Shrage, Laurie, 'Comment on Overall's "What's Wrong with Prostitution? Evaluating Sex Work" (1994) 19(2) *Signs: Journal of Women in Culture and Society* 564
Shrage, Laurie, 'Should Feminists Oppose Prostitution?'(1989) 99 (2) *Ethics* 347
Smythe, Amy et al, 'Activities Report from the Office of Gender Affairs (OGA) of the United Nations Organization Mission in the Democratic Republic of Congo (MONUC)', 10 January 2003
Simic, Andrei, 'Machismo and Cryptomatriarchy: Power, Affect, and Authority in the Contemporary Yugoslav Family' (1983) 11(1/2) *Ethos* 66
Simic, Milena and Tim Rhodes, 'Violence, Dignity and HIV Vulnerability: Street Sex Work in Serbia' (2009) 31(1) *Sociology of Health and Illness* 1
Simic, Olivera, 'Rethinking 'Sexual Exploitation' in UN Peacekeeping Operations' (2009) 32 (4) *Women's Studies International Forum* 288
Simic, Olivera, 'Speaking the Unspeakable, Remembering the Wished to Be Forgotten', *International Feminist Journal of Politics* (2011) 13(2) 247
Stake, Robert, *The Art Of Case Study Research* (Sage, 1995)
Starhawk, *Truth or Dare: Encounters With Power, Authority, and Mystery* (Harper, 1987)
Stiehm, Judith Hicks, 'Peacekeeping and Peace Research: Men's and Women's Work' (1997) 18 *Women and Politics* 27
Stiglmayer, Alexandra (ed.), *Mass Rape: The War against Women in Bosnia-Herzegovina* (University of Nebraska Press, 1994)
Stojsavljevic, Jovanka, 'Women, Conflict, and Culture in Former Yugoslavia' (1994) 3(1) *Gender and Development* 36
Sullivan, Barbara, 'Rape, Prostitution and Consent' (2007) 40(2) The Australian and New Zealand Journal of Criminology 127
Sullivan, Barbara, 'Feminism and Female Prostitution' in Roberta Perkins (ed) *Sex Work and Sex Workers in Australia* (University of New South Wales Press, 1994) 253
Sullivan, Barbara, 'Trafficking in Women: Feminism and New International Law' (2003) 5(1) *International Feminist Journal of Politics* 67
Sullivan, Mary, *What Happens When Prostitution Becomes Work?: An Update on Legislation on Prostitution in Australia* (Coalition against Trafficking in Women, 2005)
Sullivan, Mary Lucille, *Making Sex Work: A Failed Experiment with Legalised Prostitution* (Spinifex, 2007)
Sutherland, Kate, 'Work, Sex, and Sex-Work: Competing Feminist Discourses on the International Sex Trade' (2004) 42(2) *Osgoode Hall Law Journal* 139
Tambiah, Yasmin, 'Sexuality and Women's Rights in Armed Conflict in Sri Lanka' (2004) 12(23) *Reproductive Health Matters* 78
Tanesini, Alessandra, *An Introduction to Feminist Epistemologies* (Wiley-Blackwell, 1999)
Tayeb, Monir, 'Conducting research across cultures: overcoming drawbacks and obstacles' (2001) 1(2) *International Journal of Cross Cultural Management* 91
Taylor, Steven and Robert Bogdan, *Introduction to Qualitative Research Methods: a Guidebook and Resource* (John Wiley and Sons, 3rd ed, 1998)
The European Community Investigative Mission Into the Treatment of Muslim Women in the Former Yugoslavia: Report to European Community Foreign Ministers. UN Doc S/25240, annex I, 3 February 1993
Thompson, Susan, 'Prostitution-A Choice Ignored' (2000) 21(3) *Women's Rights Law Reporter* 217

Thomas, Dorothy and Regan Ralph, 'Rape in War: The Case of Bosnia' in Sabrina Ramet (ed.), *Gender Politics in the Western Balkans: Women, Society, and Politics in Yugoslavia and the Yugoslav Successor States* (Pennsylvania State University Press, 1999) 203

Thakur, Ramesh Chandra (eds), *A Crisis of Expectations: UN Peacekeeping in the 1990s* (Westview Press, 1995)

Tomsic, Vida, *Women in the Development of Socialist Self-Managing Yugoslavia* (Jugoslovenska stvarnost, 1980)

Turpin, Jennifer, 'Many Faces: Women Confronting War' in Lois Ann Lorentzen and Jennifer Turpin (eds), *The Women and War Reader* (New York University Press, 1999) 3

The Office of Internal Oversight Services, 'Report of the Office of Internal Oversight Services on the Investigation into Sexual Exploitation of Refugees by Aid Workers in West Africa', A/57/465 (11 October 2002)

UK Joint Doctrine and Concepts Centre (ed), *The Military Contributions to Peace Support Operations* (UK Ministry of Defence, 2004)

United Nations, *The Blue Helmets: A Review of United Nations Peace-keeping* (United Nations Publications, 1996)

United Nations Department of Peacekeeping Operations, 'United Nations Peacekeeping Operations: Principles and Guidelines' (March 2008)

United Nations High Commissioner for Refugees and Save the Children UK, 'Sexual Violence and Exploitation: The Experience of Refugee Children in Liberia, Guinea and Sierra Leone,' Report of assessment mission carried out from 22 October to 30 November 2001 (2002)

Vance, Carol S., *Pleasure and Danger: Towards a Politics of Sexuality* (Routledge and Kegan Paul, 1984)

Vandenberg, Martina, 'Hopes Betrayed: Trafficking of Women and Girls to Post-Conflict Bosnia and Herzegovina for Forced Prostitution' (Human Rights Watch, 2002)

Vazquez, Norma, 'Motherhood and Sexuality in Times of War: The Case of Women Militants of FMNL in El Salvador' (1997) 9 *Reproductive Health Matters* 139

Walsh, Martha, 'Post Conflict Bosnia and Herzegovina: Integrating Women's Special Situation and Gender Perspectives in Skills Training and Employment Promotion Programs' (International Labour Organization, 1997)

Walby, Sylvia, *Theorizing Patriarchy* (Wiley-Blackwell, 1990)

Waller, Marquerite and Jennifer Rycenga (eds), *Frontline Feminisms, Women, War and Resistance* (Routledge, 2001)

Warner, Daniel (ed) *New Dimensions of Peacekeeping* (Martinus Nijhoff Publishers, 1995)

Wartenberg, Thomas, *The Forms of Power: From Domination to Transformation* (Temple University Press, 1990)

Weitzer, Ronald, 'Moral Crusade against Prostitution' (2006) 43 (3) *Society* 33

West, Robin, 'Desperately Seeking a Moralist' (2006) 29 Harvard Journal of Law and Gender 1

White, Luise, *The Comforts of Home: Prostitution in Colonial Nairobi* (University of Chicago Press, 1990)

Whitworth, Sandra, 'Gender, Race and the Politics of UN Peacekeeping' in Edward Moxon-Brown (ed), *A Future for Peacekeeping?* (MacMillan Press,1998) 176

Whitworth, Sandra, *Men, Militarism and UN Peacekeeping: A Gendered Analysis* (Lynne Rienner, 2004)

Withworth, Sandra, 'The Practice, and Praxis, of Feminist Research in International Relations' in Wyn Jones, Richard (ed), *Critical Theory and World Politics* (Lynne Reinner, 2000) 149

Wijers, Marjan and Lin Lap-Chew, *Trafficking in Women: Forced Labour and Slavery like Practices in Marriage, Domestic Labour and Prostitution* (Foundation against Trafficking in Women, 1997)

Woodward, Susan, *Balkan Tragedy: Chaos and Dissolution after the Cold War* (Brookings Institution Press, 1995)

Yin, Robert, *Case Study Research: Design and Methods* (Sage, 4th ed, 2009)

Young, Iris Marion, *Justice and the Politics of Difference* (Princeton University Press, 1990)

Zacarias, Agostinho, *The United Nations and International Peacekeeping* (Tauris Academic Studies, 1996)
Zarkov, Dubravka, *The Body of War: Media, Ethnicity, and Gender in the Break-up of Yugoslavia* (Duke University Press, 2007)
Zarkov, Dubravka, and Cynthia Cockburn (eds), *The Postwar Movement: Militaries, Masculinities and International Peacekeeping* (Lawrence and Wishart, 2002)
Zarkov, Dubravka, 'Towards a new theorizing of women, gender and war' in Mary Evans, Kathy Davis and Judith Lorber (eds), *Handbook of Gender and Women's Studies* (SAGE, 2006) 214
Zatz, Noah, 'Sex Work/Sex Act: Law, Labor, and Desire in Constructions of Prostitution' (1997) 22(2) *Signs: Journal of Women in Culture and Society* 277
Zisk Marten, Kimberly, *Enforcing the Peace: Learning from the Imperial Past* (Columbia University Press, 2004)

2. UN Policies/Guidelines

Boutros Boutros-Ghali, *An Agenda for Peace Preventive Diplomacy, Peacemaking and Peace-keeping*, UN Doc A/47/277-S/24111 (17 June 1992)
Department of Peacekeeping Operations, *UN Peacekeeping Handbook for Junior Ranks* (1997)
Department of Peacekeeping Operations, *We Are United Nations Peacekeepers* (1997)
Department for Peacekeeping Operations, *Ten Rules: Code of Personal Conduct for Blue Helmets* (1997)
Department of Peacekeeping Operations, *United Nations Peacekeeping Operations: Principles and Guidelines* (March 2008)
Princ Zeid Ra'ad Zeid Al-Hussein, *A Comprehensive Strategy to Eliminate Future Sexual Exploitation and Abuse in United Nations Peacekeeping Operations*, A/59/710 (24 March 2005)
Report of the Special Committee on Peacekeeping Operations and its Working Group on the 2005 resumed session, GA A/59/19/Add.1, 59th session (New York, 4-8 April 2005)
Report of the Secretary-General, *Safety and Security of United Nations Personnel*, GA, 55th sess, UN Doc A/55/494 (2000)
Report of the Secretary-General, *Special Measures for Protection from Sexual Exploitation and Sexual Abuse*, UN Doc A/59/782 (2005)
Secretary-General, *Comprehensive Review of the Whole Question of Peacekeeping Operations in All Their Aspects*, GA Res 2006 (XIX), 19th sess,1330th plen mtg (18 February1965)
Secretary-General's Bulletin, *Special Measures for Protection from Sexual Exploitation and Abuse*, ST/SGB/2003/13 (9 October 2003)
Secretary-General's Bulletin, *Promotion of Equal Treatment of Men and Women in the Secretariat and Prevention of Sexual Harassment*, ST/SGB/253 (29 October 1992)
Secretary-General, *Seventeenth Report of the Secretary-General on the United Nations Organization Mission in the Democratic Republic of Congo*, UN Doc S/2005/167 (15 March 2005)
Secretary-General, *Report of the Secretary-General on the Activities of the Office of Internal Oversight Services*, Delivered to the General Assembly, UN Doc A/57/451 (4 October 2002)
Security Council Resolution, *Women, Peace and Security*, S/Res/1889 (5 October 2009)
Staff Regulations, ST/SGB/2001/8 (27 September 2001)
Staff Regulations, ST/SGB/2003/5 (7 February 2003)
United Nations General Assembly, *United Nations Comprehensive Strategy on Assistance and Support to Victims of Sexual Exploitation and Abuse by United Nations Staff or Related Personnel*, 59th sess, A/Res/62/214 (7 March 2008)
UN General Assembly, Investigation into sexual exploitation of refugees by aid workers in West Africa, 57th sess, A/Res/57/306 (22 May 2003)

United Nations Department of Public Information, *The Blue Helmets: A Review of United Nations Peace-keeping* (United Nations Publications, 1996)
United Nations Inter-Agency Standing Committee, *Implementation Guidelines for the Field on the Secretary-General's Bulletin on Special Measures for Protection from Sexual Exploitation and Sexual Abuse*, ST/SGB/2003/13 (May 2004)
United Nations General Assembly, *United Nations Comprehensive Strategy on Assistance and Support of Victims of Sexual Exploitation and Abuse by United Nations Staff or Related Personnel*, A/Res/62/214 (7 March 2008)
United Nations General Assembly, Comprehensive Review of the Whole Question of Peacekeeping Operations in All Their Aspects, 55th sess, A/55/305-S/2000/809 (21 August 2000)
United Nations General Assembly, *Comprehensive review of the whole question of peacekeeping operations in all their aspects*, GA Res A/59/710 (24 March 2005)
United Nations Secretariat, *Administrative Instruction on Procedures for Dealing With Sexual Harassment*, ST/AI/379, 29 October 1992
United Nations General Assembly, *United Nations Comprehensive Strategy on Assistance and Support to Victims of Sexual Exploitation and Abuse by United Nations Staff and Related Personnel*, A/RES/62/214 (7 March 2008)

3. Treaties

Convention on the Rights of the Child, opened for signature 20 November 1989, 1577 UNTS 3 (entered into force 2 September 1990)
Convention on the Elimination of All Forms of Discrimination against Women, opened for signature 18 December 1979, UNTS 13 (entered into force 3 September 1981)
Charter of the United Nations, signed on 26 June 1945 (entered into force 24 October 1945)
International Covenant on Civil and Political Rights, opened for signature 16 December 1966, 993 UNTS 171 (entered into force 23 March 1976)
International Covenant on Economic, Social and Cultural Rights, opened for signature 16 December 1966, 993 UNTS 3 (entered into force 3 January1976)
The Protocol to Prevent, *Suppress and Punish Trafficking in Persons, Especially Women and Children, Supplementing the United Nations Convention against Transnational Organized Crime*, GA Res 25, annex II, 55th sess, UN Doc A/45/49 (entered into force 9 September 2003)
Universal Declaration of Human Rights (entered into force 10 December 1948)
The Covenant of the League of Nations, opened for signature 28 June 1919 (entered into force 10 January 1920)

4. Other Sources

Autonomous Women's Center, 'The History of Feminist Movement in Yugoslavia' http://www.womenngo.org.rs/content/blogcategory/28/61/
Barker, Ann 'UN Takes Step to Prevent Sex Abuse in East Timor', *ABC News* (online) 30 August 2006 http://www.abc.net.au/pm/content/2006/s1728448.htm
Bosnia and Herzegovina-UNMIBH-Background, 12 August 2009 http://www.un.org/en/peacekeeping/missions/past/unmibh/background.html
Bromberg, Sarah, 'Feminist Issues in Prostitution'. Paper presented at the 1997 International Conference on Prostitution at Cal State University Northridge. 4 November 2004 http://www.feministissues.com/issues.pdf

Bowers v Hardwick, 478 U.S. 186, 196 (1986)

Bozay, Mehmet Kemal, 'The Balkan Experience in the Development and the Implementation of Comprehensive Strategies for Multidimensional Peace Operations: A Brief Analyses on the Bosnia and Kosovo cases', (2003) 8 Perceptions, *Journal of International Affairs* 1

Cerkez-Robinson, Aida, 'New Special Police Units to Help Fighting Trafficking of Women' *Associated Press*, 26 July 2001, 205

Channg, Mang, 'Sex Trade Flourishing in Capital', *Phnom Penh Post*, 12 February 1993, 6

Crossette, Barbara, 'When Peacekeepers Turn Into Troublemakers', *New York Times*, 7 January 1996, 9

Connell, Bob, 'Masculinities, Violence and Peacemaking', *Peace news* (online), 2001 http://www.peacenews.info/issues/2443/connell.html

Deutsche Presse Agentur, 'U.N. Investigates Alleged Sexual Abuse by Peacekeepers in Eritrea', 14 April 2005 http://www.reliefweb.int/rw/rwb.nsf/db900SID/ACIO-6BFN5E?OpenDocument

Department of Peacekeeping Operations, 'Challenges in Peacekeeping Operations, Year in Review 2005' http://www.un.org/Depts/dpko/dpko/pub/year_review05/duty_of_care.htm

Department of Peacekeeping Operations, 'List of operations: 1948-2010' http://www.un.org/en/peacekeeping/list.shtml

DPKO/OMA Statistical Report on Female Military and Police Personnel in UN Peacekeeping Operations Prepared for the 10th Anniversary of the SCR 1325 http://www.un.org/en/peacekeeping/documents/gender_scres1325_chart.pdf

DPKO/DFS, 'Guidelines: Integrating a Gender Perspective Into the Work of the United Nations Military in Peacekeeping Operations', March 2010 www.un.org/en/peacekeeping/.../dpko_dfs_gender_military_perspective.pdf

DPKO Training and Evaluation Service Military Division, 'Gender and Peacekeeping Operations In-Mission Training' (2001)

DPKO, The Standard Generic Training Module on 'Gender and Peacekeeping' (2002)

DPKO, 'Standard Operating Procedure: Public Information Activities on Sexual Exploitation and Abuse' (3 April 2006)

East Timor Institute for Reconstruction Monitoring and Analysis, 'Commentary: International Security Forces and Sexual Misconduct', *The La'o Hamutuk Bulletin* (online), August 2001 http://www.laohamutuk.org/Bulletin/2001/Aug/bulletinv2n5.html

Fleshman, Michael, 'Tough UN Line on Peacekeeper Abuses: Action Initiated to End Sexual Misdeeds in Peacekeeping Missions', *Africa Renewal*, April 2005, 16

Fourcault, Henri 'United Nations Organizational Integrity Initiative', 25 March 2004 http://unpan1.un.org/intradoc/groups/public/documents/UN/UNPAN021339.pdf

Gantz, Peter and Sarah Martin, 'Haiti: Sexual Exploitation by Peacekeepers Likely to Be a Problem' *Peacewomen* (on line), 7 March 2005 http://peacewomen.org/portal_resources_resource.php?id=1093

Guido van de Kreeke, 'Zandhaas Heeft Weer Toekomst' [Fresh prospects for foot-slogger], *De Telegraaf*, 22 August 1992, 8

Higate, Paul, 'Peacekeepers and Gender: DRC and Sierra Leone' *Pambazuka News* (online), 7 August 2004 http://www.pambazuka.org/en/category/features/23056

Higate, Paul, 'Revealing the Soldier: Peacekeeping and Prostitution' (2003) 1(5) *American Sexuality Magazine* 1

International Day of UN Peacekeepers (29 May 2010) http://www.un.org/en/events/peacekeepersday/2010/

Ledgerwood, Judy, 'The Lessons from Cambodia,' *Asian Recorder*, 16-22 April 1993, 23060

Letters: An Open Letter to Yasushi Akashi (Head of the UN Operation in Cambodia in 1994)', *Phnom Penh Post*, 4 October 1994. In Cynthia Enloe, Maneuvers: The International Politics of Militarizing Women's Lives (University of California Press, 2000)

Leopold, Evelyn, 'UN Bans Peacekeepers from Sex with Congolese', Global Policy Forum (10 February 2005) http://globalpolicy.org/security/issues/congo/2005/0210nonfrat.htm

Jeffreys, Sheila, 'The Legalisation of Prostitution: A Failed Social Experiment'. Speech delivered at the Swedish Mission side event at the Commission on the Status of Women (United Nations, New York, 5 March 2003)

Kesic, Vesna, 'Muslim women, Croatian women, Serbian women, Albanian women', *Eurozine* (online), 5 September 2003 http://www.eurozine.com/articles/2003-05-09-kesic-en.html

Kesic, Vesna, 'Odgovor Ogurlicu: Diskriminacija ocigledna vec iz naslova i opreme teksta koji zene ('lijepe djevojke') i jeftino pivo nude u paketu kao mamac za svjetsko prvenstvo u nogometu' 25 April 2007 http://www.ured-ravnopravnost.hr/page.php?id=237&type=article

Khan, Taimur et al, 'Sex Workers Project at the Urban Justice Center, Critique of the Anti-Prostitution Pledge and its Global Impact' (2007) http://www.sexworkersproject.org/media-toolkit/downloads/20070330-BriefingPaperOnAnti-ProstitutionPledge.pdf

Mackay, Angela, 'Sex and the peacekeeping soldier: the New UN Resolution' *PeaceNews* 2001 http://www.peacenews.info/issues/2443/mackay.html

Mezmur, Benyam, 'A Small Country's Big Efforts at Law and Policy Reforms' (2007) (97) *The International Child and Youth Care Network* 10

Murdoch, Lindsay, 'UN's Legacy of Shame in Timor', *The Age* (online), 22 July 2006 http://www.theage.com.au/news/world/uns-legacy-of-shame-in-timor/2006/07/21/1153166587803.html?page=fullpage

MONUC Conduct Unit, 'Issues to know: Sexual Exploitation', 27 November 2005 http://monusco.unmissions.org/news.aspx

Office of Internal Oversight Services, 'Statistics: Allegations for All Categories of Personnel Per Year (Sexual Exploitation and Abuse)', 15 December 2010 http://cdu.unlb.org/Statistics/AllegationsbyCategoryofPersonnelSexualExploitationandAbuse/AllegationsforAllCategoriesof-PersonnelPerYearSexualExploitationandAbuse.aspx

Payne et al, 'Remembering the victims of the genocide that occurred in 1994 in Rwanda and pledging to work to ensure that such an atrocity does not take place again', H.Con.Res.406, 108th congress, 2nd sess (22 July 2004) http://thomas.loc.gov/home/gpoxmlc108/hc406_ih.xml

Pezzotti, Maddalena Chief, Office of Gender Affairs, 'UNMIK Office of Gender Affairs Places Gender Concerns at the Top of Peacekeeping Political Agenda in Kosovo' (United Nations Interim Administration Mission in Kosovo, UNMIK, October 2004) http://www.peacewomen.org/assets/file/Resources/UN/dpko_unmikgenderaffairs_2004.pdf

Prosecutor v Kunarac et al, Case No IT-96-23, Judgment, 12 June 2002

Puechguirbal, Nadine, 'Training in Gender Mainstreaming in Peacekeeping Operations' (22 April 2005). Speech delivered at the University for Peace Costa Rica

Puechguirbal, Nadine 'The Feminine Face of United Nations CIVPOL in Haiti'. Paper disseminated during the course on Gender in Peacekeeping Operations, UN University for Peace 2004

SANGRAM, 'Are we not Women? Women in Prostitution, Feminist Activists, and Sex Worker's Rights Groups in Dialogue' (2008) 14 *Point of View* 1

Saric, Salko, 'Kupleraj u Mostaru' [Brothels in Mostar], *Casopis Most* (online) May 1999 http://www.most.ba/025/092.htm

Save the Children UK, 'From Camp to Community: Liberia Study on Exploitation of Children', Discussion paper, 8 May 2006

Slapsak, Svetlana, 'Zene i rat u bivsoj Jugoslaviji' [Women and war in ex Yugoslavia], *Republika* (online), 31 August 1996 http://www.yurope.com/zines/republika/arhiva/96/145/145-16.html

Sikanic, T. and Tipura A., 'Ljubav pobjeđuje podjele' [Love wins divisions], *Nezavisne novine* (Banjaluka), 26 November 2006, 7

Smith, Christopher H. et al, Hearing before the Subcommittee on International Operations and Human Rights: 'The Betrayal of Srebrenica: Why Did the Massacre Happen? Will It Happen Again?'105th congress, 2nd sess (31 March1998) http://commdocs.house.gov/committees/intlrel/hfa49268.000/hfa49268_0f.htm

The Executive Committees on Humanitarian Affairs and Peace and Security (ECHA/ECPS) UN and NGO Task Force on Protection from Sexual Exploitation and Abuse, 'Terms of Reference for In-country Focal Points on Protection from Sexual Exploitation and Abuse by UN/NGO/IGO Personnel' (November 2008)

Todorovic, Branko, 'Ways of Reconciliation in Bosnia and Herzegovina'. Paper presented at Stockholm International Forum on Truth, Justice and Reconciliation, 23 April 2002 http://www.dccam.org/Projects/Affinity/SIF/DATA/2002/page1685.html

Toonen v Australia, CCPR/C/50/D/488/1992, UN Human Rights Committee (HRC), 4 April 1994

The United Nations Fourth World Conference on Women, Platform for Action, Beijing, China, September 1995

The Executive Committees on Humanitarian Affairs and Peace and Security (ECHA/ECPS) UN and NGO Task Force on Protection from Sexual Exploitation and Abuse, 'Terms of Reference for in-country Focal Points on Protection from Sexual Exploitation and Abuse by UN/NGO/IGO Personnel', November 2008

UN Chronicle, Fifty Unforeseen Years (1998) 12 July 2007 http://findarticles.com/p/articles/mi_m1309/is_3_35/ai_54259331

UN Division for the Advancement of Women, 'Women 2000' (Department of Policy Coordination and Sustainable Development UN New York, 1995)

UNMIBH Legal Office, Guidance No. 21, 'Trafficking in Persons' May 1999

UNICEF, 'Inter-Agency Training for Focal Points on Protection from Sexual Exploitation and Abuse by UN personnel and partners: Facilitator's Manual' 2007 http://www.unitarpoci.org/media/course_extras/vaw_focal_point_manual.pdf

'UN Peacekeepers Accused of Rape in Haiti', *Reuters* (online), 23 February 2005 http://www.reuters.com/newsArticle.jhtml?type=worldNews&storyID=7717662

UNICEF, 'Inter-Agency Training for Focal Points on Protection from Sexual Exploitation and Abuse by UN personnel and partners: Facilitator's Manual', 2007 http://www.unitarpoci.org/media/course_extras/vaw_focal_point_manual.pdf

UNMIBH and OHCHR, 'Trafficking in Human Beings in Bosnia and Herzegovina: A Summary Report of the Joint Trafficking Project of the UN Mission in Bosnia and Herzegovina and the Office of the High Commissioner for Human Rights' 12 May 2000 www.ohr.int/ohr-dept/hr-rol/thedept/hr-coord-cent/info-reps/hr-reports/default.asp?content_id=5099

United Nations, 'Promotion and Protection of the Rights of Children: Impact of Armed Conflict on Children.' Note by the Secretary-General, A/51/306 (26 August 1996)

United Nations Department of Public Information, 'UN Establishes Peacekeeping Conduct and Discipline Units: Latest move in Reforms to Tackle Sexual Exploitation and Abuse' (Press Release PKO/120, 3 August 2005) http://www.un.org/News/Press/docs/2005/pko120.doc.htm

United Nations News Center, 'UN will not turn 'blind eye' to peacekeepers' misconduct, vows UN official', 25 July 2007 http://www.un.org/apps/news/story.asp?NewsID=23333&Cr=peacekeep&Cr1=&Kw1=morocco&Kw2=peacekeepers&Kw3=sex

United Nations Inter-Agency Standing Committee Policy Paper, 'Protection of Internally Displaced Persons', New York, December 1999.

United Nations Children's Fund, 'Facts on Children' http://www.unicef.org/media/9482.html

United Nations Department of Public Information, 'Former Yugoslavia-UNPROFOR' (31 August 1996) http://www.un.org/Depts/dpko/dpko/co_mission/unprof_b.htm

United Nations Department of Public information, 'Dag Hammarskjöld United Nations Oral History Collection (1995-2007) The UN Years' (9 January 2011) http://www.un.org/Depts/dhl/dag/oralhist.htm

United Nations Department of Peacekeeping Operations, 'Gender Statistics by Mission: for the month of September 2010' (14 October 2010) http://www.un.org/en/peacekeeping/contributors/gender/2010gender/sept10.pdf

United Nations General Assembly, 'Promotion and Protection of the Rights of Children: Impact of Armed Conflict on Children', Note by the Secretary-General, 51st sess, A/51/306, 26 August 1996

United Nations Office for Coordination for Humanitarian Affairs (OCHA), 'Protection from Sexual Exploitation and Abuse' http://ochaonline.un.org/HumanitarianIssues/Protectionfrom-SexualExploitationandAbuse/tabid/1204/language/en-US/Default.aspx

United Nations Truce Supervision Organization, Sec Res 50, S/801, 310th meeting (29 May 1948)

United Nations Truce Supervision Organization (3 January 2011) http://www.un.org/en/peacekeeping/missions/untso/

United Nations Peacekeeping Operations (January 2011) http://www.un.org/depts/dpko/dpko/bnote.htm

United Nations Peacekeeping Fact Sheet, http://www.un.org/en/peacekeeping/documents/factsheet.pdf

UNEF I, Completed Peacekeeping Operations http://www.un.org/Depts/dpko/dpko/co_mission/unef1backgr1.html

UNIFIL http://www.un.org/Depts/dpko/missions/unifil/background.html

Ured za ljudska prava, 'Okrugli stol pod nazivom: Argumenti pro & contra legalizacije prostitucije' 30 May 2005 http://www.ljudskaprava-vladarh.hr/Default.aspx?art=93&sec=59

Vogt, Margaret, 'The Impact of Peacekeeping Operations on Local Populations'. Paper presented at the Conference on Building capacities for Peacekeeping and Women's Dimensions in Peace Processes, Santiago, 4-5 November 2002

Voetmann, Peter, 'The Structure, Planning and Execution of UN Peace Operations' (The Royal Norwegian Ministry of Foreign Affairs, 1997) in Monograph No 10 on Conflict Management, Peacekeeping and Peacebuilding http://www.iss.co.za/pubs/monographs/No10/Contents.html

Walsh, Declan and Byrne, Nicola, 'Peacekeeper jailed for porn films', *Scottish News* (online) 22 December 2002 http://www.prisonplanet.com/peacekeeper_jailed_for_porn_films-retry.html

Women's Worlds 2011, http://www.womensworlds.ca/

Zarkov, Dubravka, 'Gender, Violent Conflict, Peacekeeping: Paradoxes of Women's Engagements'. Paper presented at the EU conference 'Women in Conflict Situations and Peacekeeping', Amsterdam, 2004

GPSR Compliance
The European Union's (EU) General Product Safety Regulation (GPSR) is a set of rules that requires consumer products to be safe and our obligations to ensure this.

If you have any concerns about our products, you can contact us on

ProductSafety@springernature.com

In case Publisher is established outside the EU, the EU authorized representative is:

Springer Nature Customer Service Center GmbH
Europaplatz 3
69115 Heidelberg, Germany

www.ingramcontent.com/pod-product-compliance
Lightning Source LLC
Chambersburg PA
CBHW060745150926
51501CB00003B/97
9783642284830